ДАДИМ ДЛЯ СТРОЯЩЕГОСЯ СОЦИАЛИЗМА В 1931 г.

8 МЛН. ТОНН ЧУГУНА

THE GREAT OFFENSIVE

Edwin A. Ross

BOOKS BY MAURICE HINDUS

BROKEN EARTH

HUMANITY UPROOTED

RED BREAD

MOTTO OF SHOCK-TROOPER

At inertia, idleness and senility, on which outmoded society thrives, let us strike, STRIKE, STRIKE.

THE GREAT OFFENSIVE

MAURICE HINDUS

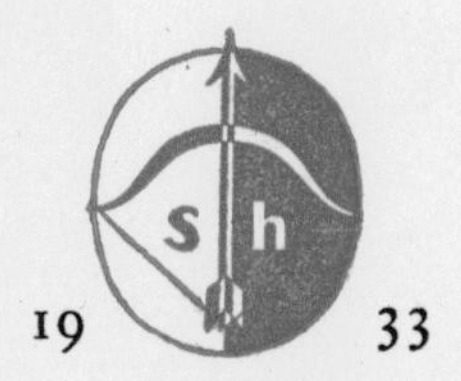

19 33

HARRISON SMITH AND ROBERT HAAS

NEW YORK

••

PRINTED IN THE UNITED STATES

CONTENTS

PART THREE

For New Adventures

INTRODUCTION

"—And supposing there is a famine in Russia," continued my interlocutor, an American business man of national renown and known for his liberalism, "what will happen?"

"People will die, of course," I answered.

"And supposing three or four million people die."

"The Revolution will go on."

"And Stalin."

"He may remain, he may go, but the Revolution will go on."

Students of Soviet Russia, with an intimate knowledge of the people and the conditions of the country, will, I feel certain, concur in this opinion. Leaders may come and go, famine may fall on the land, a breakdown there may be in the steel or coal industry, policies may change, repressions may increase, but, unless a war comes and imposes a foreign rule on Russia, the Revolution will march on. In the years of its existence it has gathered such momentum that it cannot halt. It must press forward. What I mean is that the efforts of the Communist Party and of the Soviets to recast human society and to reconstruct the human personality have gone so far that they cannot be stopped.

The difficulties and setbacks these efforts have encountered are stupendous. One can see them at every step and feel them in the very air. The Russian newspapers fairly scream with resentment at their presence, and since the conclusion of the first Five Year Plan foreign correspondents have ceaselessly and vigorously emphasized them. Aside from the food shortages and the critical condition of livestock in the country, there is the mounting severity toward elements in the population which, rightly or wrongly, have been regarded as inimical to the Revolution and obstructing its path. There is the exile of several Cossack communities from the North Caucasus, not *koolacks*, but whole communities—which means *bedniaks* as well, or the poor people who have been held up as the chief champions and beneficiaries of collectivization. There is the new passport system which is compelling thousands of families to leave the city and find new homes and new jobs in small communities, with all the heartaches and hardships attendant on such an uprooting. There is the even more momentous cleansing of the population along the frontiers of elements suspected of disaffection and involving a further forced migration of vast masses of people. There is the execution, in March, 1933, of 35 high officials in the Commissary of Agriculture. There is the arrest and trial of the British engineers and the resultant clash with England. There are difficulties in transportation, in industry, in agriculture. Indeed, the farther the Revolution advances the more stupendous are the difficulties it encounters. Truly did a Soviet leader remark to the writer: "Our Revolution has meant jumping from one difficulty to another. The important thing is not to strike a blind alley."

And yet like the tide of the ocean in the midst of wind and storm the Revolution continues to roll on and on. The Russians speak of the Five Year Plan as the beginning of a socialist offensive. Socialist or not, it has been a mighty offensive all along the line of human effort and human experience. It has pervaded all phases of human life and all processes of thought and action. It has left nothing and nobody untouched and unshaken. Peasant worker, intellectual, man, woman, child—they have all felt its shattering impact and have yielded to its transforming powers.

For purposes of concreteness and without presuming to be mathematically precise, I should divide Russian life at this moment into the following sections: consumption, or the standard of living in terms of material satisfactions; construction, or the process of developing industry; culture, or education, hygiene, refinement of manners, and civilized diversions; psychology, or the reconstruction of the human personality. If one were to express the condition of each of these in terms of curves, one would note that the consumption curve has been steadily declining, but that the construction, culture and psychology curves have been steadily ascending. If only because Russian youth is so decisively atheistic and so flamingly averse to private enterprise the human personality in Russia is markedly different from what it is in other lands.

In brief the Russians have waged their Offensive for a new world along two vast all-embracing fronts—that of economics with the aim of creating a new economic order, and that of sociology with the aim of creating a new human personality. It is on the economic front that they have encountered their chief setbacks, and it is from this front that news has been emanating of difficulties, blunders, mishaps. But on the sociological front they have met slight obstruction. Here the Offensive has swept on and on to new and ever-growing conquests. To the physical eye these conquests are not as visible as are the reverses or achievements on the economic front. But that does not make them the less real or exciting. Indeed, it is the sociological triumph of the Revolution that makes it so unique an event in human history. Within the short space of sixteen years it has so "reboiled," or "reforged," the human being in Russia that he is a new personage on this earth, with a body of new aims, attitudes and responses. It is this sociological triumph of the Revolution that makes its new Offensive so exciting to follow. It demonstrates for one thing that even in this advanced machine age it is easier to reconstruct the human personality than to rebuild an economic order.

No dictatorship is tolerant of enemies, real or imaginary, and the Russian dictatorship has been more than severe to its enemies, and some of them have been imaginary. Severity has risen and fallen with the rise and fall of mishaps and opposition. If by the word liberalism we mean tolerance of opposition, then there is not a vestige of it in Russia. But if we mean by it advanced ideas and practices in social accommodation then the Russian dictatorship has outliberalized the most liberal statesmen in the world. Witness its sanction of freedom of sexual selection, its practice of racial equality, its treatment of the criminal (not the political offender), the prostitute, the soldier, the child; above all, its exaltation of science. Such a scene as Germany witnessed on the 10th of May, 1933, when even books of scientists (of Freud and Einstein) were consigned to flames, is as inconceivable under the Soviets as is the enthronement of a Czar.

And so Russia continues to be a strange mixture of dark shadows and bright lights, of brutal methods and exalted aims, of constant hardship and assiduous enterprise, and of all the elements that make it the most dramatic spectacle in the world.

In this book I have aimed to set down as fully and as vividly as I could the nature and the meaning of the new Offensive for a new world.

Some of the subjects treated in this book, like religion, morality, the family, I discussed at length in "Humanity Uprooted." But their importance has impelled me to consider them anew in the light of the events that have transpired since the writing of that book.

MAURICE HINDUS

PART I

FOR A NEW ECONOMIC ORDER

I

LIFE

OUTWARDLY Moscow has never looked so bright as it does now. On street after street the ancient cobbles have been torn up and replaced with shiny asphalt. The shop windows on the main avenues, once so dingy and funereal, are now washed and polished till they gleam. Nor are they any longer empty as of old. The shelves inside may indeed be bare of goods, but the well-filled display windows give no sign of it. In the food shops row on row of vegetables—cabbages, carrots, tomatoes, beets, eggplants, cauliflowers, neatly arranged in even tiers, with their variety and splash of color, make a lively picture. In drapery and clothing shops, fabrics and garments are likewise neatly hung out. And though to Western eyes the shoddy quality of these goods—the cheapness of material, of style, of workmanship—may be at once apparent, for the Russian these displays are a novelty and an achievement.

Outwardly Moscow appears happy as well as bright. For the first time since the Revolution there is again a semblance of night life in the city. Hitherto only foreigners have enjoyed what meager night life there was.

Now Russians too, if they have the price, are free to partake of it. The restaurants, in which formerly one hardly ever saw Russians in the evening, are now crowded with them. The gypsy choirs, which two years ago were banned as a "disintegrating influence" out of tune with the Five Year Plan, are once again adding their gay note to the social life of Moscow. Even the dance-hall, which like a dread pest was banished from the land, is now being welcomed back. There is only one as yet, in a suburb of Moscow, but it is thronged nightly with young people who want to make merry, and there is talk of others being opened all over the land.

Indeed, Kaganovitch himself, next to Stalin the most influential person in Russia, informed Moscow Communists at a recent meeting that the plans for the reconstruction of the capital during the second Five Year Plan include a project to build several large dance-halls.

Nor do the revolutionaries any longer sniff with disdain at the fox-trot. Only rarely now does one hear it denounced as a perverter of decency or as a symbol of bourgeois sensuality. Last summer I was waiting for a train in an out-of-the-way town in the black earth region. Among others waiting were two school-teachers whom I had met earlier in the day. They were going to a near-by town to attend a "spectacle," a dramatic performance of Young Communists. "And after the spectacle," said one of them, "we'll dance. I love to dance!"

"Will they let you fox-trot?"

"Of course. For a long time they wouldn't permit it, but now they do."

There is even semi-official sanction of the once

despised fox-trot. At the before-mentioned Communist meeting addressed by Kaganovitch, some one in the audience asked him what dances would be permitted in the projected dance-halls of which he had spoken. Without a moment's hesitation, he replied: "The fox-trot." This reply, which was doubtless a shock to some of the more pious Communists in the audience, is an indication that outstanding leaders in the party recognize the need of more play for the masses and more sensuous enjoyment.

The masses, the youth especially, are taking up the idea of play with much enthusiasm. Russia has never appreciated the outdoors as much as now. All along the Moscow river, in and outside the city, the banks in summer now swarm with people, some in bathing-suits, some without. They linger for hours baking themselves in the hot sun and splashing noisily in the waters. Sun-bathing has become a universal fad. Workers on highways, on farms, on construction projects, often wear only trunks. Their bodies are dusky with sunburn and sweat rolls off them in shiny streaks. But their hunger for sun is insatiable, and day after day they expose themselves to its full blaze. As you watch these multitudes of young people you are impressed with their superb physical appearance. They show no evidence of under-nourishment—certainly not to the layman. Wiry and muscular, they hop and dash about with a cheery alertness. In all her history Moscow never has displayed such zest for sports and outdoor movement as now. Her people crowd the parks to watch or participate in games—soccer, volley-ball, tennis—and there is a movement now on foot to introduce baseball. Plans for the construction of mammoth stadiums in the cities speak eloquently of the place that athletics is to be accorded in the everyday life of the people. Among Young Communists one finds enthusiasts who glowingly predict that when the Revolution has finished its tasks of industrializing the country, Russia will become a new Greece—a land of superbly developed human beings—a land, indeed, of supermen!

And how the people rush to places of entertainment! Theaters and operas and motion-picture houses are always overcrowded. Time and again, with all the special privileges that I enjoy as a foreign journalist, I have been unable to obtain tickets to the Art Theatre or the ballet. At the doors of the "movie" around the corner from my hotel, hundreds of people wait eagerly every evening, even in drizzling rain, for the chance to go in. Never have there been so many concerts in Moscow as now, or so many literary evenings devoted to professional readings from the best of the old and the new Russian literature or to authors' readings from their own writings, published and unpublished. An outsider, seeing a performance of *Hamlet* at the Vachtangov Theatre, the most spectacular in Moscow, might conclude that the Russians, in the midst of all their strife and sacrifice, enjoy laughter and fun as much as any people in the world. The audience roars with mirth not only at the words of Polonius, but also at those of Hamlet, for in this daring and buoyant interpretation of the great Shakespearean classic Hamlet is no tall, lean, pale poet, dreamer, philosopher, but a short, plump, cunning young fellow who loves nothing so much as fun for its own sake, and whose sole ambition is to make fools of the royal suite and to capture the crown for himself. In the hands of the Vachtangov players, *Hamlet* ceases to be drama or tragedy and becomes instead a lively melodrama and a stupendous, almost hilarious, spectacle.

At every step in this straggling city one comes upon evidence of improvement in the appearance of things. Life booms and roars everywhere with the onward sweep of the Bolshevik main weapon of offense, the machine, in the form of stone-crushers, cement-mixers, tractors, trucks, all in ever-increasing numbers rumbling deafeningly along the main avenues. The newspapers exult in the completion of new factories—fifty-five of them in Moscow alone—and the renovation of nearly three times that number of old ones. Some of these, such as the Amo automobile factory, the Kaganovitch ball-bearing plant, the Freser tool-cutting shop, are proudly proclaimed among the largest and best equipped in the world.

This advance of the machine is rapidly pushing into oblivion one of the most ancient and picturesque figures in the country—the *izvochtshik* (cabman). Only two years ago there were still fleets of *izvochtshiks* in Moscow. Like gigantic shadows they lined the streets and squares around the railroad stations, the hotels, the restaurants, the parks. Their cabs were growing more rickety, their clothes more ragged, their beards more unkempt, yet, like faithful sentinels, they were ever at their posts, night after night, in rain and blizzard, watching for the beck and call of their masters, the Moscow public. Their presence, their speech, their cabs, their very appearance, were reminders, even more eloquent than the ragged churches with their fading cupolas, of the fact that an outworn world, a world with a pageantry and a glory all its own, was crumbling into dust.

The *izvochtshiks* no longer line the streets. Time and again, even in the middle of the day, I have searched for one near my hotel or in the public squares, but nowhere could I find a trace of one. Like a plant in barren soil, he is withering away. The machine is drawing unto itself the sustenance that was his. Not that there are even now enough street-cars, buses and taxi-cabs in Moscow to meet the demand of the populace. Foreigners who have *valuta*, or foreign money, to spend find plenty of Fords, Buicks, Packards, Fiats, Lincolns at their disposal day and night, it is true; but the natives who have only roubles must hunt hard to find a taxi. Often when one comes into view a great crowd will dash forth to meet it. Then the man who runs fastest, and is the first to jump inside and slam the door, commands its service. These rouble taxis, Government owned and equipped with meters, are only one-tenth as expensive as cabs, and the *izvochtshik*, knowing that as more and more taxis roll through the streets there will be less and less call for his services, sees doom ahead. Pressed by taxes as well as high prices of fodder, and denied a rationing card in Government shops, he hastens to abandon his ancient pursuit, and drifts into the factories and collective farms, or else hitches his horse to a lumber-cart and hauls brick, sand, steel, and so merges with the seething mass of proletarians.

Yet along with the invasion of the machine seems to come a growing need for natural beauty that finds expression in an increasing effort to enhance the pastoral quality of this ancient and glamorous city. Old parks are being extended, new ones opened, and trees by the cartload—evergreens, willows, maples and now and then a birch—are being planted along the sidewalks, in the yards and around the squares. For the Muscovite asks nothing better in summer than to spend his leisure at ease among the many finely arbored boulevards and parks of the city. He loves to loll around on a bench or stroll endlessly up and down the neat paths, content just to talk and enjoy the aroma of grass and trees. He is still too close to his earthbound past to feel happy amid the roar and swelter of the ever-encroaching machine.

But there is no place where one can sense the swing and the beat of the times as clearly as in the book stores. There are many of them in Moscow—one on nearly every corner in the business section of the city. An endless stream of people flows in and out of them—Muscovites and visitors from all the corners of the far-flung Soviet Empire. Inside, their loaded tables display the latest publications, row upon row of books, their paper covers challenging attention. They are living voices of the Revolution, proclaiming bravely enough, for the most part, the new ideas, new inventions, new principles, new adjustments. What the proper care of rabbits will do for the country; what proper reorganization of labor in the beet-fields will do for the production of sugar; the new kinds of homes the Soviet must build for its workers; the new type of education it means to foster; the new system of labor rewards to be introduced on the collective farms; the new principles and purposes that writers and artists are to pursue in their works; the new games the people are to play, the new songs they are to sing, the new health laws they are to observe; the classless society that the second Five Year Plan is to mold—these are only a few of the topics that the eye catches as it wanders hastily from book to book. Some of the current pronouncements such as the new principles of education and art, so eloquently championed now, were only a year ago under ban, and woe to the Soviet citizen who dared voice his approval! A year ago a protagonist of the very principles now advocated would have been denounced as a backslider, an oppositionist, a Trotskyite, a social reformer—anything but a red-blooded worthy soldier of the Revolution. And one too articulate in his advocacy might well have suffered deranking, disfranchisement, exile. Now, of course, anyone who disapproves of them is the object of that vitriolic scorn which Communists love to bestow on non-conformists.

The significant feature of all these new books is that they are dedicated to a positive purpose. Nowhere is there a subject or title suggestive of doubt, skepticism, regret or contrition. If blunders and evils are mentioned or emphasized, it is only for the purpose of giving prominence to the corrective plans and measures. Nowhere in these books is there indulgence in abstractions and speculation for their own sake. Such philosophical considerations are officially suppressed. Negative aspects are carefully avoided. Nowhere is there emphasis on negation. Only the positive and concrete is emphasized—new methods, new tasks, new purposes, final achievements. The central thought is always the deed which is as multitudinous and disparate as are the plans at hand and the interests and wants of the Soviet citizen. Nothing pertaining to any part of a project is neglected, be it deep-breathing exercises or the operation of a press punching machine.

There are also, of course, the books of fiction. But present-day Russian fiction, with few notable exceptions, is in form and in spirit as hard and heavy as the coal and steel, the factory and the farm, with which it concerns itself. Besides, there is always very little of it in stock in the book store. No matter how large the supply the store receives, it is bought up almost as soon as it is unpacked. Favorite foreign authors, like John Dos Passos, who with the rising intelligentsia has superseded all other foreign writers, including Upton Sinclair, in popularity, can be obtained only if ordered in advance of publication or through some obliging friend associated with the publishing house or the book stores. Visitors to the book shops are not curiosity seekers or window-shoppers. They come to buy books and they pay for them. They buy packs of books for themselves or the institutions they represent. There are no such eager book-buyers anywhere else in the world as there are in present-day Russia. It is the one country that does not know what "remainders" are.

Indeed, on my arrival in Moscow, as I was walking around observing shops, people, pavements, traffic, new construction, I had a feeling that Moscow was a booming metropolis and that the second Five Year Plan was pushing on in a blaze of triumph.

But this impression did not remain unchallenged. Late one evening soon after my arrival, as I was returning to my hotel, I saw a side-street crowded with men and women who were lined up two and three abreast. Some of them, evidently worn out with standing, had slumped down upon the sidewalks and gone to sleep beside their empty baskets. Others remained patiently on their feet. It looked very much like a bread-line in any American or European city, with hungry people waiting for a hand-out of food.

But it was not a bread-line. It was a meat-line. And the people waiting in it were not wards of charity. They had money. They had come, not to beg, but to buy meat, and they arrived hours before the store opened in the hope that if they came early enough the meat would last until their turn came! What is true of meat shops is true of pastry and dairy shops. Always there are crowds before their doors, always there are people waiting, waiting, waiting! Only in some of the well-organized stores operated in connection with the factories, and open only to their employees, are customers spared the ordeal of standing in line.

These queues make one realize how hard life is now at the beginning of the second Five Year Plan, how badly organized, over-strained and ill supplied are the institutions that minister to the everyday wants of the people, and how acute is the shortage of commodities which they had hoped they would have in abundance on completion of the first Five Year Plan. These queues set at naught the gay boasts of unthinking Communists and the dismal premonitions of the no less unthinking capitalists who at the inception of the original Five Year Plan had imagined that on its conclusion Russia would take her place among the most advanced and prosperous nations of the world. The Russians have launched the slogan: "To catch up with and to surpass the capitalist countries" in production and in consumption. Whether or not they will ever realize the aim of their slogan remains a question. But at present they are still at an impressive—even a prodigious—distance from their goal. In fact, the beginning of the second Five Year Plan, despite the external sparkle of Moscow, which as the most favored city of the Soviets has received special attention, despite the imposing construction in progress throughout the country, and despite the ever-expanding cultural opportunities in city and village, finds Russia face to face with a crucial food problem, a problem more extensive than it has ever been since the days of the famine. The rations of meat and of fats have not been so meager in a whole decade!

In Moscow the rations of sugar, even for workers, have been cut from one kilo to eight hundred grams a month. Nowhere is there an adequate supply of tobacco or matches or even cigarette paper. Many Muscovites who smoke are saving their newspapers, like peasants in the country, in order to use them for cigarette paper. On main street corners, boys stop pedestrians and offer them a light for five copecks. And if you give a Russian porter in a hotel or at a railroad station a piece of soap, a packet of the cheapest cigarettes, or a can of sardines, he will reward you with the lowest bow you have ever witnessed. He will prize it far more highly than a tip in money, however generous.

I know Russians who have been vainly seeking to buy an overcoat for three years. There simply are not enough overcoats to go round. In a city like Kiev, in the autumn of 1932, the daily rations of bread for workers were cut from two pounds to one and one-half, and for white-collar folk, from one pound to half a pound. Except in some of the well-organized shops, it is difficult to buy even handkerchiefs or towels or bedding in Russia today. And every time I look into a five-and-ten-cent store in America I see scores of articles of which the Russians have never even heard. Such a store would be to them a miracle of miracles and a boon of the highest order. So far as I know even now, at the end of the first Five Year Plan, Russia is not manufacturing either fountain pens or cameras, and the great dream of Russian school-children is to come into possession of a good pencil. It is impossible to go into a Russian drug store and buy a bottle of iodine or mercurochrome. Only hospitals and dispensaries are well supplied with the common drugs. There is a shortage of every conceivable commodity in the country, from food (now and then, in some places outside the industrial centers, even of bread) to footwear, from safety pins to good ink—a shortage of everything in fact except possibly cosmetics!

Judged, then, in terms of everyday material satisfactions, the first Five Year Plan, which is the first step in the Great Offensive for a new society, a new world, and a new human personality, has not only failed to improve, but has actually lowered, the material standard of living. The machine, it is true, has swept forward with rapid and tumultuous strides. In the years between 1923 and 1927 there were few automobiles in Russia, and these of foreign make; there were few home-manufactured tractors and no home-made aëroplanes. But peasants and workers had substantial and sometimes ample supplies of meat, eggs, cheese, and butter. They had begun to eat as never before in all their history. Now Russia has scores of the most modern and best equipped factories in the world. All over the land one hears the whine and roar of new machines. Gigantic smoke-stacks are constantly rising above the earth. Huge brick structures take shape before one's eyes. But of the things that the people need for their bodily comfort there is less and less.

In the original schedule of the first Five Year Plan, the cost of living was to be reduced by 14 per cent. The people in the city were to consume 27.7 per cent more meat, 72 per cent more eggs, 55.6 per cent more milk, and country people were to increase their consumption by 16.7 per cent more meat, 45.2 per cent more eggs, 24.7 per cent more milk products. Yakovlev, the Commissary of Agriculture, in a long, highly statistical, and eloquent address before the Communist Congress in 1930 assured the Russian people that at the end of the first Plan they would have twice as much meat and milk. But neither the original schedule of the Plan nor the inflated promises of the oratorical Commissary of Agriculture have materialized.

It is this decline in the material welfare of the people that conveys an impression of gloom to so many foreign visitors in Russia. They see the queues in the shops and restaurants and railroad stations. In talking with Russians they hear endless complaints of shortages of indispensable commodities, and they conclude, naturally enough, that the Revolution and even the Five Year

Plan have been failures. Russians themselves, including Communists, are not loath to voice disappointments. The reasons for this visible slump in the standard of living will become evident in subsequent chapters. But it should be said here that to view either the Five Year Plan or the whole idea of national planning and Socialist reconstruction in terms of immediate material rewards, particularly in a country as complex as Russia, is only one way of appraising them. Such a point of view fails to take into account their vastly greater significance as a step toward national development and social transformation. Viewed in terms of such aims, the Offensive becomes a historic phenomenon. It will go down, in Russian history at least, as the most daring task or adventure ever embarked upon; and the story of it, especially when surveyed in the light of prevailing internal and international conditions of the country at the time it was launched, will read like an extraordinary legend. The price the Russian people have paid for this adventure is beyond calculation. But the aim and the achievement in terms of ultimate purposes and possible promise are likewise beyond calculation.

II

MACHINES

THE ARITHMETICAL RESULTS

IT WAS, in 1928, a year of trouble and torments. Russia's international affairs were in a dismal plight. England had broken off relations, America persisted in her policy of non-recognition, France continually sulked, Poland never ceased to make wry faces, China forcibly broke into the Soviet embassy in Peking and the consulates in other cities, raided them, and ousted the Soviet representatives. No nation save possibly Germany, then a republic, and Turkey evinced any sympathy, and neither was too openly nor too abundantly friendly; no credits were in sight save in limited amounts from Germany and Italy. No help was forthcoming from anybody, anywhere.

Internally the picture in 1928 was no more cheering. The Communist Party was then riven with dissension. Trotsky was ousted; his followers in their hundreds, among them the ablest men in the country—orators, executives, writers, engineers, economists—were exiled to remote parts of the land, and the Right opposition was continually threatening a fresh disruption. The peasants were growling with dissatisfaction, the *nepmen* (business men) and the intellectuals were recalcitrant, and some of the latter, though a much smaller number than the hysterical Soviet Press would have the world believe, were actually effecting sabotage. There was little skilled labor in the country, and very few engineers experienced in building modern industrial plants, and few leaders to manage such plants once they were built. The country itself was backward and had barely recovered from the cumulative ravages of the World and civil wars, which had reduced industrial output to one-fifth and agricultural to three-fifths of normal. In brief, Russia was alone, disunited, impoverished.

It was in such a setting that the first step in the Offensive was launched. In their discussions of the first Five Year Plan, many foreign observers have assumed that it is something complete within itself, like a business order to be filled within a certain time, in a certain amount, and in a certain way, and at a certain price. The Plan is that only in its mathematical formulas. In all other respects, and especially in its underlying purposes, it is a phase in a historic process, a means to an end, or merely a move in the Offensive to remold civilization. The final aim of this Offensive is a classless society, in which for the first time since primitive days, so runs the theory, there shall be no classes and no causes to create them. There shall be no private ownership of the *means of production*, or the machine, and no chance for any human being to employ or exploit any other human being. Eventually in this society the state is to disappear, and the task of preserving order or enforcing social discipline, should it be necessary, is to devolve on productive organisms. The human experience promised in this classless society is most challenging. All men are to be socially equal, and are to have an equal chance to work and to live in comfort. There is to be no unemployment, for society shall plan to produce only as much as it shall need, and the work involved in the process of such production will be evenly distributed among the whole working population. There are, therefore, to be no cycles of prosperity followed by cycles of depression and all their attendant evils. There are to be no racial feuds and no religious faith. All men are to have abundant opportunity to cultivate whatever talents they may be endowed with. Always they are to enjoy economic security and all the compensations that it implies.

Trotsky denounces the notion that any one nation even as large and potentially as rich as Russia can build a classless society. Stoutly he proclaims that such a society can come only when the whole industrial world has gone Soviet. Stalin and his followers, however, sternly repudiate Trotsky's position, and the Communist Party in Russia is acting upon the assumption that Russia alone can eventually build a classless society—but only after she has forged into being a mighty industrial machine which can produce in abundance all the goods that the nation might need. This machine, under Socialist control, so Russian leaders hold, can function more successfully than under capitalist control. Lenin was most emphatic and outspoken on this point. "Productivity of labor," said he, "is in the last analysis the chief and most important element in the triumph of the new society. Capitalism has lifted productivity to a point unheard of under feudalism. Capitalism can and will be decisively beaten by Socialism, through the power of Socialism to create a much higher productivity of labor. Either to perish or to catch up with and outstrip capitalist nations in economic effort; to perish or to push full steam ahead—thus has history put the question."

Before anything else, therefore, Russia must have an industrial machine of her own as well built as in any capitalist nation and functioning much better. But Russia under the Czars, while becoming more and more industrialized, had remained primarily an agricultural country with 80 per cent of the people living in villages and working the land with primitive implements, and with the coal, iron, power, machine-building industries nowhere near well enough developed to satisfy the nation's needs, and with only a bare beginning of a chemical industry. Hence, before Russia could hope to challenge the supremacy of a capitalist society in production, she had to have an industrial machine of her own, and the first Five Year Plan was merely the first step in the process of building up such a machine.

Economically the general aim of the Plan was intensively to industrialize the country; to effect, in a period of five years, an industrial progress which other nations had achieved in decades. Constantly, and with great assurance, Russian leaders proclaim that the rate of industrial development which they had set out to achieve, and had actually been achieving, has never been approximated by any other country. They credit it all to the magic beneficence of Socialist construction and to the program of national planning that it presupposes. Without under-estimating the value of either, an outsider, on sober reflection, cannot help being ruffled by this assertion. He cannot help asking himself how much the idea of Socialist construction and all that it implies would have availed Russia if Europe and America had not saved her the trouble, the time, and the expense of developing the industrial machine? Nowadays, any nation, no matter what its system of government, can build an up-to-date steel plant or an automobile factory more easily and more rapidly than at any time since the rise of the industrial age. In all their boasts of the rapidity of their industrial growth the Russians never once allude to the fact that the capitalist world has saved them the experimental stage of industrialization. They can take everything ready-made. All they need do is engage competent engineers, as they have done, and buy modern machinery, which they have also done, and the tractor and automobile and chemical plants rise into being.

It is because Russia has leaped and not grown into industrialization that she has had such success in building factories and such difficulty in operating them. It is easy to buy machinery ready-made in Germany, America, or England; it is not so easy to develop a worker competent to run the machines. In capitalist countries industrial skill developed with the rise of mechanization; in Russia it had no chance to develop because the machine was imported ready-made.

The significant feature in Russian industrialization is the fact that Russia has had to undertake it with scarcely any financial aid from the outside, and not under private but under government initiative. In Japan the government has played a big part in the country's industrial development. But Japan had the abundant support of bankers and financiers in other lands. Russia has had to carry out her ambitious program with her own hands and her own resources. One cannot stress this point too vigorously. In the early days of the Plan the Russians did not appreciate the immense difficulties they would encounter. Overcome with fervor, they did not realize the hardships and the sacrifices the Plan would impose on them. They regarded it more as a journey to a festival than as a grinding task, the most grinding any nation had assumed in recent times. It meant digging ditches and blasting rock and hauling brick and lifting steel and being exposed to wind, rain, cold, and subordinating personal comfort and enjoyment to the tasks of the moment. But they were brave and resolute, for they knew that without a machine of their own they were doomed to failure and collapse.

While the ultimate aim of the Offensive is the achievement of a classless society and the immediate building of an industrial machine, there were two pressing purposes which came to dominate every move in the Offensive. One of these was national defense.

Since their rise to power the Russian leaders have been overcome with an irrepressible dread of war. They had memories of the presence of foreign armies on their soil in the early part of the Revolution—armies from Japan, England, America, France, Poland, Rumania, Italy, Serbia, Czechoslovakia—indeed from most of the nations of the world, including the richest and the most powerful, and they dreaded a repetition of the experience.

Once, an obscure Polish official was quoted, in an obscure Polish publication in Volyna, as saying that it was Poland's mission to unite the whole of the Ukraine into one body—and Moscow at once shook with nervousness and indignation and began to see blood. True enough this official was echoing an ambition which Polish patriots had in earlier days openly professed. But Poland was so harassed with internal troubles and dissensions that it seemed absurd to imagine that she would deliberately launch another war against Russia merely for the sake of occupying the Ukraine. Yet the Russians raised a mighty cry that another war threat was hanging over them and that the masses had better be prepared for the worst or the capitalists would blow them to atoms.

Periodically the Russian papers were uncovering somebody who was striving to muster diplomatic and military support for an attack on them. The refusal in those days of Poland, France, Japan, and the Baltic States to sign non-aggression pacts increased Russia's uneasiness. Now that these nations, with the exception of Japan, have signed such pacts, the old dread has abated but has not disappeared. Indeed, with the Japanese army hovering about the Russian frontiers in Siberia, and the Nazi leaders in Germany openly espousing the idea of the conquest of southern Russia and its colonization with Germans, Russia is likely to become more fearful than ever.

If fear of war has been an emotional burden for her—a strain on her nerves—it has also been a stimulus and a challenge. Writers on Russia who appraise Soviet achievement in terms of arithmetical formulas fail to comprehend her social and national aims. They fail to perceive, for example, the stress of the first Five Year Plan on military defense. The Russians talk continually of "catching up with and outstripping capitalist countries" in production and in distribution—and of the Five Year Plan as the first decisive step in that direction. But for the present, at least, they have been actuated by military considerations more than by any others. They feel that they have won power at a frightful cost of blood and substance, and they would so fortify themselves in the quickest possible time with all modern weapons of warfare—from tanks to chemicals, from bombing-planes to gas-masks—that no enemy or enemies, however formidable, could wrest this power from them. National defense has been, and still is, one of their foremost concerns in all industrial plans and programs.

Only slightly less momentous has been their aim to industrialize agriculture—of itself a stupendous undertaking. By 1929, the second year of the first Five Year Plan, the Russians had rearranged their program so as to hasten the manufacture of agricultural implements. They were determined to put the machine on the land within the shortest possible period, and sweep the peasant into industrialization as quickly and completely as they had the city dweller.

Thus Russia set out to achieve immediately, through her Great Offensive, two simultaneous aims: military defense and mechanization of agriculture.

Now that the first step in the Offensive has been

finished, and the second step, the second Five Year Plan, has been begun, what has been her success in these and in other aims? And, more important than the facts themselves, what is the significance, to Russia and the world, of this vehement attempt to recast the mold of a civilization and to reconstruct the human personality?

The Offensive has not cooled the Russian ardor for speech-making, but the nature of the speeches, like the subjects with which they deal, has undergone a startling change. The speakers may or may not run true to ancient form and begin with a vitriolic tirade against Western culture, against Trotzky and his followers, against the Right opposition, and against the Socialists in Germany and England. If they do, it is the only bit of oratorical flamboyance they allow themselves. For the rest their speeches are essentially reports and interpretations of existing plans and conditions, very much like the reports of presidents of big corporations or universities, except that invariably the Soviet speeches are much more exhaustive. Statistics are as prominent features of these speeches as are quotations from Marx or Lenin, and the statistics are more than mere tables of figures. They scintillate with a fire that is exciting and captivating. In days when people feel acutely the shortage of dairy foods, meats, manufactured goods, emphasis on figures or statistical accomplishments are especially welcome. They convey a sense of triumph and hold forth promise of happier times. They are to the Russians what football scores or results of any athletic event are to lovers of sports, or what stock-exchange reports are to gamblers in stocks, and sometimes what pulse and temperature of patient are to nurse and physician. They pulsate with hope and triumph, also with anxiety and panic.

There lies before me a set of recent speeches by outstanding Soviet leaders, and I quote from them the following figures, which speak for themselves. It is well to state here that the Plan was condensed into four years and three months. Originally it called for the building of only 12,600 railroad cars in its last year. Actually, in 1931—the third year of the Plan—20,000 cars were built. In the output of tractors, the Plan has done well, having lifted production in 1931 to 40,000 units. Only 825 locomotives were supposed to be turned out in the last year of the Plan, but as early as 1931, 812 rolled out of the factories. In 1913, Russia manufactured in factories 17 million pairs of shoes, but in 1931 the figure rose to 76.8 million pairs, exceeding the schedule for the last year of the Plan by 16.7 millions. In 1913, Russia manufactured 27 million pairs of rubbers; in 1931 the number had grown to 63.9 millions, or 2.9 millions more than the last year of the Plan was supposed to yield. In 1913, Russia manufactured 94,000 tons of soap; in 1931, she manufactured 189,000 tons (and yet the demand far exceeds the supply). In oil production in 1931 Russia marched far ahead of the Plan and became second only to the United States. In machine-building she is fast approaching second place, and in the manufacture of agricultural machinery she is rapidly moving toward first. Since that was one of her chief immediate aims, the array of figures is especially significant. During the period of the first Plan, Russia turned out from her own factories the following implements:

105,800	tractors
13,690	combines
62,400	tractor threshing-machines
173,650	tractor ploughs
3,229,150	horse-drawn ploughs
103,960	tractor grain-drills
501,730	horse-drawn grain-drills
37,500	binders for tractors and horses
29,520	tractor mowing-machines
9,330	beet diggers
15,370	flax gins
56,550	horse-drawn threshing-machines
3,340	cotton-picking machines
7,000	potato diggers
9,600	potato planters

According to Soviet reports, Russia also manufactured manure-spreaders, hay-rakes, cotton-drills, corn-harvesters, corn-crushers, flax-drills, hay-loaders, silo-cutters. All of these machines, as well as tractors and combines, Russia had never before produced on her own soil. In addition to the above machines, Russia had built, in the first three years of the Plan, 402 grain elevators.

The most striking revolution, statistically of course, has occurred in agriculture. Originally the first Plan called for the collectivization of only one-fifth of the present holdings; in reality three-fifths of them were collectivized, and the lands of these, together with those of the state farms, now embrace four-fifths of all the land under cultivation in Russia. In other words, only 20 per cent of the land is now being held by individual farmers.

But these triumphs, even in terms of statistics, tell only a part of the story. With the exception of the manufacture of agricultural implements, they apply chiefly to the first three years of the Plan, years of extraordinary effort. Since then there has been a slackening in the rates of growth, though construction and development have gone on with unabated energy. Let the reader bear in mind the importance of heavy industry in any program of national development, for it is heavy industry that serves as a base for all other industry. Here the Plan, at its finish, has fallen short of its intended mark. Coal, pig-iron, steel, and rolled steel are the four mainstays of heavy industry. This is what has happened to their output:

Coal.—The original Plan for 1931 was for 53 million tons. The "control," or revised figures, raised it to 83 million tons. The actual amount mined was 59 million tons. For 1932 the original schedule was for 75 million tons. The control figures boosted it to 90 million tons. Actually, during the first nine months of 1932, only 47 million tons were mined; and by the end of the year the total was 64 million tons, much less than even the original Plan called for. (Yet it is well to remember that in 1913 only 28.9 million tons were obtained.)

Pig-Iron.—The original schedule called for 10 million tons in 1932, but the control figures reduced it to 9 million tons. Actually 6 million tons were produced for the year.

Rolled Steel.—The original schedule called for an

output of 8 million tons. The control figures for 1932 reduced it to 6.7 million tons. Actually 4.25 million tons were produced.

Steel.—The original Plan called for an output this year of 10.4 million tons. The control figures for 1932 cut it to 9.5 million tons. Actually only 5.8 million tons will be found to have been produced.

Since coal, iron, and steel are the materials most needed in industry, a drop in their output must result in a slump along a good part of the line of ready-made machines. This is felt most severely by the automobile industry. Lack of sufficient steel is one reason, though by no means the only one, for the failure to fulfil the original requirement, which called for 130,000 cars in the final year of the Plan, or to realize the last "control" figures, which reduced the number to 75,000. Nizhni Novgorod, which is the seat of the new Ford factory, was supposed to produce, in 1932, 30,000 machines; but, owing to a variety of circumstances, among them insufficiency of steel, turned out in the last eight months only 2,400 cars. The combined output of all the factories in Russia for 1932 was 26,700 automobiles.

It is well to remember that actual production of automobiles did not begin until the latter part of October, 1931. (In 1930, Russia made hardly any cars—she assembled only 8,550 of them.) At present the Amo automobile factory in Moscow and the Nizhni Novgorod plant each turns out 65 cars daily. A third factory in Yaroslavl has likewise begun operations and is manufacturing five-ton trucks. And so, while neither the original schedule of the Plan nor the revised figures has been fulfilled, Russia at the end of the Five Year

Plan does find herself in possession of an automobile industry, with three huge factories, built and equipped in the best modern manner, kept continually at work. She has been more fortunate in the tractor than in the automobile industry. In 1927-28 only 1,279 tractors were manufactured. The Five Year Plan called for the manufacture of 91,000 units. Actually 105,850 units were turned out.

The reasons for the slump in the final period of the Five Year Plan are many and varied, the chief ones being lack of competent labor, bureaucracy, poor transportation, absence of adequate supplies, and—most important of all—the world financial crisis, and the depression of the standard of living. The world crisis had cut deeply into Russia's income of *valuta*, or foreign money. This in turn necessitated a reduction in imports of machinery and in the hiring of foreign experts, and simultaneously an increase in exports. The Russians had their financial obligations to meet, and if they could not get as much for grain as they had thought they would at the time they assumed these obligations, before the crash in world prices, they had to make up the loss by an increase in the export of grain.

What was true of grain was true of lumber, meat, butter, sugar, and a host of commodities for which they could find a market in foreign lands. In 1931 and 1932, Russian butter, eggs, cheese, wine, caviar, sometimes meat, could be bought in Berlin, London, and other European cities in unlimited quantities, but not in Russia. In spite of an acute shortage of animal fats at home, Russia continued to export these foods because she would not default her payments abroad. Harsh as this procedure may seem, the Russians reasoned simply enough that it was more important for them to forego the consumption for the time being of certain foods and other commodities, than to invoke distrust and eventual boycott of foreign industrialists and financiers. They would do everything to continue building up industry, for without it they could not hope to carry out their ambitious social program and—what to them was a more immediately pressing need—build up their national defenses. Anything rather than weaken the country's military powers and invite danger of overthrow from without.

Yet Russian workers, with all their class consciousness, are still human beings. If they hear that at a certain place there is more meat and sugar and tobacco than in the factory in which they are working, they pack up and move. Hence the colossal turnover of labor in industry. With all their propaganda and discipline, the Communists have been unable to check this disrupting force in the factories. In Stalingrad and in Kharkov, in the tractor factories, workers come, receive training, and then disappear, and new workers have to be trained anew, consuming precious time of foremen and skilled mechanics and thereby slackening output. At a conservative estimate the turnover of labor in these two plants was at least 25 per cent in the final year of the first Five Year Plan. In the Don coal basin it has become a chronic affliction. According to the *Pravda* of October 16, 1932, in a group of metal factories in the Urals, which employ 61,000 men, 206,000 workers have had to be hired in the past three years, and 203,000 have left their work-benches. Again and again the Russian newspapers print devastating reports of the turnover of labor in industry, and the principal reasons for it are inferior living conditions and the ordinary human urge to go where these can be bettered.

The constant shift of labor from place to place has been one of the chief causes of the failure of Russian industry to lift productivity to the level prescribed by the Offensive. This in turn has contributed to another drawback in Russian industry, the lowering of cost of production. Molotov, the Soviet Premier, devoted most of his speech at the Communist Congress in January, 1933, to a discussion of these shortcomings in Russian industry and methods for overcoming them. That is one reason why the first year of the second Five Year Plan is being dedicated to a consolidation of gains—tightening of organization and discipline with a view to increasing productivity of labor by 14 per cent, lessening cost of production by 15 per cent, and improving the quality of the output.

Nor can the Russians boast of the high quality of their manufactured goods if they are to be measured by European and American standards. Their tractors do not stand up as well as American tractors. Articles of everyday consumption are notably inferior to those of European or American make. How often has a Russian asked me if I could spare him a toothbrush, saying that his own lost its bristles after it was used a few times! Their shoes, likewise, wear out more easily than in the old days, though their overshoes are among the best in the world.

Recently, on a visit to the city of Kiev, a friend told me that he went into a shop and bought a pair of shoes.

He tried on only one shoe and, since it fitted well, he told the clerk to pack up the pair. On reaching home he discovered that one shoe was longer than the other. He took the shoes back to the store, where the clerk was willing enough to change them, but on investigation it was discovered that there were one hundred pairs in stock of the size which my friend had bought and in every one of them one shoe was larger than the other! This incident, of course, is not typical of the whole shoe industry, but it is indicative of lax management somewhere. Nor is the shoe industry the only one that suffers from extreme incompetence.

Consider this evidence of confusion: there are four cities, Kolomensk, Bryansk, Lugansk, Kharkov, all of which manufacture locomotives of the same model, size, shape, and weight (96.5 tons). Yet the Lugansk factory uses for each locomotive 130 tons of metal; the Kolomensk, 125 tons; the Kharkov, 117 tons; and the Bryansk, 127.

Consider also the following: In the *Pravda* of July 24, 1932, there is a letter from Grozny, Russia's booming oil town in the south. The writer says that the Palace of Labor in that city was put up at a cost of millions of roubles, and yet only a year after it was finished it needed major repairs. For one thing, the lavatories had no provision for ventilation. After rain the mud around the palace was so deep that it was impossible to get up to the building. Likewise, a workers' club which was put up in the town did not have a single lavatory, and the new dormitories that were built for workers failed to admit adequate sunlight. Hardly a day passes but letters telling of similar things appear in the leading

Russian newspapers. Writers all over the country report such failings at length, and the Press everywhere prints these reports, grieves over them, and roundly scolds the leaders and organizations that have allowed carelessness and incompetence to get the best of them.

It is easy to point out the deficiencies in the industrial organization of Russia. One does not have to search for them; they are on the surface and open to anyone who wants to see them. Foremen, workers, editors, Communist leaders, and commissars never tire of denouncing them. In the light of these shortcomings the Soviet aim of "catching up with," not to say "outstripping," capitalist nations in production seems for the present at least a mere chimera. It will require many a Five Year Plan to discipline the Russian industrial machine so that it will function as harmoniously and as bountifully as the American or English industrial machines. As for service, anyone who has tried to buy apples or soap in a Russian store, or has lived in a Russian hotel, or has eaten in a Russian restaurant, knows only too well how vast is the distance which Russia must traverse before she is even within sight of the achievement of capitalist nations. She has not yet begun to understand the elementary principles of service.

But then, five years is a short space of time, and, when one remembers this, one marvels not at obvious shortcomings but at outstanding achievements that are all the more remarkable in view of such drawbacks as the backwardness of the Russian people, their lack of experienced technicians, the comparative absence of credits from abroad, the clash with the Chinese in Manchuria in 1929, when they attempted to seize the

Chinese Eastern Railroad, the constant dread of war in the West and in the East, and, most important of all, the general shortage of sugar and animal fats.

The first Five Year Plan has given Russia a metal industry which she never had before, together with a wholly new coal and iron center in the Urals and in Siberia. It has given her an automobile and tractor industry, and a tool and machine-building industry which mark such advances over the past that they may be called new, and which make it possible for her to manufacture for the first time in history her own equipment for electrical and metallurgical industries. It has given her a network of shops for the manufacture of agricultural implements, and a new chemical industry with plants scattered all the way from the south to the arctic circle. It has given her an aviation industry with factories in Moscow, in Nizhni Novgorod, in Voronezh, and in Siberia. It has expanded her textile industry so that it is no longer centered in the north in the Moscow region, but has reached out to eastern Siberia, Central Asia, and the Muggan steppes on the Persian border. It has given her fifteen hundred new plants, some small and some as large as any in the world. The story of the industrial development of the Urals (which may some day challenge comparison with the Ruhr) and of Siberia reads like a heroic epic. Indeed, this struggle for a new industrial machine has changed the very face of Russia, has converted her into a land of steel and iron and motors and engines and smokestacks and aeroplanes. Though still very vaguely planned, the second step in Russia's Great Offensive proposes to carry on the work of the first in an ambitious manner. It proposes to increase electrical power six times, machine-building three and a half times, coal production two and a half times, automobile manufacturing at least ten times, and also to treble the output of commodities. These are sweeping aims, and even if pitched so high that they must inevitably fall short of full realization, they are symbolic of a will and an energy to push on with the fight.

That is one reason why a statistical approach to this Offensive tells so little of its importance for Russia and for the world. The failure to achieve scheduled production in heavy industry is, in my opinion, not nearly as telling as the fact that Russia has achieved a heavy industry, which, however badly manned at present, is in its equipment comparable to the best in the world. The offensive in terms of statistical formulas is one thing, and is quite another as a symbol of a new age and a guide to a new destiny.

Consider what all this has meant to Russia in military defense. I happened to be in Russia on November 7, 1932, and attended the celebration of the fifteenth anniversary of the Revolution. The Red Square was packed with thousands of soldiers all grouped in military formations. It was a dim day with clouded skies, but the square was bright with the multitudes of gray uniforms. The parade began with unit after unit of soldiers—well clothed, well drilled, with perfect poise—passing by in review before Lenin mausoleum on the top of which had gathered the small group of men who rule the country: Stalin, Bukharin, Kuibiyshev, Kalinin, Kaganovitch, Ordzhonokidse, Voroshilov, and a few lesser satellites. In their slovenly attire and in their caps

—not one of them wore a hat—they were a dismal contrast to the magnificently dressed soldiers and officers parading before them with dignity, rhythm, and vigor—infantry in gleaming helmets, their guns thrust forward, their bayonets fixed; cavalry mounted on high-spirited horses; artillery with rattling carts and bulging guns. Then from near-by streets there rose a roaring clatter and fleets of tanks, following along in as rhythmic formation as the columns of soldiers, rumbled over the square—little tanks and big tanks, slow-moving and speeding at forty miles an hour; caterpillar tanks and eight-wheeled tanks; tanks with chauffeurs visible and tanks rolling along like mechanical monsters, their drivers hidden within; tanks with small guns and tanks with big guns sticking out of their sides like quills on a porcupine.

And even as the tanks were thundering past the mausoleum, high overhead sounded another roar as squadron after squadron of aeroplanes, likewise lined up in magnificent formations, came swooping over the square. In watching this parade, the most impressive demonstration of military defense that has yet been publicly witnessed in Moscow, one got an impression of tremendous power.

Indeed, with her tractor and aeroplane shops, and her automobile plants and her far-flung and rapidly expanding chemical factories and her man-power of many millions, Russia is on the way to becoming a formidable military figure. "We are manufacturing our own aeroplanes," exclaimed Kaganovitch in a speech printed in the *Pravda* of February 19, 1933, "our own tanks, armored cars, artillery, etc. Having fulfilled the

Five Year Plan in four years, we have, *tovarishchi*, added to our Budenny cavalry (horse cavalry) a technical cavalry, a flying cavalry, a crawling cavalry, a swimming cavalry, a diving cavalry."

True enough, Russia renounces war. At the Disarmament Conference in Geneva, she has repeatedly declared herself ready to scrap her armament if the other nations would do likewise. There is nothing she dreads more now than war, for nothing would so seriously interfere with her plans of social and national reconstruction. But she will not be caught unawares. Rightly or wrongly, she feels herself isolated and disliked. Whether she deserves to be disliked is beside the point. The fact is that she is conscious of isolation and dislike, and, with dictatorship rampant in Europe, with Nazi leaders openly boasting that they hope to conquer and colonize some of her richest territories, and with Japan spreading her legions of war through Manchuria and other parts of China, she feels all the more keenly the need of maintaining military vigilance on all of her far-reaching frontiers. Unless the world will come to terms with her on disarmament she will not lessen but will intensify her efforts to strengthen her military forces.

III
MACHINES

THE HUMAN EFFECTS

VIEWED as a symbol of a new age the Great Offensive has made Russia predominantly an industrial nation. Of course agriculture plays a leading part in Russian national economy, but it is second in value of output to industry. In 1928 industry provided 48 per cent of the nation's output of goods, and in 1932 this percentage leaped to 70. Henceforth, in spite of all mistakes and shortcomings in industrial production, the world must regard Russia as an industrial and not primarily an agricultural country.

Behind Russia's enormously increased industrialization is her machine-building. In the old days the machines which Russia built were limited in number, and the best ones came largely from factories owned by foreigners, British, French, American, Belgian, and German. So limited was the output of these plants that as late as 1913 Russia imported, chiefly from Germany, nearly one-half of her ploughs, even the light ones which peasants worked with one horse or one cow.

Until the Five Year Plan was in operation, Russia had never made any turbines, tractors, combines, or die- and gear-cutters. Now, for the first time in her history, she is making these and a host of other complicated machines. She still is importing foreign machines and if more credit were extended would import much more. But she is no longer helpless without foreign machines. It is true that she often makes them badly—with parts missing, or not fitting well, or breaking easily; but, after all, she is still new and inexperienced at the task. It is true also that she is still untrained in the task of tending the machine. As Dr. Alcan Hirsh, American chief consulting engineer to the Soviet chemical industry, has so often said to Russian political and industrial leaders: "The machine has no class consciousness. It does not care whether it is handled by a capitalist or a Communist. It wants decent handling. If it does not get it, it goes on strike against the Communist as quickly as against the capitalist." There is no lesson that the Russian leaders and workers need so much to learn as the one embodied in these words. They have been so eager to make records, to exceed scheduled programs, and to have an excuse for boasting that they are "catching up with and outstripping capitalist countries," that they have sacrificed quality to volume in the making of the machine, speed to caution in its handling.

Yet, even with these shortcomings, they have reached a point of independence at which, if necessary, they could continue their internal development with their own mechanical resources. It will not be as easy as some of Russia's political leaders imagine, but it is infinitely easier now than it ever has been in Russian history. In fact the old Russia could never have done it. Prior to the days of her Offensive, a war, a blockade, or an international boycott would have been disastrous. It still could cause serious trouble, but at worst it would only hamper, not halt, further industrial growth. If she were engaged in a war today, Russia could manufacture practically all her own armaments including chemicals.

Of even more dramatic significance is the fact that this Offensive has wiped out nearly all individual enterprise. All industry, all wholesale trade, all retail trade, with the exception of the bazaars, are under the iron rule of the Soviet State. Never before in history have such gigantic enterprises been built and exploited by governments. It was not easy to smash private enterprise, even in the land of the Soviets, where there was so much less of it proportionately than in any other modern nation. It required no small measure of ruthlessness and audacity. Visitors to Russia in the years 1929 and 1930 who mingled with Russians must still carry poignant memories of the arrests, evictions, and confiscation of the property of shopkeepers and other private enterprisers. Without officially liquidating *Nep*, the government proceeded systematically and mercilessly to liquidate the *nepman* and his properties. It resorted to every legal pretext its finance inspectors could conjure up to achieve this liquidation. It imposed back taxes on shopkeepers, accused them of violating certain laws and of engaging in exploitation. It rolled up income-tax figures in excess of gross incomes, knowing beforehand that the *nepmen* could not pay them. It did this merely as an excuse to confiscate properties in shops and homes and often enough to exile the owners or put them under arrest.

But whatever the methods and the motives of the Soviet government, now private enterprise is gone. Except for the bazaars there is none left in all Russia. I do not know of a single privately owned restaurant or hotel or book shop anywhere in the country. The government is supreme master of all economic enterprise unless one includes in this classification the 35 per cent of the peasants who still cling to private tillage of land. But these are subject to such stern discipline that they constantly find themselves compelled to fit their chief transactions into the Soviet National Plan.

The recent decree allowing individual peasants and collectivized farmers and handicraftsmen to sell in the open market does not seriously interfere with the purposes of the new offensive. It is stated specifically in these decrees that the transactions are to be between producer and consumer. The middleman is barred. With the abolition of grain collections and the levy of a grain tax on the peasant, bazaar trade, at least for the time being, is destined to expand. The peasant will have more to sell. No doubt there will be adventurous souls who will seek to circumvent the laws and buy and sell at a secret profit. But they know that, if discovered, they will be dealt with mercilessly. Agents are at all bazaars watching sharply for such vendors, and so harsh is the prevailing official hatred of private trade that the laws against speculation are sure to be invoked in all their severity against any offender who may be apprehended.

Whether or not a nation's economic development can proceed as well or better under the Russian scheme of state control is a question which only time can answer. But for the Russians there is no road back, so long as Soviet Russia remains Soviet. Individualist enterprise, in my judgment, will return, if at all, only in the event of foreign conquest of Russia in war, or after an internal crash which will allow Russia's individualist neighbors to divide and absorb her territories and impose private business. Even then this could be achieved only through frightful human slaughter, for neither the worker nor the new youth would yield to such a change without desperate resistance.

The fact is that the very desire for individual enterprise has become paralyzed and atrophied. In speaking to Russians who in the old days conducted shops of their own under the Czar and under the *Nep* one hears vociferous criticism of the manner in which the state is conducting its business. The government certainly has as yet been unable to organize trade on a basis even remotely approximating the efficiency of private enterprise in old Russia or in other lands. In striking testimony to this fact are the ever-present queues. One can understand why there would be queues in places where there is a shortage of commodities—in meat shops, milk stores, pastry bakeries. But one can see no excuse except plain inefficiency for queues in the post offices. There certainly is no shortage of postage stamps or registry receipts. Yet all too often the simple matter of buying postage stamps in a Russian city, or sending off a registered letter, becomes an ordeal. Nor can one understand the reason for the queues at the so-called *Torgsin* stores, where the best foods, textiles, and other consumption goods are sold on a gold basis. There are seldom shortages in such places; yet, whether at the fruit stands, meat counters, or in the textile department, one sees everywhere these dismal queues. The time that people waste and the discomfort that they endure!

People grumble vociferously at the slow and wasteful methods of service. But even such people, especially if they were once in business for themselves, have lost all desire of returning to it. They know only too well that as long as Russia is Soviet they will be outcasts and pariahs. They will be hated, ostracized, repressed. If they were given a chance to resume private enterprise they would shrink from it with horror. They know the confusion and despair of "liquidation" and they would not care to run the chance of going through it again. Only the rare kind of adventurer who lives for the moment and cares nothing for the future might respond to the bait if it were once more thrust forward. But those latter are scarce. Many former business men have already recovered their citizenship. A good many more are on probation and are on the road to enfranchisement. At last they have regained or are about to regain self-respect, not only for themselves but for their children, and they would be horrified at having to lose it again, which they would if they returned to private trade. "Never for all the gold I might gather," exclaimed a builder of mansions in the old days.

As for the young generation, there is nothing that it so profoundly despises as private enterprise. I have yet to meet a university student who would not regard it an insult if he were advised to embark on a business or a professional career of his own. Nothing is more remote from his mind. With the very air he has been breathing he has imbibed the idea that no sin a man may commit, no disgrace he may bring upon himself, is as sinister as "exploitation" or private business. No inducements, however promising, could lure him into it. "Wouldn't you really enjoy having a private practice of your own?" I asked once a group of medical students. They laughed me to scorn. They plainly regarded it as tantamount to bringing back the old civilization with all its evils.

"How many men does your father employ in his factories?" a Russian college girl once asked an American girl whose father was a well-known manufacturer in an eastern state. "About 40,000," responded the American girl. Thereupon the Russian girl exclaimed: "And aren't you ashamed of having a father like that?" To her, reared in an atmosphere of loathing for all private enterprise, it seemed that a person who had as many men in his employ as this girl's father had sunk to the lowest depth of degradation.

If the Soviets were to fall today, the one idea that would be sure to survive them is that of national planning. It is not an original idea with them: the whole Marxian concept of economics presupposes above all else balance between production and consumption. But they have given the idea color and drama. They have endowed it with a fresh importance and a new hope. Hoover, with all his hatred of "Bolshevism," was once moved to speak of a "twenty-five-year plan" for America. Hitler, with all his phobia against Communism, proposed, on his ascension to power, the inauguration of two four-year plans for Germany. Not an economist or industrialist of note but has pondered over its meaning and possibilities. Not a diplomat or statesman but has taken it to heart. Meanwhile, the idea of national planning has had far-reaching effects on the mind of the Russian people.

In the first year of the Plan I was visiting a collective farm in the province of Tambov. The name of the farm was "Friendship," and an appropriate name it was, for everything on the place, from the far-stretching orchard and winding stream to the sweep of forest and the rolling meadows, spoke of cheer and comfort.

A group of Pioneers, boys and girls from a near-by city, were spending their vacation there. One evening they built a bonfire and gave a public celebration in honor of the Five Year Plan. Peasants from near-by villages came by hundreds to attend the event. It was an impressive occasion. The fire blazed and crackled and shot tongues of flame into the dark, and the Pioneers in couples and in groups, all barefooted and in tight-fitting gymnasium costumes, sang and danced and gave recitations expressive of the ideas and purposes of the Plan. Before each act the leader would announce what it was about: pumping oil in Baku, hewing coal in Donbas, rolling steel in Leningrad, operating power stations in Siberia and in southern Ukraine. Whatever the audience might have thought of the Five Year Plan, there was no denying that it enjoyed immensely the performances of these children in the open field. Simultaneously it gained a vivid if incomplete conception of at least one thing—the nationwide sweep of the Plan.

And this is most significant. It has deepened Russia's national consciousness. There is not a peasant in the country who has not heard of Magnitogorsk or Dneprostroy or the Stalingrad and Kharkov tractor plants or any of the other outstanding industrial enterprises. Disappointed as he may be with the results of the Plan in so far as it has failed materially to improve his personal condition, he nevertheless is conscious of a new effort and a new movement in the country—the attempt to knit it together with rail and wires and all else that the modern machines make possible.

When any single enterprise is finished it becomes a matter not only of local but also of national importance. The opening of Dneprostroy was signalized by the presence of delegations from all over the country; and by meetings, concerts, lectures, above all dramatic performances, likewise all over the country. Indeed, the idea of planning is intensifying a newly developed national consciousness and is, in the rising generation, stirring up a spirit of patriotism which Russia has never known. True enough the Bolsheviks abjure patriotism. They regard it as a bourgeois vice, an emotion whipped up falsely by the bourgeoisie to fool the masses into fighting for them. But they certainly are whipping up a similar emotion in Russia. At least it is everywhere present. The difference, from their point of view, is this: in Russia the emotion is dedicated to a holy end and they don't call it patriotism; and in bourgeois countries to an ignominious purpose, and they do call it patriotism.

The Plan has also wrought a real transformation in the Russian attitude toward the machine. The outgrowth of this attitude must be traced back to the early part of the Revolution, when the machine was already spoken of as a conquering hero. But the Five Year Plan and the bringing of vast supplies of foreign machines and the building of hosts of them at home have crystallized and solidified it.

In the old days Russia scorned the machine. The old government was afraid of it. The machine stirred new wants, new ideas, new dissatisfactions. It held within it the seed of death to autocracy. The landed gentry likewise had only contempt for it. The machine was a dirty thing, vulgar and grinding, and interfered with the ease and grace of living. The rising industrialists in the country wished for the development of mechanization, but they had not the social standing of the landed gentry nor their political power.

As if to give moral support to the prevalent contempt for the machine in good society, Tolstoi, like Gandhi of today, denounced it as a distorter of human values, as a perverter of human emotions. The machine, he shouted, had made men greedy, hard, and vicious, and was a weapon of torture and death.

The peasant likewise had a whole-hearted contempt for it. It was something alien and brutal, out of tune with his daily work and his daily life. What Russian has not thrilled to the folk song *Dubinushka* in which the peasant makes merry sport of the Englishman who when confronted with a task beyond his powers proceeds to invent a machine to perform it for him, while the *muzhik* in a similar predicament merely bursts into song?

The coming of the Revolution, and especially the

Five Year Plan, completely reversed this attitude. The whole scheme of reform which Sovietism and the Five Year Plan embody—the reconstruction of the nation's economic life and the remaking of the human personality—is rooted in the triumph of the machine. And so it has come to pass that the machine has become an object of reverence in Russia. All former objects of reverence—religion, private possessions, the home—have lost or are losing their appeal. But the machine stands out as an object of ever-growing veneration, the great miracle and the great deliverer of the mass.

Intimate knowledge of the machine and continuous contact with it are changing the Russian mind. Since the beginning of the Five Year Plan ten million people, men and women, chiefly from the villages, have been drawn into industry. Schools are springing up by hundreds all over the country, especially devoted to educating students in the use of the machine. Millions of books, posters, pamphlets, and charts are pouring out of the presses to help along in the process. All Russian public schools since the coming of the Plan have been polytechnicalized, and are known as labor schools. In all of them manual training, locksmithery, foundry, and machine-shop work are compulsory. The study periods in the schools are supplemented by visits and a certain amount of actual work in neighboring plants. All this is done to develop workers for the factories. But this process is transforming the Russian mind, making it more disciplined, more sophisticated, more restless. The peasant or the woman who has been in contact with the machine will never again be the same as before.

The mere word "Plan" suggests a new approach for everybody to the problem of living. Hitherto man as an individual may have focused his ambitions, tastes, ideals, upon a well-conceived personal plan, but in the aggregate as a nation he was willing enough to follow a policy of *laissez-faire*. He was guided by immediate needs and was scheming in the best way he could for the perpetuation of the prevailing order of things. His "I" was his kingdom. Everything might begin and end with his "I."

The Plan puts an end to all this. It envisages the recasting of society into a new mold. Man's "I" is no longer the center of things. It is an organic part of the aggregate—or, as the Russians say, of the mass. In the basic things of life the individual cannot sunder himself from the mass without inviting disaster and even destruction. In the chief calculations of the government it is the mass that counts, and everything that man as an individual needs—from bread to shoes, from books to headache powders, from museums to theaters, from automobiles to highways—comes to him by the grace and the force of the Plan for the mass. He may cherish whatever ambitions he chooses, indulge in whatever joys, cut whatever capers he likes, so long as these are not in conflict with the basic interests of the mass. If he wants more shoes than his neighbor, cares to visit a theater more often, prefers red neckties and brown shirts, no one will stop him provided his earning capacity permits the enjoyment of these things and the supply of goods planned for the nation make these available for him.

That is why the idea of planning has assumed such

momentum in Russia. The Plan is the life-blood of everything and everybody. Everything you do is part of the Plan. You dig a ditch, you plant potatoes, you heave bricks, you blast rock, you study medicine—it is all part of the Plan; you buy shoes, you decorate a house with pictures, you install a telephone, you eat canned tomatoes—it is all the result of the Plan. "Nurseries," reads an announcement on a poster in a village kindergarten, "should be put to the service of the Plan," and lower down on the poster comes the explanation of the meaning of these words: "By keeping the children in the nurseries, mothers can make their full contribution to the fulfilment of the social program of the Five Year Plan."

No wonder Russia is so Plan-conscious, and no wonder that the Plan has become the great idea, the great purpose, and the great passion of the young. There is no schoolhouse, co-operative farm, or factory that has not a plan of its own which fits into some other plan and which, like a rivulet that flows into a river on its way to the ocean, does not in the end become part of the one Plan. I have seen dances and songs and games and plays that center in the idea and the emotion of the Plan. Indeed, the Plan has become an incentive and a triumph. It supplies a stimulus that is not unlike that of private profit in an individualistic society.

It has done more. It has helped immensely in the process of energizing the Russian masses. Sadly enough did they need such energizing, for laxity is one of the legacies that the old order had bequeathed to the Revolution.

Some years ago Mr. E. J. Dillon, who had lived long

in Russia, wrote a book under the title "Russian Traits." It is an incisive study of the weaknesses in Russian character. Suggestive enough are the titles of the opening chapters, which are: "Lying," "Fatalism," "Sloth," "Dishonesty." Two sentences culled at random are even more revealing: "This combination of fatalism, with paralysis, indifference and grovelling instincts gives us a clue to the marvelous endurance of the masses, whose mode of life is at times more bleak, cheerless and less human than that of the grazing monks of Mesopotamia described by Sozome, whose sufferings were at least the result of choice." And again: "The extent to which fatalism, shiftlessness with all the other vices of which they are the source, have eaten into the Russian character can with difficulty be realized by those whose knowledge of the people is not derived from personal experience." Yet a number of years later when Paul Milyukov was visiting Harvard University and the Russian professor of literature there asked him which book on Russia in English he regarded as the best, Milyukov replied: "Dillon's 'Russian Traits'." This reply illustrates the tendency of old time Russian intellectuals not only to recognize but to magnify the weaknesses of their people. Russian literature groans with the burden of these weaknesses. Turgenev in his novel "On the Eve," wishing to portray a character with capacity to act promptly and effectively, selects a Bulgarian. The heroine of the novel in speaking of this Bulgarian in a letter to a friend says: "When he speaks of his fatherland he grows and grows, and his face becomes handsome and his voice is like steel, and it seems as though there were not a man in the world before whom he would lower his eyes, and he not only talks, he acts and acts." And again: "Here at last is an upright man, here is someone on whom I can rely. This man does not lie, all the rest lie continually." In much of the old Russian literature from Pushkin to Chekhov the outstanding characters are chiefly dreamers, idlers, talkers, who often go to their doom because of a lack of talent to act properly and decisively.

The coming of the machine to Russia had begun to develop a tougher breed of man, and such writers as Gorky and even Chekhov have given us full and fitting portraits of this man. Yet to this day idleness and lassitude are pronounced features in the character of vast groups of Russians, and because of this a school of scientists in America are of the opinion that Russians are foredoomed to such traits because of the geography of the country. Professor Elsworth Huntington of Yale University has written at length on this subject. Speaking of the Russian peasants he says that "they are inert, submissive and unenterprising" and in answer to the question as to what has made them so he says: "Passivity, dreaminess, lack of initiative, docility, carelessness of detail and the tendency to put off until tomorrow appear to be Russian characteristics closely connected with the long, cold, monotonous workless winters."

It is only too true that masses of Russian peasants have lived a life of enforced idleness in winter and that this has had a vitiating effect on their mentality. One can find evidence of it at every step in the Russian village. "Why don't you join a collective farm," I once asked a peasant who lived in a squalid hut in the province of Tambov. "Why should I?" he replied defiantly. "Having my own land I work it as I please in summer, and in winter when cold comes, I just lie on the top of the oven and spit at the ceiling. But on a collective farm I couldn't do that—I'd have to work all the time." I would not pick this man as typical of the Russian peasant, but there is no doubt that one reason so many peasants frown on collectivization is because it implies discipline and regularity of work in summer and winter.

And yet the exceptions to the tendency to passivity and idleness are so many and so pronounced, especially nowadays, that one cannot help distrusting Professor Huntington's theory. Surely Siberia would fall within Professor Huntington's climatic zone and yet the Siberian peasant is noted for his energy, his decisiveness, his spirit of adventure. Besides, even in the old days thousands of young men from the villages would in winter scatter over the forests, the lakes, the factories—and work. Certainly the Russian peasant woman is noted for her industriousness. There never was a more hard working woman than she. In winter she not only does the housework and attends to chores in the barns, but devotes her spare hours to weaving and spinning.

And what of the seven million Jews and six million Germans who had lived in Russia for generations? Whatever their failings no one would ever accuse them of idleness and lassitude. Then there is the *koolack*. Several years ago Eisenstein, the Russian motion picture director, after long and arduous work, released a picture on collectivization. One of the villains was a *koolack*, and what a monster he was—fat, lazy, gluttonous, brutal, as scummy a creature as ever trod this earth. Of course in real life one hardly finds such creatures, not even in Russia. The *koolack* may at times have been cruel in his treatment of the poorer peasants, but he never was the fat, lazy, gluttonous monster that Eisenstein depicts him. But then, in a motion picture anything is possible, even in Russia, especially if propaganda and not truthfulness to life is the sole purpose. In real life the *koolack* was among the hardest working, the thriftiest and most progressive farmers in the village. It was he who would always cry out to the *bedniak*: "If you worked as hard as I do you too would be prosperous." He was a prodigious indefatigable worker.

Now if the Russian climate is supposed to sap energy out of human beings and make them shiftless and unreliable, how then can one explain such a phenomenon as the *koolack*? As late as 1928 there were, according to Soviet figures, over one million of them.

An inquiry addressed to Viljahlmur Steffansson, the noted explorer, on this subject has elicited from him the following reply:

"As to evidence, reasoning and conclusions the Huntington statement is so different from my experience and views that I yielded to the temptation of beginning what is already an extensive and promises to be a long correspondence with educators, officials, and general residents of those parts of Canada which have the type of winter climate which Huntington believes so inimical to Russo-Siberia. Later I hope for an extensive publication of the results but as yet I can report on only one class of evidence, that which has come in from a questionnaire sent by General MacBrien, Commissioner of the R.C.M.P., to (I believe) all those commissioned officers who are now within easy reach of the mails and who have been stationed for one or more full winters in the debated climate.

"Two replies accord in general with the Huntington view—they report what he reports, reason as he does and conclude with him. Nine officers are opposed with similar emphasis. No one questioned takes a middle ground. Both of those for and most of those against claim to speak not for themselves but for most or all others who have been similarly placed.

"I do not quote the pro-Huntington letters since they are in effect a paraphrase of him. As typical of the anti-Huntington letters I select that of an inspector who has been stationed under the climate allegedly conducive to the Huntington Effect for four years and who incidentally has served one year of that time farther north than any other commentator on the Huntington views. He says in part:

" 'I did not find it depressing during the cold dry period, i.e., in the month of February, after the sun had become reasonably high. On the contrary, I noticed the temperature at this time had a most exhilarating effect.' "

Professor Huntington himself supplies an explanation about Canada. "Why," says he, "has not a similar climate produced a similar result in Canada? It has to a certain degree among the French Canadians, but there are two great differences between Canada and Russia even if we eliminate race. One is that the cultural level of the Canadians is so high that they do not suffer from idleness in any such degree as the Russians, and in the second place, the Canadian climate is far better than that of Russia because it is much more stormy. This sounds absurd to many people, but variability of weather from day to day is one of the important factors in promoting health and activity. It so happens that the coldest agricultural region of North America is one of the parts of the earth's surface where cyclonic storms are most frequent, so that the best kind of climatic variability is highly developed. The U.S.S.R. on the contrary, by reason of the size of Asia, is rarely penetrated by cyclonic storms in winter, and the weather is extremely monotonous, or else is broken by rare storms so violent that they do more harm than good." Perhaps he means only what the French called Canada, which we now speak of as Ontario, Quebec and the Maritime Province.

In a subsequent passage Professor Huntington, realizing that exceptions to his theory of the effect of Russian climate on character are too obvious and too flagrant to ignore, and in particular with regard to the women in the Russian villages, softens his judgment with the following words: "But the Russian climate would not be so bad if the *mode of life* were different. This is evident in the Russian women." (Italics are mine.) This, I would add, is also most evident in the Siberian men. The reason for the difference is precisely the one Professor Huntington mentions—difference in the mode of life. The Siberian peasant hunts and fishes and cuts wood in winter. He is always active and does not grow soft and lax as does the average Russo-European peasant. The same is true of the Russian woman. She is never idle. This is also true of the Jews, the Germans, the *koolacks*. They are industrious folk.

But idleness induces inactivity not only in Russia but in other lands regardless of climate. It becomes a habit, and like all habits feeds on itself. When I worked on a farm in northern New York there were about two months in winter when we had little work—nothing but chores—and we used to idle away our time sitting around the stove, reading, playing cards, drinking cider, eating popcorn and apples, and above all talking. The people I worked for were not Russians or other foreigners but sturdy Americans whose ancestors had come to this country so long ago that they did not know the exact year. Yet comparative inactivity during those two months in winter made us all so lax that whenever chore time came around we would watch the clock and postpone our departure to the barn by five minutes and then five more, and sometimes by half an hour. We had lost our zest for work, and we hated to get up from the floor or the chairs around the open fire. But we experienced none of this lassitude during the wood-cutting season. We were ever alert and ready to fell tree after tree and log it home.

Professor Huntington ignores completely the old social background of the Russian peasantry, their poverty, their isolation, their ignorance, and the comparative absence of material or other stimulations which stir man's energies into action. In speaking of the Canadians Professor Huntington advances the theory that in their case the influence of climate has been offset by greater variability in the weather and by a higher cultural level of the population. "They have far more animals to care for, and the men take care of them. The men have to break out the roads and go to the distant villages on errands and the habit of reading is widespread." Saying this Professor Huntington inadvertently admits that it is the social condition and not necessarily climate that determines alertness and industriousness. If the social condition is conducive to activity men are alert and industrious even in a cold dry climate which is supposed to make them lazy, and if the social condition is conducive to inactivity men become lazy even if they live in a climate that is supposed to make them energetic and active.

The Russian peasant had lived in a world that fostered idleness and inactivity. But that world is dead. Whatever the Revolution may or may not have achieved, it has completely changed the peasant's environment. It has brought a higher level of culture to him, so that now he can and does read books and newspapers, and what is equally significant, it has been assiduously prying him out of his ancient habits and his ancient lassitude. The whole of Russia is plastered with posters and banners continually urging people to be more active, more energetic, more productive. I must repeat that the bringing of the machine to the Russian city and country has brought a new driving force in the life of the people —a force that cannot be dodged or defied. What is shock brigadiering, and socialist competition, and stewardship over factories, and schools and farms, and physical culture, and Pioneers and Young Communists, but an earnest and desperate effort to shake the Russian populace into a new attitude toward life and work? Certainly the conditions, including the blunders of the Communist

Party which have resulted in a lowering of the material standard of living, have hampered the efforts to energize the people. But this is something else, which has nothing to do with climate.

And what is true of so-called Russian laziness is true of Russian mechanical inaptitude. There are any number of American engineers who were or are in the employ of the Soviet government who are firmly convinced that it just is not in the Russian to become mechanically minded. There are of course other engineers who are of a contrary opinion. Nevertheless the notion is widespread that it just is not in the Russian to learn to handle tools. Yet one only has to go to any Russian store where toys and embroideries are sold to see how skilful the Russians can be with tools. It seems to me that there is nothing that the Russian cannot fashion with carving knife out of a piece of wood. In the museum of the city of Poltava in the Ukraine there is an extraordinary collection of parts of wagons and ox yokes and the high bows that peasants use in their harnesses on which are carved all manner of delicate and fantastic designs. The Russian peasant is highly skilled with tools, only the tools he has had for ages have been simple and primitive. Now with the advance of the machine he is beginning to handle a new tool—complicated and heavy.

It is the first time in his life that he has had such a tool placed in his hands, and naturally enough he is clumsy with it. He mishandles it. He ruins it. But what reason is there to suppose that in time he will not learn to operate it as skilfully as he now wields his carving knife and buzz-saw and chisel? The experience of

Russian immigrants in American industry alone warrants an optimistic conclusion. In the steel, coal and machine building industries thousands of Russian peasants have learned to work as well as any other people. Under the tutelage of American foremen and mechanics Russian peasants, fresh from their primitive villages, have learned how to operate well complicated and delicate American machines, not only in industry but on the land. Whatever the grievances the Canadian government may have against its Russian doukhobors, who are ordinary peasants, none of its officials will deny that they are among the best farmers in the country. They have cleared wildernesses in Saskatchewan and British Columbia and have converted them into most fertile fields and orchards. Indeed, these doukhobors are noted for their mechanical skill and even Canadian farmers when things go wrong with their machines gladly turn for help to doukhobor blacksmiths and mechanics. If Soviet industry and agriculture had commanded as able teachers as do Russian immigrants in America and in Canada the progress of Russian industry and agriculture would have been far more gratifying.

The Offensive, however, to make Russia a modern nation industrially is slowly breaking down the old inertia and the old lassitude. It is bringing a new discipline and a new appreciation of regularity and promptitude. The Russian is still lax and has a long distance to travel to become the equal of the American or the Canadian in efficiency and alertness, but the Offensive is driving him on and on, at times with a fury that pains and dismays.

Granting however that eventually Russians do become as skilled workers and managers as are Americans and Germans and other so-called mechanically minded people, have they resources enough in the land to enable them in the end to reap satisfying rewards for all the sacrifice that they are now enduring? In view of recent pronouncements of certain American geographers that the paucity of Russia's resources dooms her to perpetual and comparative poverty, it is well to make a survey of these resources.

IV
MACHINES

THE NATURAL RESOURCES

IN THE opening chapter of his illuminating book, "The Northward Course of Empire," Viljahlmur Stefansson recounts the history of man's lack of faith in northern lands. By "northern" here is meant not lands in the extreme north but those lying immediately north of lands already settled and found habitable. The Greeks and Romans regarded the people living north of them as inferior to themselves and as doomed to perpetual inferiority because of the "supposedly hostile climate of the lands of the north." As wise and learned a man as Tacitus expressed the firm belief that no human being would voluntarily choose to live north of the Alps because, as Stefansson says, the climate there was "supposed to be disagreeable, and the soil sterile," a conception which would surely draw guffaws of amusement from modern Frenchmen as well as from anyone who has ever visited France.

The Moors in ancient Spain, Stefansson further informs us, were convinced that the foggy and chilly climate of England was "inimical to high development, and nothing much was expected of such a country and such a people," and "today," adds Stefansson, "there can be found as many people to agree as to disagree with the contention that Britain has for a century been the foremost land on earth." Stefansson instances a man named Robertus Anglicus, a teacher in the university of Montpellier in the 13th century, who was dubbed a visionary because he did not share in the current belief that England was a barren land.

As a more recent and striking example of the tendency of man, even of the wise and the learned, to undervalue the potentialities for civilized living in northern countries, Stefansson cites the peace negotiations between the French and the English on the conclusion of the French and Indian wars. Both the French and the English wished to hold the island of Guadeloupe, because of its economic importance. The French offered the British Canada in the place of this island, but the British refused on the ground that, aside from some furs and codfish on the Newfoundland banks, Canada held forth no promise of substantial wealth. As astute a man as Benjamin Franklin admitted, in a pamphlet which he wrote, that this island was more valuable than Canada, but he advised England's acceptance of Canada because of its proximity to other English possessions. Yet now, how many readers of these lines even know where the island of Guadeloupe is located?

The United States' purchase of Alaska from Russia furnishes another dramatic example of man's innate reluctance to appreciate the possibilities of northern countries. Every boy and girl who has read American history knows how vehemently Secretary Seward and the Republican Party were denounced by the Democrats for this transaction. America paid for Alaska $7,200,000 in gold; and in gold alone America has dug out of that territory at least fifty times as much as its original cost.

The unwillingness of man to see in northern lands anything but a bleak wilderness has abated somewhat with the advent of new discoveries, but it has not yet disappeared. The reasons for its persistence are as numerous as they are intriguing, but this is not the place to examine them. Anyone who wishes to go into the subject further might well read Stefansson's "Northward Course of Empire." It is a brilliant and informing book, and indirectly helps to explain the distrust with which some geographers view Russia's reputed wealth in natural resources. Distrust is rather a mild word, for these geographers deny, on so-called scientific grounds, that Russia has an abundance of such resources and hence they doom her to perpetual impoverishment.

For example, Professor W. Elmer Eckblaw, of Clark University, who has spent four years with the MacMillan expedition in Greenland, and who visited Russia on the occasion of the International Soil Congress in 1930, in speaking of Russia's mineral resources, says: "Russia is relatively deficient in iron, coal, copper, lead, zinc, tin, nickel, nitrates, and sulphur. She has practically inexhaustible stores of manganese, platinum and petroleum." Professor Elsworth Huntington of Yale concurs in Professor Eckblaw's judgment. "Russia's economic situation," he says, "is very precarious because the supplies of coal, iron and other metals are not only small in proportion to the vast size of the country, but badly distributed." If these pronouncements are true, then no matter what Russia's government or what the social and political aims it espouses, she never can attain a high industrial development. She never can build up a high steel-and-iron civilization, and her people never can hope to rise to the standard of living commensurate with such a modern civilization.

The evidence on which Professor Huntington bases his judgment he does not give. Professor Eckblaw, however, bases his on data gathered by Russian geologists who coöperated with geologists of other nations in making an inventory of the world's available supply of minerals and of its productive capacities. By his own admission this "was done before the war." Presumably Professor Huntington bases his opinions likewise on pre-war data, for it is inconceivable that he would be so decisive in his opinions had he been following the new Russian literature on the subject of resources, particularly the publications of the various scientific societies. Whatever else the Soviets may or may not have been doing, they have been most assiduously combing their vast territories for natural resources. The difference between the efforts in this direction in the old days and now is enormous. The Russian Geological Society was founded in 1882 and was made up of six members. Though the number of these had risen to fifty in the pre-war days, their equipment was comparatively poor. They had at their disposal only a few prospecting drills of more or less primitive construction. Of course they were not alone in their study of the nation's natural resources. Private enterprises engaged in similar work on their own account and quite extensively. Now, however, the Geological Society has 5,956 members, 868 of whom are geologists and the others prospectors, hydro-geologists, geo-physicists and chemists. They have at their disposal 743 prospecting drills of various kinds. The Society has stations and substations in all parts of the country, and all the work of investigating and prospecting for natural resources is in its hands. In 1931 it had 2,000 surveying parties in the field; in the following year, 2,500, with a personnel of 80,000 workers; and its labors have borne ample fruit.

Only a short time ago I read in the Russian press of the discovery by Russian scientists of a mountain range in Yukatia, eastern Siberia. No one had ever before observed this mountain range, and it had never appeared on any map. Whether or not it has any natural riches is not yet known, but it is a possibility. In the Kazakstan Mountains in Central Asia a few years ago, other Russian scientists chanced upon the plant *tauzagys*, rich in rubber content. About 40 miles away from the Tashkent railroad, in the mountains, they found 15 million bushes of this shrub growing wild. Experiments have shown that it can be cultivated in the North Caucasus and in the Central Black Earth region, though the rubber content of the plant in these areas is not as high as in its native soil in Turkestan, where it averages 13.9%, a percentage higher than that of any other rubber plant as yet discovered. The second Five Year Plan includes the cultivation in Russia of more than 150,000 acres of this plant.

Similar advances have been made in chemical science, a field which, in pre-war days, was of little consequence in the economic life of the country. Professor Eckblaw mentions the fact that Russia has no nitrates. Neither has America. But during the war, Germany learned to extract nitrates from the air, and the rest of the world has followed her example. Countries that can afford the installation of the necessary machinery are now making their own nitrates out of air. Russia has four plants for this purpose, all newly built and largely by American engineers.

Raw materials for a Russian chemical industry are constantly being discovered in various parts of the country. The potash deposits, for example, in the Northern Urals, though known in the old days, were never examined extensively, and not much was done to make use of them. Now there is a booming city in that region—Berezniki—with a highly developed chemical industry. The estimated half-billion ton of appatites in Khibini, as well as the 2 billion tons of sodium sulphite in the Caspian country, which, according to Dr. Alcan Hirsch, are of a very high quality, are recent discoveries. Without wearying the reader with detailed accounts of the finds that have been made in the chemical field in recent years, it may be stated simply that there have been many and in substantial amounts. It is true that for her drugs and dyes Russia still depends largely on foreign supplies. That is why the shortage of drugs, even such common ones as iodine and ether, is so acute. But unless present plans miscarry, Russia hopes within the near future to become one of the largest manufacturers of commercial fertilizers in the world. In the old days she manufactured no commercial fertilizer.

Consider now what has been happening in the coal industry. In the pre-revolutionary days Russia's chief source of coal was the Donetz basin, which supplied from 80 to 90 per cent of the output of the country. The Moscow, Kuznetsk, Ural and Karaganda deposits were known and worked, but not extensively. It was also known that there was coal in northern Siberia. Fritjof Nansen and other travelers saw outcroppings of coal along the Yenisey River. But no effort was made to ascertain the kind and quality and possible amount of this coal. Since the coming of the Revolution, and particularly since 1928, these and new fields, formerly utterly unknown, have been carefully surveyed and prospected, with the result that the total amount of coal now available for exploitation has increased from the estimated 220 billion tons in 1913 to more than 11,000 billion tons in 1933, or from 3 to 14 per cent of the world's supplies. Among the coal fields previously unknown or undeveloped are the Pechora deposits along the river of that name, the Bureya deposits in the Far East along the Amur River, and the Tungusia deposits in northern Siberia in the basin of the Yenisey River. Among these might be included the 60 billion tons of known deposits of Yakutian brown coal in the basins of the Lena, Vilui, and Aldan rivers which were practically untapped. And the end is not yet. Professor M. Prigorovsky, one of Russia's leading geologists, feels certain that other large stores of coal will be uncovered within the coming years.

The story of the city of Bobriki, some 150 miles south of Moscow, well illustrates what may happen in a territory in which new minerals are discovered. Three and a half years ago there was no such city. There were only vast plains without a single smokestack, without the sound of an engine, save possibly the whir of a tractor in a nearby field. As early as the 'nineties, a German business house had discovered coal there, and had opened up a cement plant. But soon it closed both plant and coal mine because experts considered the coal too poor in quality. During the world war another effort was made to mine this coal, but it, too, was a feeble effort. According to Professor Prigorovsky, a real survey of this territory was begun in May, 1918, after the Soviets had come into power. The survey disclosed that, in addition to coal, the region was rich in fire-clay, gypsum, phosphates, raw materials for cement, for bricks, for ceramics, as well as in high-grade quartz sand for the manufacture of glass; while only a short distance away, in the old province of Tula, there was good iron ore with a 46 per cent iron content. Now Bobriki is a fast growing city with a whole network of new factories already built and a number of others in process of construction.

What is true of chemicals and coal in Russia is true of iron, of copper, of zinc, of lead, of other minerals. New discoveries are constantly augmenting the known supplies.

A case in point is that of the so-called Kursk Magnetic Anomaly. Though it was discovered in 1874, old Russia did nothing to exploit it and very little to ascertain its possibilities. Exhaustive geologic surveys were made in the period between 1919 and 1926. In 1931 the surveys were renewed by a staff of scientists of the Geologic Society. Boring to a depth of from 120 to 150 meters, they discovered an ore of as rich an iron content as that of the Kirvoy Rog district, long famous for its rich iron deposits. The first shaft for the mining of this Kursk ore has already been sunk. Indeed, in the Kursk Magnetic Anomaly the Russian scientists believe that they have discovered one of the greatest iron treasures of the world. Professor Gubkin, a member of the Academy of Sciences and Russia's most celebrated geologist, says of these deposits: "A preliminary calculation allows us to assume that the iron ores of the Kursk Magnetic Anomaly will in all probability double the world's supplies, deferring by many centuries the menace of a civilization bereft of iron." Professor Gubkin and his colleagues may or may not be unduly optimistic in their estimates. In either case the future will tell. But completely to leave out of account the possibilities of the Kursk territory—which, incidentally, is most conveniently located, being halfway between Moscow and the Donetz coal fields—as Professors Eckblaw and Huntington seem to be doing, is to be unwilling to face actualities.

That the mineral resources of Russia, particularly of coal and iron, are badly distributed—or rather, are not as advantageously located as they are in the United States—is true, at least for the present. Russia, as already explained, has built two huge steel mills, one in Magnitogorsk in the Urals, and one in Kuznetsk in Central Siberia. The Magnitogorsk steel mill depends chiefly on the coal of Kuznetsk, and the Kuznetsk steel mill depends chiefly on the iron from Magnitogorsk. The two are about 1,400 miles apart. This means that, other things being equal, the production of steel in these two plants will be more costly than in America, Germany, England or any country where coal and iron are found in close proximity. But when the Karaganda coal mines attain the output that is expected of them, Magnitogorsk will no longer depend on Kuznetsk for the bulk of its coal, and Karaganda is only half as far away from Magnitogorsk as is Kuznetsk. Likewise, when the iron ore near Kuznetsk is properly worked it will no longer be necessary to ship such ore all the way from Magnitogorsk. But even if Magnitogorsk and Kuznetsk were always to depend on one another for coal and iron, respectively, the Russians feel that for purposes of national defense alone they are more than justified in making steel in these two places instead of buying it outside, even if production outside be cheaper than at home. In time of war both Magnitogorsk and Kuznetsk, strong in the distances that separate them from foreign lands, would be almost impregnable. Besides, making steel at home obviates the need of paying for it with foreign money, goods, or gold; and it provides work for armies of men.

But if the coal and iron are not everywhere placed within close range of one another, the Russians have no occasion, for the present, at least, to worry over possible shortages of either. In the Official Publications on the Five Year Plan (Vol. II, Part II, page 11) there is this significant statement: "There is no doubt that the fuel resources of the USSR are sufficient for the industrialization of the country on any scale." What is true of coal is certainly true of iron. Unless one assumes that the Russian geologists who coöperated in the making of the program of the Five Year Plan, and who have done all the prospecting and estimating of available mineral resources, are deliberately falsifying the facts, one must accept the foregoing statement as true—especially in the absence of evidence to refute it.

How recent discoveries are continually changing the Russian figures as to the mineral resources of the country the reader can glean from the following table prepared by the Russian Geological Society.

	Jan. 1, 1914	Jan. 1, 1929	Jan. 1, 1933
Iron (millions of tons)	2,056	6,174	9,378
Lead (thousands of tons of metal)	483	1,003	3,500
Zinc (thousands of tons of metal)	893	1,501	6,584
Copper (thousands of tons of metal)	988	1,630	15,000
Manganese (millions of tons)	167.9		555.1
Coal (millions of tons)	220,000	553,732	1,100,000
Potash (millions of tons)	?	?	50,000
Phosphates and appatites (millions of tons)	12,279	?	17,401

According to the tabulated estimates, Russia now has available for exploitation more than four times as much iron as she had in the old days, five times as much coal, eight times as much lead, seven times as much zinc, fifteen times as much copper. Not all of these minerals are being exploited. The deposits of copper in the Lake Balkash region are still safely resting in the earth. The efforts to build a new modern city and to put up smelters there have encountered serious setbacks. John Calder, the Detroit engineer who built the Stalingrad tractor plant and helped in the construction of a number of other imposing industrial enterprises, and who was entrusted with the task of building a new city and erecting the smelters in the Balkash district, made so little headway with his work that he withdrew from the assignment. Nor would any one venture to suggest that present Russia has already become, or is sure in the near future to become, a highly industrialized modern nation comparable to Germany, America and England. She is far from it. The magnitude of the task of industrializing the country, the inexperience of leaders and workers, miscalculations, accidents, international tension, political blunders which have resulted in a degradation of the material standard of living—these and other purely human shortcomings, not shortage of mineral resources, are making the achievement of the task difficult and painful.

If in their estimate of Russia's mineral resources Professors Eckblaw and Huntington seem to content themselves with general statements unsupported by available data, their appraisal of Russia's agricultural resources as comparatively sparse is bolstered by elaborate and extensive explanations. "Half of Russia," says Professor Eckblaw, "lies north of the sixtieth parallel, and is a land in which nothing can be grown of any consequence for either food or clothing or any other human need." He asserts moreover that the country suffers from a shortness of the growing season, and, what is equally serious, from "an acid soil in which the upper thicknesses, down to a depth of a foot or more, are leached of the humus, with the consequence that the soil becomes too acid for the production of most crops."

Professor Eckblaw summarizes his position very dramatically by declaring that if we lay out the base of a triangle from Leningrad to Odessa, the western boundary of Russia, the northern leg from Leningrad through Perm and Omsk to Atchinsk, and the southern leg from

Odessa through Rostov to Atchinsk, "we have a territory which embraces 15 per cent of the area of Russia and 77 per cent of the population, and the Soviet government itself with its unlimited powers cannot extend the area of agriculture or the area of habitation very far beyond the triangle . . . beyond that northern boundary crops of a food-producing nature cannot be grown."

As to the acidity of the Russian soil, it is well to remember that man has struggled with acid soils for more than two thousand years and has managed comfortably to survive the ordeal. The soils of the whole eastern United States and of the original timber regions are more or less acid; yet that does not prevent Indiana, Ohio and New York states from being fairly productive agricultural territories. Professor Eckblaw would have Russia return to the ancient strip system of farming as the sole means of escape from ruin. "Through long ages . . . the Russian peasants have found, just as the farmers of Scandinavia and northern Germany and the midlands of England have found, that the land must be cultivated in strips, ridged up in the middle, and trenched on either side, the more rapidly to drain the land and retard undue acidity. Only by the strip method of agriculture can the land be farmed successfully and permanently."

Yet I know of not a single Russian agriculturist of importance, in or outside of Russia, who does not hold that the strip system of farming was the bane of Russian agriculture. I know of nothing that has involved such a waste of time and human and animal energy as the continuous travel of each peasant to and from his strips of land which sometimes lay just outside his village and sometimes were twenty and thirty miles away from his home. Nor do I know of anything that so grossly vitiated Russian grains as the weeds which grew abundantly on the ridges or in the dead furrows that separated one strip from another. As one travels in the Russian countryside one often sees whole villages on sunny days washing and drying their grains on huge sheets of homespun linen in order to cleanse them of weed seed and other impurities.

If it were true that the strip system is the only way in which northern lands can be farmed successfully, then certain Russian peasants such as the so-called Stolypin homesteaders, as well as the landlords who long ago abandoned this ancient system, should have sunk into pauperism. On the contrary, they were among the most prosperous farmers in Russia. During the past nine years I have been visiting at frequent intervals a number of large farms in the northern part of the black earth belt. Some of these are among the best farms in the country, and one is the model farm of its district. It was founded by peasants who had been in America and who on their return home had brought with them a large supply of American machinery. There is no strip system on this or any other of these farms. They grow wheat, rye, oats, barley, potatoes and other root crops as well as fruits and berries and some of the best tomatoes in Russia. Yet I never heard a single agricultural expert or foreman or even an ordinary peasant worker associated with these farms complain that the abolition of the strip system of farming has in any way impaired the productivity of the land.

I am not even sure that Professor Eckblaw is correct

in assuming that the reason farmers in northern countries have been working their lands in strips "ridged up in the middle and trenched on either side," was to prevent or retard undue acidity. In all my experience with Russian peasants I have never heard any of them say so. Nor have I ever known a Russian soil scientist who would agree with Professor Eckblaw. Professors Tulin and Pryanichnikov, the latter a member of the Academy of Sciences, and both associated with the Moscow Soil Institute, repudiate it as a theory without foundation in fact, at least as far as the Russian peasant is concerned. He had been ridging up his land, not as means of overcoming acidity, but for the purpose of draining it of undue moisture. That was why the practice was confined chiefly to White Russia and to Poland, regions noted for their lowlands, and was not customary in other parts of Russia having acid soils. Russia has her share of such soils, just as Germany and England and especially Denmark have theirs; but she is seeking to combat acidity, not through a primitive method of farming but through the application of certain chemicals.

Professor Eckblaw betrays all of man's ancient distrust of northern lands by declaring that outside of the boundaries of his triangle very little if any agriculture is possible. Yet according to his own estimate, 23 per cent of the Russian population of 37,000,000 people, almost as many as comprise the whole of France, live outside his triangle. Of this vast region only certain sections depend for food on other parts of the country. A map drawn up by Dr. Marbut, chief of the Division of Soil Survey of the United States Department of Agriculture, shows that millions of acres of the best black

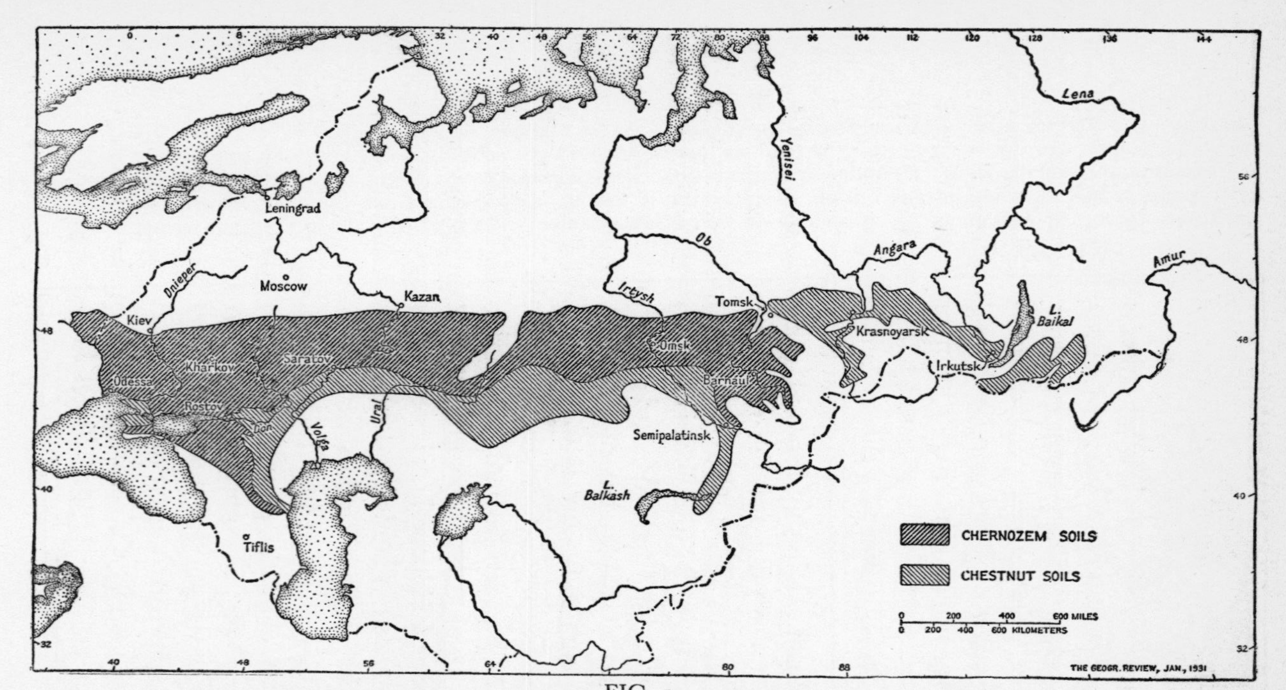

FIG. 1

FIGS. 1, 2, 3: THE BELTS OF CHERNOZEM AND CHESTNUT SOILS IN RUSSIA AND THE UNITED STATES AND THEIR RELATION TO WHEAT PRODUCTION

Fig. 1 shows the general distribution of the belts in Russia. The areas within the belts locally incapable of use for grain are not distinguished. Probably they do not exceed 20 per cent of the area in European Russia, and not much more in Siberia.

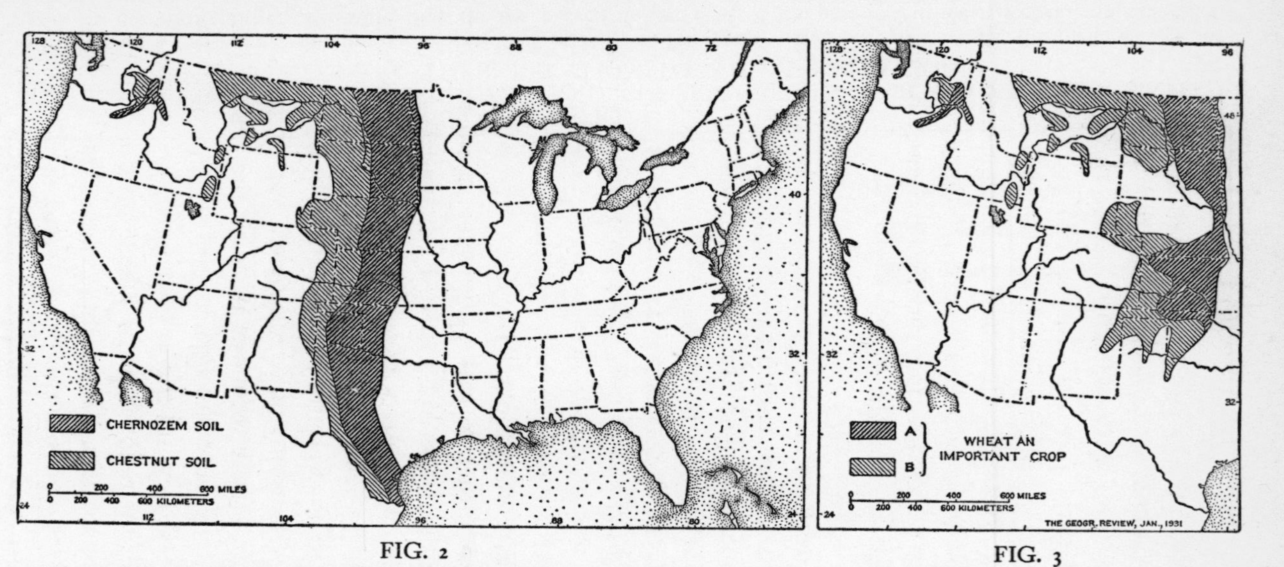

FIG. 2

FIG. 3

Fig. 2 shows the belts in the United States. Limitations imposed by climate in the south and by locally unsuitable soils in Nebraska and South Dakota are apparent in Fig. 3, which shows those parts of the belts where wheat is an important crop. A represents first-grade chernozem soils where wheat is important; B represents chestnut soils and inferior chernozems in which wheat acreage and production are less than A. Scale of maps approximately 1:36,000,000.

(Reproduced by courtesy of the editor of the Geographical Review and Dr. F. C. Marbut.)

earth of Russia lie east and north of Dr. Eckblaw's triangle. This reckoning also leaves out the whole of the rich Crimea, the Caucasus, central Asia, the Far East, as well as all of the north of Russia. That half of Russia, indeed more than half, lies north of the sixtieth parallel is true. But it does not follow that the lands beyond this parallel are wholly unproductive. In Norway agriculture has been carried as far north as the 70th parallel, and in Canada beyond the 65th.

I have before me a document which bears significantly on this subject. It originally appeared in the Geographical Review of January, 1933, and was written by W. D. Albright, who is in charge of the experimental farm at Beaverlodge, Alberta, and of the experimental substation at Fort Vermillion, which is within one degree of being in winter the coldest known place in North America, with a record of 78° below zero. In 1930 Mr. Albright was commissioned by the Canadian Department of Agriculture to make a journey north through the full length of the Mackenzie River valley, visiting the experimental substations of Roman Catholic missionaries and in general ascertaining the agricultural possibilities of that country. His article bears the suggestive title, "Gardens of Mackenzie," and at the very beginning the writer astounds us with the report that since its establishment the agricultural settlement of the Peace Country, beyond the 55th parallel, has won four international championships in wheat production, two in oats, three in peas. "A volume," says Mr. Albright, "might be written about the Peace." At Fort Fitzgerald, most northern town in Alberta, within a few miles of the 60th parallel (beyond which, according to Dr. Eckblaw, nothing can be grown for food or wear), Mr. Albright found "neat plots of wheat and oats. . . . Roses bloomed the year of planting, wintered successfully with protection, and bloomed again in 1931." He also saw lilacs, zumbra, cherries, pin cherries; while raspberries, gooseberries, strawberries, blackberries, black and red currants ripened in 1931. Potatoes had grown there for forty years, and one settler had gathered 920 bushels from three acres. In the Oblate Mission at Simpson, beyond the 60th parallel, the author dined on home-produced eggs, butter, milk, and onions. At Fort Norman, close to the 65th parallel, despite a frost in June of 1932, potatoes were better than they had been the year before, cabbage averaged eight pounds a head, and there were peas and lettuce all summer. At Good Hope, beyond the 65th parallel, Mr. Albright found fields in which for the past sixty-six years potatoes had been produced without the use of fertilizers. All kinds of stable vegetables flourished there, the cabbage averaging twelve pounds per head. At Thunder River, 80 miles north of the arctic circle, grew wild raspberries, strawberries, red and black currants, while "lettuce was being thrown away by the armful." Even at Alkavik, somewhat farther north, lettuce, carrots and potatoes grew successfully last year, and barley and oats ripened. Just south of Alkavik, at McPherson, the Hudson Bay manager grew lettuce, spinach, radishes and turnips. Of the latter vegetable the manager said that he could produce tons.

If this kind of agriculture can thrive in the Mackenzie valley, there is no reason to suppose that it cannot thrive in the valleys of the vast Siberian rivers, provided, of course, that the settlers are equally intelligent and enterprising. There are marshes and morasses in the plains of these north-flowing rivers, but explorers who have journeyed over them have found not a little evidence of the presence of fertile lands. We have the testimony of Captain Joseph Wiggins who discovered the Kara or northern sea route to Siberia. He journeyed up the Yenisey River for more than 1,800 miles, and while he complains of mosquitoes, he also speaks of dense forests above high and sloping banks, of large bushes of currants, raspberries, blackberries "loaded with fruit," of abundant strawberries and fine large mushrooms that made him long for a stewpan and a good fire. In addition to berries aplenty, he saw also wild flowers—heart's-ease, forget-me-not, wild rose, anemone. In his diary he speaks of "quiet, gentle, meek-eyed reindeer" in little herds, and also of splendid horses. "Any number of cows were to be seen, but few sheep, although the pastures are very rich." He saw considerable hay-making, with the hay consisting "of rich grass mixed with large clover, buttercups, sorrel and many other flowers." At Doodinka, which is near the 70th parallel, Captain Wiggins reports that "the right-hand bank was still steep and was called the rocky bank and the left shore was flat and called the meadow bank." Just above the arctic circle, at Kureika, he saw trees "in good leaf, and grass two feet long."

A more recent traveler, the well-known Fritjof Nansen, who journeyed up the whole length of the Yenisey, tells us in his book, "Through Siberia—the Land of the Future," that he found much civilization along the banks of this famous river. At Turukhansk, a most northern town near the 65th parallel, he found good cattle on a monastery farm, and coursing southward, he saw in one place "a whole herd of cows on the bank." Nansen was of the opinion that the territory a long way to the north was good for cattle raising and dairy farming. "There is splendid deep soil rich in mold, and if the forests were cleared and the land brought under plow it would certainly give a good yield. . . . Beside grass, root crops thrive well for a great distance to the north and in any case the kind of farming that we see in our Norwegian mountain valleys might be carried on here with great advantage. . . . *But the turn of these regions will come and cattle raising and dairy farming especially are bound to flourish here. What a rich country, what immense possibilities!*"[1]

In a country like the Yeniseisk province, which also lies outside of Professor Eckblaw's triangle, Nansen found that "wheat, rye, oats, barley, flax, hemp, buckwheat, potatoes are cultivated . . . a good deal of hay is made." The yield is smaller than it is in Norway, "and this," he says, "cannot be due to the soil, since it is certainly far better, for the most part, in any case . . . but must rather be due to higher and more developed farming."

The fact is that isolated Russian settlers and Czarist exiles had practiced farming in a desultory manner in various parts of the North. But as the country was thought quite uninhabitable, neither the old government nor the people bothered to make a systematic study of its agricultural possibilities. Now such a study is being

[1] The italics are mine.—M. H.

made on an expansive scale. A special division in the Department of Agriculture, known as the Northern Sector, is in charge of this work, and in the last three years it has opened experiment stations all along the European and Asiatic north. Some of these stations—such as those in Obdorsk, Sumarovo, Yartsovo, Igarka, Rotchevo, Maryan Mar, all close to the arctic circle or beyond it, and also Pokrovskoye, which was opened in 1928, and Pechora, which has existed since 1908—are specializing in dairying, vegetables, and, whenever possible, in grain growing. Other stations like those in Lovarosovo, Hapgan Mar, Nizhne-Kolymsk, Bulunsk, Anadyr, Penzhensk, and Volosyansk, the latter two beyond the 70th parallel, are concentrating on reindeer and other possible arctic livestock. More and more land is being plowed and more and more crops are being planted. In 1932 the area put under cultivation in the far North was 364,000 acres. In 1933 it was increased to more than 600,000 acres, and in 1934 it is planned to put at least one million acres under the plow. The crops planted are, in the order of their importance, winter grains, potatoes, spring grains, silo plants, grasses and a large variety of vegetables, such as cabbage, beets, carrots, radishes, turnips, onions, potatoes, peas, cucumbers, tomatoes, kohl-rabi, and lettuce. This outdoor farming is being augmented in the North by the extensive development of hot-house gardening.

The Russians may of course find that the agricultural possibilities of the arctic lands are limited. But the work that they are now doing there will in time yield a body of experimental facts, the most extensive of any yet assembled, which will enable scientists to draw definite conclusions as to the kinds of farming that may be legitimately pursued there. To pronounce judgment on the subject at present, in the absence of a body of reliable evidence, is merely to indulge in prophecy. Yet whatever the outcome of these efforts to develop agriculture on an ever increasing scale in the arctic regions, the lands there are not universally as bleak and barren and useless as Professor Eckblaw paints them, especially in view of such possibilities as are offered by the rising reindeer industry.

Several years ago, in the company of Dr. Horsley Gantt of Johns Hopkins University, I made an extensive journey in northern Finland. We went beyond the arctic circle and everywhere we encountered lovely inns, clean and cheery and comfortable, and excellent food. Everywhere and at practically every meal we were offered smoked reindeer, which we instantly liked and ate with as much relish as any meat to which we had been accustomed. Slowly but persistently reindeer meat is finding a place in man's daily diet, not only in Finland, but even in America.

The history of the reindeer in Alaska provided a most timely and valuable lesson for Russia. It was in 1891 that the first ten animals were imported to Alaska from eastern Siberia. The original purpose of this importation was to help the Eskimos solve their food problem. In 1892 more animals were imported, 171 head. By 1902 the number brought over, all from eastern Siberia, mounted to 1,280. Now Alaska boasts the possession of a million reindeer.

In the introduction to United States Department of Agriculture Bulletin No. 1089, "Reindeer in Alaska,"

E. W. Wilson, formerly chief of the United States Biological Survey, writes: "The reconnaissances already made indicate that Territory [Alaska] has available grazing sufficient to carry between 3,000,000 to 4,000,000 reindeer. The annual surplus from that number would yield a meat product each year worth more than the precious metals mined in the Territory and second only to the fisheries as a permanent producing asset." In a hearing before Congress, Mr. Wilson put the possibilities even higher, in expressing his opinion that the output of reindeer in Alaska would amount to 1,250,000 carcasses a year.

The Russians figure that on the basis of available pastures in their arctic regions they can comfortably feed 30,000,000 reindeer. Now they have only 2,500,000, some of which are of the best breeds in the world, and some of the poorest. These animals have been for the most part in the hands of nomads who never learned the proper care of livestock, and who have been helpless in the face of the diseases that have been ravaging their herds. Anthrax, though unknown in the Far East, is prevalent in the European and middle Asiatic North, and has for years been exacting a heavy toll—causing the death annually of 200,000 reindeer. The hoof disease has further swelled the mortality of the animals. That is one reason why the number of reindeer in Russia has remained almost stationary for some years. But now efforts are being made to combat disease. There is a Reindeer Institute in Leningrad which is devoting itself to the study of the animal with a view to ridding it of disease and improving its breeds. The various experiment stations scattered all over the north are pursuing a similar aim. Vaccination against anthrax has already been introduced on a massive scale, with the result that mortality from this cause has been reduced to about 35,000 head a year. The Russians have of course much to learn about the proper care of reindeer. But they are willing to learn it because they are beginning to realize its importance in the economic development of the country. The time when reindeer can supply a substantial part of the country's meat and fur and leather may be far off. But in the meantime, the tending of the reindeer requires little outlay of capital, little human labor, and makes possible the exploitation of lands that are fit for nothing else but pasture. If the Russians ever bring the number to 30,000,000, they can slaughter annually 10,000,000 head, which will be no small item in the nation's supplies of food and clothing.

Professor Elsworth Huntington, whose pessimistic opinion has been quoted previously, presents impressive figures to show the low productivity of Russian agricultural labor. "In the United States," he says, "as a whole the return from similar work is about six times as great, and in Iowa twenty times as great. If prices of all products were everywhere the same, the average production per man on the farms would show approximately the following ratios":

Russia	1
Mississippi	5
United States	11
Iowa	22

These figures tell a pathetic story that is only too true. But Professor Huntington puts the blame on Russian natural conditions. "The hope of relief," he says, "through improvement in agricultural methods or the cultivation of unused lands is far less than is generally supposed. In no other country is there such a huge area of rich black soil as in Russia. Yet this superb soil does not yield large crops per acre, because it suffers from extremely low temperature and drought. . . . Fertilization does not help nearly so much as might be supposed, for fertilizers produce great benefits only when kept moist most of the time. . . . In Russia the fertilizing process is checked not only by many months of frost but by long dry spells in both spring and fall." These are sweeping statements and there is truth in them, but not the whole truth. Fertilizers do, indeed, little good unless sustained by a proper amount of moisture. But the low temperature and the drought of which Professor Huntington speaks are not as nationwide as his words imply. Southeastern European Russia and western Siberia are the chief sufferers from drought. But even there one can count on three years out of every five in which there is sufficient rainfall for fair or good crops. With the use of fertilizers, which Russia is only now on the point of manufacturing on a large scale, the yields in these good years could be substantially improved. Likewise, complete crop failure is less frequent than one would infer from the writings of Professors Eckblaw and Huntington. According to Professor Pryanichnikov, heavy and widespread drought comes about once in every ten years. Usually the droughts are regional. In 1931, for example, the lower Volga and a large part of Siberia suffered from drought, but the Ukraine had one of the best crops in years. In 1932 the Ukraine suffered from drought but the Crimea did not.

Then there are some parts of the country, White Russia, for example, and the adjacent parts of the Ukraine, which even in the days of the big famine in 1921 had bountiful crops. Nor are the Moscow, Leningrad, and other northern regions subject to severe drought. Moreover, as Dr. F. C. Marbut has pointed out, "rainfall is much used as an indirect means of arriving at the productivity of a region, but is liable to lead to erroneous conclusions, for production depends on effective moisture during the growing season rather than on absolute amount of rainfall. . . . *The dark chestnut-colored soil shows by the darkness of its color that it has supported a good cover of grass and hence that in spite of low rainfall the effective moisture is sufficient for that purpose. . . . Stronger evidence than any yet brought forward is necessary before it can be concluded that nature has deceived man by presenting him an unproductive dark-colored soil developed under low rainfall. Until more data has been accumulated we must still conclude that the extension of wheat growing in Russia depends on the Russians rather than on Russia.*"[1]

Nor do Professors Eckblaw and Huntington make allowances for the possibility of irrigation in the drought areas and in deserts, or for the possible drainage of Russia's immense swamps and marshes. On the border of Afghanistan the Russians are now digging and blasting out canals to divert the waters from the river Vaksh, which has its source in the Pamyr Mountains, onto a vast tract of land, a quarter of a million acres, where they hope to grow Egyptian cotton. Right in the heart of Siberia in the Barnaul region, between the rivers

[1] Italics are mine.—M. H.

Irtysh and Ob, there is a vast territory of good land, estimated at about ten million acres, which the Russians hope some day to irrigate. Then there is the project to divert water from the Volga onto lands that are subject to drought. And there are other possibilities of irrigation which for the present are not even engaging the attention of the Russians.

What is true of irrigation is true of drainage. Russia has about half a billion acres of marsh land, especially in the north. Not all of this land can be drained, but a good deal of it can be prepared for farming. In White Russia, for example, there are about ten million acres of swamp. Some of it has already been drained. I have seen state farms on this drained land; they are among the best in White Russia.

Professor Huntington's statement that Russia has about reached the limit of her usable lands no Russian agronomist will accept. For it ignores completely not only the possibilities of irrigation and drainage of vast tracts of good farm land, but of the application of dry farming methods to areas which have never yet been touched by the plow. According to Dr. Marbut, Russia's first and second-grade wheat land alone (on the basis of her black and dark-brown soils) amounts to 854,503,040 acres, as against 234,565,920 acres of similar land in the United States. In other words, Russia possesses, in potential wheat soils alone, an area more than twice as large as her total acreage now under cultivation for all purposes—an area more than three times as large as the whole wheat-growing acreage of the United States. It is true that much of this land has to be improved. But that hardly implies that the land is not available. The contention that the temperature in these regions is too low is incorrect, for experience has shown that good wheat can be grown there, and no one, says Dr. Marbut, "can seriously maintain that the growing season is too short for the safe ripening of spring-grown grains." Even north of this wheat region—in the Yeniseisk country in Siberia—grain grows well, as it does also in the Peace River country in Canada, above the 55th parallel. In fact, as far north as the Russian black earth belt extends, it is possible to grow the choicest of grains. It is not days but hours in the growing season that count—*hours of sunlight*—and in summer these increase with each degree of latitude.

So it would seem that Professors Eckblaw and Huntington sadly underestimate the immense importance of the black lands in human history. It was not until man learned how properly to make use of them that he was able to store up a surplus of bread stuffs. Russia, and the rest of the world too, have yet much to learn about the best way to treat these lands in order to whip out of them all that they can yield. There is still very much that even America can discover about dry farming, which after all is of comparatively recent origin. Russia, having the largest area of black lands in the world, some of it is of the finest quality that there is, can look forward with more than justifiable hope to the day when from these lands alone she will gather harvests more than ample for all her needs in spite of her fast growing population.

In this connection it might be well to consider the contention of Timoshenko and of Poletika, both Russians living outside of Russia, that the Russian wheat belt suffers from an abundance of alkali and from the disintegration of soil structure which is a result of continuous cultivation. The trouble with this theory is that there is no evidence that disintegration is taking place; and, as Dr. Marbut asks, why is there no such breakdown of the soil structure in Canada, the United States, and the Argentine, where wheat is grown on soils of the same character as Russia's? For the present, at any rate, this appears to be no problem. Here, as elsewhere, the critics of Russian resources, whether agricultural or mineral, are making mountains out of mole hills. Or, to state the case more specifically in the words of Dr. Marbut: "No Russian pedologist has ever stated that the presence of alkali in the chernosem [black earth] and chestnut colored belts will seriously interfere with their use in grain-growing. Furthermore, the extent of the area so affected has been grossly exaggerated."

Thus have been overemphasized the limitations that nature has imposed on Russian agriculture, whether in the form of drought or low temperature or acidity of the soil. Her critics dismiss completely the value to Russia of her northlands, which may yet become important meat producing centers. They disregard the possibilities of irrigation and drainage, which are already reclaiming substantial acreages, and which, if pursued with energy and intelligence, can reclaim immense territories of farm land. But even within Dr. Eckblaw's triangle there are tens of millions of acres which with slight or substantial improvement can be put to use. I have yet to visit a Russian village whose adjacent wastelands could not be used for gardening or fruit growing. White Russia alone has millions of acres of swamp land some of which has already been drained to make excellent farm land.

In speaking of the extension of the wheat growing area in Russia, Dr. Marbut says that its success depends on Russians and not on Russia. This comment is applicable to all phases of farming in the country. Neither Professor Eckblaw nor Professor Huntington seems to appreciate the truly wretched condition of Russian peasant agriculture, yet evidence of it can be seen at every step in the Russian villages. There is little intensive farming, and what there is needs to be completely overhauled. In 1923, on my first trip to Russia, I made an extensive journey through the Tartar territory in the province of Kazan. As I wandered about in the villages, noting the comparative absence of gardening and fruit growing, I could readily understand why the famine of 1921 was especially severe in this country. Only the mullahs and the Russian settlers there had gone into gardening and fruit growing, and they were not as badly hurt by the famine as were the natives. Severe as was the drought, some gardening was possible. The instruction in gardening which they are now receiving is bound to make an enormous difference in the lives of these millions of Tartars, in times of plenty as well as famine.

In any earnest study of Russian agriculture one cannot emphasize too vigorously the low productivity of Russian land which is directly attributable to bad methods of tillage. How often have I seen peasants setting cabbage plants too close together on the theory that the more plants they put into the ground, the more cabbage they would harvest! Nor was this quaint theory of theirs limited to cabbages.

Truck farming in Russia is in its infancy. It is now being developed on a large scale not only in the environs of every city, but on lands adjacent to factories and military encampments as well. In every case, the success of these truck farms has depended entirely upon the skill shown in their management. Russian fruit growing, too, is in need of improvement. Americans who have traveled on the Volga late in summer will remember the bags and baskets of apples which peasants offer to passengers on the boats. Invariably the fruit is spotty and wormy. No American grocery man would dare display such fruit before his customers. In the days when I worked on a farm in northern New York I was instructed to throw away apples which in Russia would have fetched a high price in any bazaar. And what shall be said of peasant livestock? If farmers in America housed their cows in such windowless manure-cluttered barns as those of the Russian peasants, no board of health even in the most remote communities would permit the sale of milk from those cows. Nor do the peasants, with some notable exceptions, know the barest rudiments of cattle feeding.

Russia's lack of agricultural enterprise has some very definite bases. One of these is the limited variety of crops that can be cultivated on her lands. Russia has been growing corn in the south, but she has nothing comparable to America's corn belt. Nor can she ever become a land of citrous fruits. She has neither a California nor a Florida nor a Texas. But a greater diversity of grass and vegetable crops than she now grows is certainly possible. An example of this is the very small amount of lettuce grown in the country. This is principally because the people, even in the cities, regard lettuce as mere grass. Accustomed to a simple diet of small variety of foods, the Russians are loath to acquire an appetite for new foods, particularly vegetables.

What Russia needs above everything else is more intensive farming. There always has been too little of it in the country. The amount of vegetables, fruits, dairy products, eggs and meats, could be increased many, many times under a system of well directed intensive agriculture. Seeding of meadows and pastures, rotation of crops, commercial fertilizer, silos, incubators, hatcheries, scientific selection of seed, scientific breeding of livestock, insect-destroying chemicals, decent plowing and decent preparation of seedbeds, proper and timely sowing and harvesting—these and many more are the things that Russian agriculture requires. If since the beginning of 1929 the food situation in Russia has been steadily growing worse, with the winter and spring of 1932 and 1933 bringing distress and privation to the North Caucasus, to parts of the Ukraine and to Kazakstan, the fault is not of Russia but of Russians. Mismanagement of collectivization by local officials, and even more by the Central Committee of the Communist Party, constitutes a sad—indeed, the saddest—chapter in the Revolution. In another place I shall deal fully with this subject. Here I wish only to emphasize that if in the future Russia remains a poor country with a low standard of living, with famine visiting this or that part of the land bringing in its train demoralization, disease and death, the blame will rest not with nature but with man, with the Russians themselves. Nature has placed at their disposal abundant mineral and agricultural riches, and it is their task to make such use of these as will enhance their every-day welfare and happiness.

V

VILLAGE

THE PEASANTS HAVE THEIR SAY

AUGUST was nearing its end. In Moscow the days had grown gray and chilly and the skies were heavy with autumn rains. But in the Ukraine summer still lingered. The sun was bright and warm, the skies blue and limpid, and peasants walked around barefooted and in light clothes. It seemed like a new world here, outwardly serene and cheerful, with no trace of the somberness of the north in man or nature. Pastures were fat with grass, mowed clover-fields shimmered with verdure, and the stubbles of harvested wheat had not yet been nipped by frost or flattened by rain or storm. Herds of cattle browsed lustily in far-stretching pastures, and the whitewashed villages set against the black earth shone like stars in a dusky sky.

A glorious land the Ukraine is—rich in color and substance and famed in song and legend for its wit and ardor, its stalwart men and its pretty women. No people in Russia speak with so melodious an intonation as the Ukrainian, or dance with such sprightly abandon, or laugh with such gay heartiness. They love fun and play, and the Ukrainian *diadko* (uncle) is an incomparable host. Food and drink, if he has it, he will heap up before the visitor, and how he will sulk if his hospitality is not accepted to the utmost limits of one's appetite! No wonder Russian writers from Gogol to Gorky have written of the Ukraine with such rapture.

And yet in Moscow people spoke anxiously of the Ukraine. So-and-so had sent flour, cereals, cheese, or a flank of beef to a friend or relative in the Ukraine—a procedure which sounded as absurd as the proverbial carrying of coals to Newcastle, especially since the Ukraine was the one section in the country which in 1931 had had a bountiful crop. Stories without end circulated as to what was happening there—of peasants who had lost heart and were engaging in sabotage in the fields; of peasants who had eaten up all or most of the grain that they were allotted for seed; of peasants who were fleeing from the land, alone or with their families. Cheerless, disturbing stories! Certainly Ukrainian peasants wandering the streets of Moscow, alone or with families, were a common and arresting sight.

Once I passed such a family, man and wife and three children, who had spread themselves comfortably on the sidewalk around the corner from my hotel and were partaking of a meal of bread, herring, and apples.

"Why," I asked the man, "did you come here?"

"And why not?" he answered with defiance.

"There is work in the fields in the Ukraine; the papers are talking a lot about it," I answered.

"Let others do the work," he answered gruffly.

"The devil with work in the fields," rasped the woman. She was big-boned and ruddy-faced and there was wrath in her voice. "What good does it do to work?" she continued with rancor and eagerness to speak her mind. "You work and work and then they come, these commissaries, and take it away from you!" Her loud speech attracted pedestrians, among them a youth in cap and sandals, with the smear of a downy beard around his pointed chin.

"You ought to be ashamed of yourself for talking like that," he chided her aloud, and then proceeded to tell her that people like her and her husband, who flee from the land because of certain setbacks, are cowards and defeatists. The man, unperturbed by the verbal lashing, continued to eat in silence. But the woman, though ordered by her husband to refrain from answering, turned hotly on the youth.

"If you think it is a joy to be on a collective farm when you see with your own eyes pigs dying because commissaries did not leave enough food for them, go there yourself and get all the joy you can out of it."

"Such an uncultured tribe," muttered the youth in disgust, and walked away.

The youth's harsh words might have cast aspersions on the revolutionary zeal of these peasants, but it did not discredit their tale, which only bore out the gossip that floated about the city. The Ukraine was in distress. This land of rich soil and brilliant sunshine and sturdy people had become what the Russians termed "a critical sector on the agricultural front," and not through any visitation of nature; indeed, in spite of nature's benevolence.

It was therefore cheering to see the country, on our arrival there, so bright and peaceful, with nowhere in the outward appearance of things a suggestion of havoc or distress. We had come, a colleague and I, for a leisurely wandering visit. We knew that the people we should meet in fields and villages would be glad to talk, for there is nothing peasants love more than to tell of their woes and everything else that may come to their minds. They may start out with a recital of grievances against officials high and low, but as they talk on, emotion and imagination get the best of them and they wander off into gossip and comment about neighbors, strangers, themselves, the whole gamut of their daily experiences.

We stopped first in a district outside Kharkov, the capital of the Ukraine. We ascended a hill, and after getting lost in a heavy brushwood we emerged into a clearing on a hillside and almost bumped into a herd of pasturing cattle. It was a small herd, with the cows for some reason crowded close together—a superior breed of cows, with big bodies and fat flanks, a few with low-hanging udders testifying to their high milk-giving capacity.

There was a herdsman near by, a tall man in winter cap and heavy boots, whose broad sun-baked face wore that taciturn expression which comes to people who live alone and spend a great deal of time in the open. He was followed by a surly dog and two children. Peasant fashion, he began to talk. He did not ask us who we were or where we had come from, those preliminaries to which most outsiders must submit on first meeting peasants. He talked about himself. He had always been a herdsman, but never in all his life had he had such a small herd as now. The year before there had been twice as many cows under his charge. But in the preceding winter fodder got scarce and many people, fearing their cows were going to die, butchered them. Others had theirs taken away as meat collections for a price not one-twentieth as high as that prevailing in the open market. And so what was he to do? He was being paid by the head, and how could any herdsman make a living on a herd of twenty-five cows, even if the rate per head was high? He could not. That was why he was abandoning his life-long occupation. A friend of his had written that there were plenty of jobs in Dneprostroy, where they had built a big dam. This friend, who had gone to work there, and had food and tobacco and matches and sugar and good shoes, had invited him to come along, and he was going. As soon as it got too cold and wet to keep cows out in the open he would go to Dneprostroy. He had made up his mind, and nothing could induce him to change it—nothing!

His were significant words. They spoke eloquently of why people from the villages have been flocking to cities and factories, and why shouldn't they? So much has been written and preached about the sovereignty and supremacy of the proletarian, and of the special privileges conferred on him, that even peasants in back woodlands, when faced with repressions and reverses, become ambitious to find their way into some industrial enterprise and join the proletariat. That achieved, the best in the land in food, in manufactured goods, in amusements, in education, is theirs, and they are done with grain collections, taxes, reprimands, worries over fodder for livestock, and many other annoyances which they now have to face in the villages. This, of course, drains agriculture of energies it cannot spare, particularly in these times of feeble organization and loose division of labor on the collectives. But the peasants, especially the older men, are too self-centered to care.

We left the herdsman with his dog and two children and descended the hill. We crossed a boggy lowland and followed a winding road that undulated along a range of hills until finally we came to the village of K——. A winding village it was, with a double row of whitewashed cottages each separated from the other by a rail fence and a gateway, and each fronted by a yard with an open well, a garden, and now and then an orchard. It was midday, and there were few people about. But dogs barked furiously, those mean Ukrainian watch-dogs that are kept on chains and ropes all day, and sometimes all night, and who never see or hear a stranger pass by but they swell with fury and leap ahead as far as their chains will let them, ready to sink their fangs into human flesh. But, knowing the nature of these dogs, we had armed ourselves with stout sticks and went our way unmolested. We came presently to a brick building with large windows and a spacious open yard.

It was obviously a school-house. We entered the yard in time to see a well-dressed youth dip a drink of water out of an open well. We spoke to him, and just as we were on the point of asking him what class he was in he informed us that he was the principal. He looked too juvenile for such a position, but he assured us that he was twenty and a Komsomol. This was his first year of teaching and he had two assistants, both girls. Would we come in and look around? Only we must be charitable in our judgment. They had universal education in the village, but were short of books, paper, and other supplies. Still, they did the best they could.

With a boyish eagerness he led us into the schoolhouse. It was clean and spacious and the classrooms were hung with innumerable posters and lithographed portraits of leaders of the Revolution. His assistants were as pleased as he by our presence, for no foreigners had ever visited their school-house, and they had never seen Americans. It was obvious that they felt honored! We visited one of the classes. The teacher was a young woman, short, with sharp features, light brown hair visibly sprinkled with gray, and a resonant voice. As we entered, the pupils, as though obeying a standing order or an instinctive impulse, instantly arose and exclaimed, "Welcome, *tovarishchi*," then sat down again. They looked well fed and clean, and stared at us with a solemn curiosity unbroken by titters or whispers. The teacher was so excited that she couldn't go on with the recitations and dismissed the class for a special recess. She wanted so much to talk to us, she said, and if she held her class we might go away and she wouldn't have the chance. Where had we come from, and what were we doing, and how did we like Soviet schools? Did we not think the students looked clean and orderly? And they were bright, too, only they had so few books and so little paper and so few crayons. They were doing too much social work—helping to dig potatoes or pull up weeds. They shouldn't be burdened with such work during the school season, should they? But there were new decrees out, and maybe now they wouldn't have to any more. Then she paused, grew reflective, and now and then cast furtive glances at us, like a little girl who had a secret to tell and wondered if she should. She remained silent for so long that my companion and I rose to go. But she implored us to stay. She wanted to talk to us, she said. Would we believe that the night before she had been thinking of committing suicide? Luckily she wasn't alone. If she had been she mightn't be alive now.

Her eyes glistened with moisture and her face reddened, but she didn't cry. She was obviously making an effort to control herself. We wondered what it was that had made her so desolate. Was it personal disappointment or political troubles? We knew well enough that in these days of the Socialist Offensive, with the Revolution mercilessly battering down anyone in the way of its onward march, a broken heart was no rare phenomenon either in city or in village. Yet she was teaching school. If she or her parents had sinned against the Revolution, she wouldn't have held her position, certainly not in the Ukraine, where political vigilance was even more stern than elsewhere. We waited for enlightenment, and it came quickly enough.

It was not that she had any grievance against the Soviets, the party, or the school. Nor was she dismayed over the condition of the peasantry in the Ukraine. Peasants grumbled incessantly, but as a little girl she had been through worse times in the famine region. It was a personal misfortune that was crushing her—and would we listen to her? She was so sad, so broken up!

Perhaps she was wrong in allowing a personal disturbance to overcome her. That's what the principal had told her. This was a time of strife and battle, he had argued, and people had to muffle inner tribulation and concentrate on the social task at hand. But she couldn't do it. Revolution or no Revolution, she couldn't subdue her inner turmoil. Perhaps she was foolish, but how could she help herself? The year previous she was teaching in a village fifty versts away, and on her first day there she was introduced to a bookkeeper, a thin, withered man with a small beard, who was much older than she. He was an unprepossessing soul and quite homely, but she at once fell in love with him, and, would we believe it, all night she had lain awake thinking of him and of how lonely he had looked, and of how she would have loved to cheer and strengthen him and make him happy. She had never been in love before—never; and she was so exalted. At last she had met the man who could stir her deepest emotions. She lay awake wondering if he were thinking of her and missing her as much as she was thinking of him and missing him. She could hardly wait for morning, and, as soon as she could, she went to see him, just to convince herself that she had not been mistaken. And the moment she saw him she knew that she hadn't, she knew that she had fallen in love. And, to her immense joy, he told her he had fallen in love with her, too, and asked her to marry him. They lost no time in getting married, and they were very happy. Then they were both offered work in this village, she as a teacher and he as a bookkeeper, and they moved over. They had a nice room and were completely happy until two days previous, when he was taken suddenly ill. He grew feverish, and complained of pains, and she rushed for the doctor. But the doctor was nowhere to be found, so she woke up a member of the collective farm and had him hitch up a team of horses and took her husband to a hospital in the near-by city. When they got there he was unconscious. The doctor examined him and said he was going to die. He had double pneumonia, and his heart was weak. If the doctor had struck her on the head with an axe he couldn't have stunned her any more. She felt as though she were sinking into the earth. She asked the doctor how much longer he might live, and he said possibly two more days. The day before he was still alive, but this was the second day, and she couldn't bear the thought of his being dead. There was no telephone near; and even if there was she wouldn't dare call up the hospital. She would go there in the evening—and if he was dead what was the use of her living on? If only she too could die!

She stopped, shook her head, and struggled heroically to retain her composure. Her eyes shone with tears, yet she didn't cry. My companion and I sought to console her, but she didn't seem to hear us. She sat hunched up at her table, her chin in her hands, and stared outside at her pupils, who were scampering about in the yard. Then a boy peeped through the door and asked if he might come in. As if awakened from a trance, she at once stood up and resolutely told him to call in the class. When the pupils crowded in, panting and excited, she lost no time in resuming the interrupted lessons.

The boyish principal accompanied us to the Soviet,

and just as we reached it the chairman came out with a bicycle. A bicycle—the dream and ambition of every youth in the land! The chairman was short and stocky, with a bony face and solemn gray eyes. He wore a cap, which he did not remove when we entered his office. An informal, loquacious man, he invited us to sit down, and began to talk. He had been in the village only a year, and what a year it had been! When he arrived, the peasants were in a truculent mood, for his predecessor had committed a blunder which had infuriated them. An awful fool, that chairman! Once, on learning that a peasant, who was then a *koolack*, had secretly slaughtered a hog with the obvious intent of evading the law, which required that the hide be sold to the government, this chairman at once proceeded to the offender's home and confiscated not only the hide, but the hog. The peasant protested and made excuses and denied any intent to cheat the government. But the chairman was determined to set an example to the whole village of what would happen to any man who butchered an animal in secret, and refused to return the hog to the owner. The next day every peasant in the village slaughtered his pigs, big ones and little ones, and for a whole year they refused to raise any more.

As we listened to him we thought of a similar instance we had encountered in a village in the black earth section, where an elderly couple had had their only cow taken away as a meat collection, with the result that the peasants of the village would raise no more cows.

Illuminating incidents these, for they tell so much of the power the peasant still has, and may always have, to wreak vengeance on the community and on the nation.

This young chairman was hopeful, because the collective farm in the village had definitely weathered its worst crisis; and that was what counted most in these days. The individualist farmers might grumble and complain, but if the collective flourished all would be well, for the new social benefits to the community depended on the collective. Even in this village, it was the collective that maintained the community dining-room and supplied meals to the teachers and other social workers, and made it possible to offer a hot meal a day to the school-children. And the better the collective worked, the greater would be the incentive to its members to keep up their enthusiasm, and the sooner would the individualists join, abandoning once and for all their parasitic existence.

He went down with us to the community dining-room, which was located in the house of an expelled *koolack*. The very sight of the house made one wonder what sort of *koolack* was the man who inhabited it, for it was a small, incommodious place, with a low ceiling, bare furniture, and a sagging roof. Several women were at work preparing supper. They had just slaughtered a steer, and two of them were dressing the meat, while the third was busily preparing tomatoes and other vegetables for soup. They were so sorry we had come when there was nothing cooked in the kitchen, but if we would wait they would cook us something, only with their wood fire it might take some time. If we were in a hurry, they could give us bread and milk. We told them that bread and milk were all we wanted, and soon they brought us a plate heaped with huge slices of fresh black bread and deep earthen bowls filled with milk. They begged us to stay for supper, when they would have meat and soup and potatoes, but we chose to move on.

We passed village after village and peasant after peasant in the fields and on the road, carting hay, straw, bricks. They were husky men with broad faces, swarthy from sun and wind, and with those sharp, luminous eyes for which the Ukrainians are noted, eyes that reveal much and conceal even more. An old woman, thin and wrinkled, stopped us. She wore dilapidated shoes and a ragged shawl slung carelessly over her shoulder, but she was a cheerful soul, and at once began to converse with us, punctuating her speech with hearty chuckles. Where had we come from? Where were we bound for? Such nice clothes we had—where did we buy them, and how much did we pay for them? Then she proceeded to enlighten us about herself. She lived in the village only a short distance away to our right, she said, pointing to where a church steeple rose above a clump of evergreens. If we would accept her humble hospitality, we might come and spend the night in her home. She would ask the neighbors in and we could talk with them. They would tell us things—oh, indeed! Peasants had much to tell nowadays. There were grain collections, meat collections, milk collections. Everything was collections now. That's why so many people were going to cities and factories. There were no collections there. Workers were getting everything, even sugar. What a blessing to be a worker! If she was young she would go to a factory and become a worker.

Then, rapidly changing the subject, she asked us if in the region from which we had come the people ate horseflesh? No? Ah, that was splendid! Then we were not Tartars? Thank God! She didn't think that we were. Tartars ate horseflesh—liked it better than beef—that's the kind of creatures they were. The previous spring two of them had come to her house and offered to buy her colt for meat. They offered her five hundred roubles, but she was furious and told them they couldn't buy it for two thousand roubles. Other peasants might be selling their horses for meat, but not she! She wouldn't see her lovely little colt killed—it was so white-faced, so tame, and so friendly. Better she should see it die of starvation than be turned into meat. But she wouldn't let it die and yet she had no feed—no hay, no grain, and only a little straw. So she went to the director of the farm for homeless children right opposite her village and said to him, "Those Tartars want to buy my colt. They offered me five hundred roubles, but they want to butcher it for meat, and I want it to live. Will you take it? You have hay and straw and you can feed it. When it grows up, keep it as your own and put it to work." The director agreed to take it, and she herself led the colt to the farm and left it there in the barn.

Two days later the director sent her two little pigs from a freshly born litter. They were pretty little pigs, and she wondered what she would do with them, since she didn't have feed enough to raise them. But she had a neighbor who had a cow that gave milk, so she asked him if he would raise the pigs in partnership with her. This he did, and now the pigs were five months old, big and fat. As soon as cold weather set in, they could butcher them and would have fat for the whole winter. Wasn't she lucky, though? She didn't have to worry about food any more. Nor did her neighbor. Now if only she could get a pair of shoes—and she pointed at the ones she was wearing, full of holes at the bottoms, their cracked and ragged tops held together with strings in place of shoelaces. She had gone to store after store, she said. She had even been in Kharkov at a store there, where there were lots of shoes. But they wanted gold or dollars, and where could she get gold or dollars? The devil only knew what was happening! Things had come to a pretty pass when a poor woman like her couldn't buy shoes with her own money, the money she got for anything she sold!

She chattered on and on glibly, wittily, loquaciously, enjoying immensely the chance of talking so freely about everything. Then she talked of her children. She had a boy of eighteen, and he wanted to go into the Red Army. He said he would get good clothes there, and shoes and an education. But she didn't know whether or not to believe him. Had we heard anything about the Red Army? Of course she hated armies, because in time of war they had to fight, and if her son was in a war he might get killed, and then what good would the good clothes and good food and good education do him? But he had a mind of his own and wouldn't take her advice. Her son was tall and handsome, she told us, liked by everybody. In the old days he could have married the prettiest girl in the countryside, and the richest. But now there were no rich people. It was a sin to be rich, and it was unsafe too. They called you *koolack* and confiscated your property, and sent you to

she marry a speculator, not even if she had to die unmarried.

But her former husband wouldn't move away. He said he would wait until she'd changed her mind . . . and she swore she never would . . . and any fool would know that, headstrong as her daughter was, she would stick to her word, and so what was she, a poor mother, to do? Oh, if only we could come to her village! She would cook supper for us and we could talk to her son and her daughter and her daughter's former husband and pass the evening so pleasantly!

VI
VILLAGE

MORE PEASANTS HAVE THEIR SAY

A FEW DAYS later we were in *Poltavshchina*, the very heart of the Ukraine. This is the so-called Gogol country, and within its boundaries are the villages of Dikanka and Rehsitilovka and others the very names of which drip with melody and of which Gogol wrote with such humor and ecstasy. Here native custom and tradition still abound. Even the poorest peasants wear white linen blouses with splashes of red embroidery on collars, cuffs, and bosom, and women flaunt homespun skirts and roomy waists with loose sleeves lying in folds, like swathes of freshly mowed grass, and likewise splashed with rich embroidery. Here the speech of the people is softer, the voices more tuneful, the manner more suave, the hospitality heartier and more majestic.

We passed village after village, and finally reached the village of R——, which we heard had been especially hard hit by the events of the previous winter. It was a large village, spreading like a triangular shawl over several versts, with the customary double row of cottages, all whitewashed and with stately shade and fruit trees overhanging the thatched roofs. Save for the puffing of an engine in the little power station, no mechanical noises disturbed the pristine calm of the place and no smoke-stacks rose above the earth. Children, half naked and sunburned, were merrily at play in the yards and in the street, and as we walked along we discerned nowhere in the outward appearance of things any trace of want and desperation. It was a quiet village smelling of earth and grass, and with a pastoral charm all its own.

We passed a garden facing the street and saw a woman picking tomatoes, the last of the crop, little and shrivelled and red, lying on the ground or hanging loose on withered vines. We stopped and spoke to her, and she instantly looked up, hastened to adjust her kerchief, apron, skirt, and asked us if we would like to go into the house, where it was cool and where we could rest. Short, plump, and muscular, with vivacious eyes and a cheerful manner, she started for the house, and we followed along. As we entered we marveled once again at the cleanliness of the Ukrainian peasant. The clean-swept cottage was freshly whitewashed inside, and its windows were darkened with cloth so that flies would not come in. Even the oven was spotless, so unlike ovens among peasants in the north, which are always thick with soot. In the corner, draped in richly embroidered linens and hung over with freshly cut willow twigs, were two shiny ikons. She asked us if we were hungry, and would we eat tomatoes and bread? Then she proceeded to talk.

She was a member of the collective farm, but the garden was her own, and thank God that it was! At least she was assured of vegetables. Once she had owned a cow and a pig. Now she had neither—no stock at all except a few chickens—and how could she keep a cow or a pig when she had no feed and the collective farm wouldn't give her any? It should, but it didn't. All the feed went away to the city.

As she was talking, another woman came in, a neighbor, a huge red-faced woman, with an excited expression on her face. She saw us go into this house, she said, and she thought she could come in and tell us everything that had happened. Perhaps people on the outside didn't know anything about it—visitors were so rare—and we might tell them so they would know how scandalously they had been treated—they, such hard-working folk, with no desire to be *koolacks* or to do wrong to anybody!

Interrupting and supplementing one another, the two women raced on with their narratives. One allotment of grain was taken from their collective farm, and another, and a third. They begged the collectors to remember the lean months of spring, when their grain-bins would be empty. But the collectors paid no heed. When winter came and the bottoms of their grain-bins began to show, they went to the Soviet officials begging for help, but they were told that they would have to scrape along as best they could with their own resources—and they had no resources. They were furious. They had been fooled. They had been promised help if they should run short of grain, and now they were told that they would get no help. From day to day the supply in their grain-bins was getting lower and lower. Still no help from the Soviets. They grew panicky. Soon they would be without bread. Hunger was coming. What would happen? Their potatoes were likewise few, and so were their cabbages. Hunger! Hunger! Could it be possible? Would they starve and swell up and die, and their children too?

So, because the Soviet was too lazy to do anything, they got together and took things into their own hands. They appointed delegates, put their money together, collected the things they could sell, and sent these delegates off with them to the north Caucasus, White Russia, the upper Volga, where they had heard grain could be bought. Trains were overcrowded. Tickets were difficult to buy. Always there were such long queues of people waiting at the windows. But their men and their delegates waited. They lay around the railroad stations. If they had to stand in line for hours, only to be told when their turn came that all tickets were sold, they didn't get discouraged. They had to get bread, even if it took a week or two, or a month, to obtain a ticket. They could not go back home empty-handed and face their wives and children. Finally they returned, one with a sack of rye, one with a sack of ground oats, one with a sack of corn meal—and so they managed to tide over the lean months. But they had had a bad fright.

Now they didn't know what was going to happen in the coming year. They all got an allotment of grain from the collective farm, enough to last them until January. They would get more after January. At least, they were hoping they would. But if they didn't, what would happen? How could Moscow and Stalin expect them to put their hearts into their work when they were treated like that? Ah, what fools, what fools Russians were! No greater fools in the world!

When we left them the sun was already setting and people were hurrying home from the fields. We walked on, and presently passed a yard in which three women were threshing millet with flails. They were a mother and two daughters. They stopped as we drew near and hailed us. They knew who we were, for the news of our presence had, they assured us, already traveled from one end of the village to the other. Jestingly they asked if we could help them thresh, and, taking them at their word, we picked up their flails and proceeded to batter away at the sheaves of millet. Peasants from near-by cottages came out and watched us and made merry comments on the way we handled the flails. The women begged us to let them finish the job, but, once started, we held on to the flails until we had threshed the last of the sheaves. There were more guffaws and comments and outpourings of good humor. Only when we asked the woman if she belonged to a collective farm did the mood of the people change. She didn't, she answered tartly, and why should she? To be sure, it was all the same. If you were an individualist they took your grain away, and if you were a collectivist they took your grain away.

"Last spring," she continued, "my husband got sick and I had no sugar, no white bread, and no meat to give him [foods, incidentally, which, because of their rarity, are regarded as luxuries in the Russian village and are supposed to possess curative powers], and how could he recover on bread made from the wastes in flour-mills?"

"It is the only kind we had for several weeks," interposed a haggard old woman who was standing by with her rough hands folded over her stomach.

"And so my husband died," continued the widow.

"Stop, mother," cried one of her daughters.

"I won't," she retorted. "Look at her," she raced on, pointing at the protesting girl. "She is a consumptive. You wouldn't think so, but she is. She's picked up this summer since we've had garden foods and cereals from the new crop. But if we face another winter like the one we had last year, she'll get worse and she'll die."

The girl, embarrassed and angry, fled into the house.

"It is bad here, very bad," murmured a bearded man with a flushed face and a broad nose that rose out of his beard like a beet out of the earth.

"On our collective farm nineteen horses died last winter and spring because we had no food for them," volunteered a youngish man in tall boots and with a whip in his hand.

"He ought to know; he is the stableman," some one else remarked.

"And the others that are left aren't much good now—they are so worn out and underfed—can't pull much," broke in the bearded man once more.

"Now look." Still another man spoke up and pointed to the valley below, where a herd of cattle, sprayed with the last remnants of sunshine, were browsing amid tall coarse reeds. "You can count the cows out there easily, can't you? That's all there are, I can assure you. But three years ago if you came here you couldn't count the cows in that pasture, there were so many of them. Everybody had a cow then."

"Even I had a cow," murmured the widow.

"And why mention only cows?" interposed the bearded man. "Nearly everyone had pigs, too, and now who can keep a pig?"

"I can't," asserted the widow.

"And I can't either," another man volunteered. "I am in the collective, and we don't get enough feed for a pig or a cow of our own."

"That's true enough."

"What can we do?" questioned the widow angrily.

"There is nothing to be done, nothing," answered the bearded man with resignation. "It is finished; life is finished for our kind. Maybe our children will enjoy it—maybe. But as for us—good-bye"; and he motioned sadly with his hand.

Others nodded their heads, some of them murmuring dolefully: "True enough, true enough."

We sauntered on, and everywhere heard the same story. To these stalwart men and women collectivization, instead of being the boon it had been pictured, had become a misfortune, and they were desolate. They had reaped none of the rewards they had been promised. Instead, they had only suffered privations.

Of course, they were thinking only in terms of immediate returns. But that is the way of a peasant, especially when he embarks on a new venture. He is neither business man nor philosopher. He has no long-range view of life. He judges the world about him in terms of what he sees and experiences, and for the moment he sees none of the blessings which collectivization promised.

It was dark when we started back toward our hotel.

The yards in which people had congregated were now deserted. So was the street. Few of the cottages were lighted up. People were retiring for the night—weighed down with distress and discouragement.

Yet no sooner had we reached our hotel than we discovered that there was another world in this village—miles and ages apart from the one we had just been visiting. It was the world of the revolutionary youth. We were invited to spend the evening with them, and we went. What a contrast they were to their elders! The public buildings which were at their disposal were brightly lighted. Halls and rooms were humming with movement and echoing with chatter and laughter. Here no one was chanting dirges. Here the voice of confusion had not penetrated.

One of the public buildings was a museum. The keeper was a man of about forty, with a flushed face, brilliant eyes, a stooping back, and a ringing voice. He welcomed us with explosive eagerness. He had been looking all over the village for us, he said, and he was so delighted that we were back. He had much, very much to tell and to show us. He was one of those self-educated intellectuals in the village who are known as "social enthusiasts." Seldom members of the party, they become absorbed in some social task and the whole village knows them. Always they are apostles of culture. This man was more than an apostle; he was a high priest of culture. Every other word in his speech was a derivative of the word culture. The museum, he assured us, was a temple of culture, and it was all his creation, and there was nothing on earth that peasants needed so much as culture. If they had had more of it earlier they wouldn't be grumbling and wailing so loudly now. They would realize that in the upbuilding of a new civilization mistakes and setbacks cannot be avoided, and that a year or two was nothing anyway. Today things might be bad; tomorrow they might be good. Yesterday they had no museum in this village; now they had one.

Everything comes in time, if only people are cultured enough to understand it. The year before, for example, he was without boots, he told us. This year he had boots. It was not easy to buy them. He had to wait for several months before they arrived. But in the end they did arrive. It was the same with everything else. In time peasants would have everything—how could they help it with Magnitogorsk and Kuznetsk and Dneprostroy and all the other vast building projects coming to a finish? But ah, this peasant! He had no eyes to see, and all because he had absorbed so little of the new culture. He had to absorb more, and the museum would help him.

Talking rapidly and excitedly, he showed us around the exhibits. Here were samples of the old culture—church vestments, church draperies, church crosses, church ikons which still bore the marks of the gold and jewels with which they had been studded; photographs of houses of former landlords, officials, clergymen; reproductions of paintings, showing the life of the peasant in the old days; photographs of scenes in the civil war, with Whites and Reds and bandits alternately coming and going and slaughtering one another. And here were the exhibits of the new culture: mounted birds and animals and insects native to the region; the various types of soil in Russia and what they were best fitted to grow; collections of rocks and fossils and all manner of tools dating back to the Stone Age; diagrams showing the course of social work in the community, explaining hygiene, telling the story of the war on illiteracy and advantages of collective tillage of the land, drawings of children in schools learning how to make and operate tractors, turbines, engines, and exhibits of apparatus that they themselves had fashioned. With profuse apologies he explained that there were many things which the museum was lacking. But he was searching around for new exhibits. In another year or two he would have a museum second to none in communities of the size of this village.

He pushed us into another part of the building and pointed with pride to shelves of books, old and new, chiefly in paper covers, with numbers and labels on their backs and arranged according to subject. This was a library on the history of the revolutionary movement in the village, and it was he who had built it up. He proceeded volubly to expound the meaning of the various subjects into which he had divided the library, and, pulling out book after book and opening them, he explained their contents. Some one suggested to him that perhaps those books were not as interesting to us as he thought they were—and he, as if abashed at such a possibility, asked us if indeed we were being bored. We intimated that we had not time to examine every book in the library or have its meaning explained, and he politely excused himself and proceeded to inform us that there was a third cultural activity in which he was engaged and which would surely interest us. It was music. He had never studied it in a school or with a teacher, but he had always loved music and had organized a balalaika orchestra and we must hear it play. He turned to one of the boys in the room and asked him to rush out and "mobilize" all the players at once. The boy forthwith dashed out, and soon returned with the news that the orchestra had been "mobilized" and was waiting in the music-room.

Still talking about the part of music in the life of a cultured people, our enthusiast piloted us to the music-room—a large room hung with posters and set with rows of backless benches on which the players had gathered. They were boys and girls in their teens, some of them barefooted, with balalaikas of various makes and sizes. Posed before them on a low platform, with set face and all the dignity and earnestness of a prima donna, their leader waited until all eyes were on him, and then he waved a little black ruler. At once the orchestra strummed away with a zest and a verve that seemed to make the very room lighter. When they finished one piece they played another, and then a third. The enthusiast seemed joyously set for a whole evening's program when the party secretary appeared. He was a serious youth in the early twenties, with a low voice and of slow but emphatic speech. He invited us to go with him to see the other cultural institutions in the village. But the orchestra leader protested. We must stay, he pleaded, and listen to a few more numbers—the best ones in his repertoire. We were not bored, were we? We assured him we were not, and it was true. There was a lilt and a melodiousness to the playing that was a welcome relief from the woes which we had heard in our afternoon rambles in the village. But the secretary was decisive. We must see the other things—and see them now when they were in full swing. This was the working season, and people might go home early to rest for the next day's labors. Finally, the two compromised on our remaining to hear just one more number, the Budenny Marching Song, which no secretary of the party, however preoccupied, would deny himself the pleasure of hearing rendered by a competent choir or orchestra.

When it was finished, we proceeded to the theater, followed this time by an ever-increasing group of onlookers—young people. The theater was an imposing structure and spread over a vast space of ground. It was still unfinished, but doors and windows had already been put in and it was now in use. It had a spacious auditorium with fifteen hundred freshly varnished wooden seats, and a huge stage with all the devices necessary for theatrical production, including good lighting. Then we were shown through the other rooms —meeting-rooms, study-rooms, a lounge-room, and of course a buffet. A theater without a buffet is as unthinkable in Russia as a theater without a stage. By winter, the secretary assured us, the whole structure would be finished and the theater would be the center of culture in the community.

There was a rehearsal in progress, and we remained to watch it. The actors were local workers, students, and teachers, and the coach was a professional actor from Kiev. Tall and thin and gray-haired, with a melancholy face and a lusty voice, he read line after line of the play, which he had his actors repeat after him, imitating him in gesture, inflection, posture, and movement. Our presence did not disturb him. He did not even bother to ascertain who we were. With a heroic fervor he continued his rehearsal. The secretary informed us that he had at one time specialized in Shakespearean plays, and had even talked of putting on one or two of them during the forthcoming winter, with himself taking the leading parts. The play he was now rehearsing was one of those numerous propaganda plays which deal with the relations of parents and children in the village and which was supposed to show young people how to awaken a revolutionary consciousness in recalcitrant parents.

Even as we were watching the rehearsal, young people began to dribble in singly, in couples, in groups. They were washed and dressed up, with many of the young men wearing collars and ties and the young ladies in dresses, not of homespun, but of manufactured cloth, and with white or red kerchiefs on their heads. Some of them were attracted by the rehearsal. Others had heard of the presence of Americans there and had come to take a look at them. Still others were members of the village choir, which was having that evening its bi-weekly rehearsal. When the dramatic coach became aware of the presence of the singers, he dismissed his actors and turned the stage over to the choirmaster, who was a local school-teacher.

The latter, a short, stubby man with a large head and piercing eyes, seemed to take his task as seriously as did the dramatic coach or the party secretary. He too had a low voice, but he spoke little and never once mentioned his cultural mission in the community, though the keeper of the museum, who presently joined us, assured us that this choir was a mighty pillar of culture in the village.

He assembled his choir on the stage, about forty voices, men and women, and led off in a song—an old folk-song of local origin, light and tuneful and with the usual repetitious refrain. When this song was finished, he began another at once, and followed this with still another. Meanwhile more and more people were coming in, and the end of each song was greeted with loud applause. All the songs were of local origin—old songs, some with a dash of humor which evoked hearty laughter. Several times the choirmaster wanted to stop, but his ever-growing audience clamored for more and more, and he readily obliged them. Not once, however, did he sing a revolutionary song, this not out of lack of regard for revolutionary music but out of a desire to demonstrate to us the high quality of the folk-tunes that had grown out of the soil of Russia.

It was past midnight when we returned to our hotel, and we were torn by conflicting emotions. We couldn't forget the men and women who had so plaintively unburdened themselves to us, and fresh in our minds were the young people we had just seen. They sang and played and studied and planned and hoped, and cherished no notion of defeat or collapse. Surely they too endured hardships. We had eaten in the restaurant in which many of them were taking their meals, and seen that, although there was bread in plenty and cereal soup and cucumbers and tomatoes, the rations of meat on the days it was served—and on most days it was not —were slight and made up of tough meat. There was no

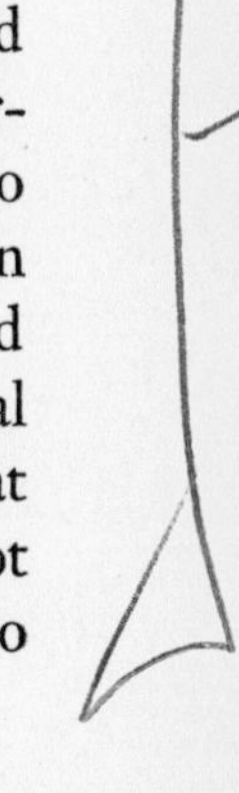

pastry in the place, and very little sugar. We had been in the stores and had seen little but chinaware on the shelves. Shipments of goods in small amounts were coming in every day, but these were snatched up as soon as they arrived. Yet these young people took it all in good humor, as though it had to be but would not last forever. They had their museum, their orchestra, their choir, their schools, their theater, and they were getting culture and having fun and encountering adventure. And what else does youth need?

Yet the grievances of their elders were real and overpowering and demand the closest scrutiny. Indeed they constitute the saddest aspect of the Revolution.

VII
COLLECTIVES

LATE in the summer of 1931, I strayed into a village in the black earth section in which an agricultural conference was being held. Leaders of collective farms, party secretaries, Soviet officials, had gathered to discuss problems of the forthcoming sowing season. These problems were all the more pressing because for the first time this district had achieved almost universal collectivization. Only a bare 5 per cent of the peasants still clung to their individual land allotments. All the others had merged their lands with collective farms.

The most exciting subject of discussion was the sowing of the sunflower. This humble seed, disdained in English-speaking countries, is assuming ever-growing importance in Russia, particularly in a district like the one I was visiting, because it is especially suited for cultivation of this plant. The sunflower seed supplies an oil that is used universally in cooking and in baking, a godsend in these days of acute shortages of animal fats, and it supplies a wholesome food for poultry. Above all, it is a luxury to Russians of all classes, who love to shell it and eat the kernels.

As this district was subject to periodic drought, there were years when the sunflower crop burned up. How to combat this visitation of nature was a problem which an experimental station had been seeking to solve. At last it discovered a solution—if the sunflower were planted in the autumn instead of in the spring, as peasants had been accustomed to doing, it could withstand drought more successfully. A representative of the experimental station was in attendance at this conference, and read a long report on the findings of the station. When he finished, discussion was called for, and delegate after delegate hailed the discovery with pride and elation. Then a resolution was introduced calling on the assembly to carry the recommendation of the experimental station into immediate practice. It was passed with unanimous and hearty acclaim.

As I was watching this conference, I could not help thinking of other meetings I had attended in villages at which, for purpose of increased land fertility, peasants were urged to introduce changes in their methods of work. I recalled a meeting in the part of Russia where I was born, at which the subject of rotation of crops was under discussion. It was in the days before collectivization. Clearly and concretely and with the help of slides, a visiting *agronom* was seeking to impress his audience with the advantages of proper rotation of crops. The peasants listened with eagerness, but when called upon to express their opinion on the proposed changes they shook their heads and uttered only words of disapproval. The best that they could say for the scheme was that it might work well in America, Germany, or Denmark where farmers might have more land and were rich enough to buy modern machines, fertilizers, and seeds. But for them in far away Russia, in their particular village, it was risky to embark on experiments. Supposing they failed—then what? There was the question of hay, for instance. True enough, they never seeded their meadows and the hay they cut was rough and sour. But it grew of itself. They never had to tend it, and even in bad years they had some hay. Under the new system they would have to plough up their meadows and then keep on seeding them, and they were too poor to buy the seed. Besides, suppose it didn't grow well or was visited by drought—then what? No, they could take no chances, and not a single peasant in the whole community would take the advice of the *agronom*—this in spite of the fact that the ancient three-field system of farming, whereby they used one field for spring crops, another for autumn crops, and allowed the third to lie fallow, was one of the outstanding curses of Russian agriculture.

There were peasants, chiefly in the Ukraine, in the northern Caucasus, and in Siberia, who had copied methods of farming from neighboring landlords. The German colonists likewise were superior farmers. That was why they were originally invited to come to Russia. These farmers had acquired machinery and managed to wrest substantial yields from the land. They had choice livestock and knew how to tend it. But they were small in number, no more than four or five per cent of the whole peasant population. They were largely the so-called *koolacks,* who later paid a tragic penalty for whatever success they had achieved in farming. The vast masses of Russian peasants had always feared radical departure from established practice. They had memories of lean and famine years, and they would not risk an innovation lest it result in failure and leave them desolate.

In spite, therefore, of lectures, motion-pictures, promises of bountiful yields and richer living, they preferred to plod on in their own ancient way. They ploughed poorly, sowed poorly, harvested poorly. Few would ever break up the lumps of earth in their fields and prepare a proper seed-bed. Their care of livestock was notoriously faulty. In winter they fed their cows little or no grain, and consequently obtained little or no milk. They housed livestock in windowless barns which, with some notable exceptions, they cleaned twice, or, at most, four times a year. The conditions under which they produced milk were preposterously unsanitary. They allowed pigs to fend for themselves, and though this method developed native breeds that were strong, alert, and combative, it did not produce much meat.

Viewed from any angle, it was obvious that Russian farming as practiced for ages by the vast majority of peasants needed a drastic overhauling. Collectivization provided a way of achieving it with dispatch and without undue resistance from peasants. They might object, prophesy failure, refuse properly to carry out orders, but the net result was always some small gain, and if the results were promising they never again would offer objections. The conference which I was attending was eloquent testimony to the ease and speed with which reforms could be launched under a system of collectivization where there was centralized control of the land. If the peasants in this district had held land in individual possession, each of them free to till it as he thought best, the introduction of such a comparatively simple change as seeding sunflowers in autumn instead of in spring would have required years of strenuous campaigning, and, even then, some peasants would have persisted in their old methods. One has only to visit the sections in which German farmers live, and observe the difference between crops and livestock on the German farms and on the peasant farms, to assure oneself of the inexplicable stubbornness with which the *muzhik* clings to his ancient ways of working the land. Very rarely does he follow the example of the Germans.

In my judgment, collectivization has been a most beneficial thing for Russian farming. It eliminates a multitude of crying wastes which are inherent in Russian individualist landholding—wastes in seed, in labor, in human and animal energy. It wipes out at once the ancient and ruinous division of land into long and narrow strips with their adjacent weed-growing ridges. Under proper management it can, as in the case of the above-mentioned district conference, at one stroke discard ancient methods of tillage. It can raise fertility of soil to a height unattainable under ordinary Russian conditions.

Through the abolition of small landholding and the creation of large-scale farms, it makes possible the universal introduction of the best modern agricultural machines. It provides an easy method of weeding out scrub breeds of stock and their replacement with the best breeds obtainable. Above all it guarantees open-minded management which can readily apply anything new that science and experience advise. Merely as a method of farming, collectivization is economically as sound as the building of new schools, new factories, new homes.

The Communists, of course, had powerful political motives in launching this movement at the time they did. They wanted to deal a death-blow to private enterprise in the village as they had done in the city. They had embarked on the Five Year Plan for the purpose of laying the groundwork of a new society in which private enterprise was to have no place, and here in the village and all over the country were twenty-seven million farmers holding their land and their stock and their implements in private possession, and threatening to sharpen the conflict between village and city and thus defeat one of the main purposes of the Revolution.

There was a further and more immediately pressing consideration which made the Communists impatient to spur on collectivization. In the years of 1926 and 1927 and 1928 they had engaged in nation-wide conflicts with peasants in their efforts to obtain food for the cities and army. Under a system of individualist farming the unruly peasant managed often to find a way of deceiving government officials. He would hide his grain and his stock as he had been doing, and leave the government official empty-handed. Prohibiting the sale of grain and other products to private traders did not necessarily make him deliver these to the government, especially as the government could pay him little in goods.

And here they were with the Five Year Plan on their hands and with millions of new workers to be taken care of. These workers had to be assured a good living, or those who had come from the village would run back home, and the industrial program would suffer setbacks and perhaps collapse. Clearly they could afford to take no chances nor spend much energy on conflicts with peasants. But collectivization, once it was achieved and entrenched, offered an easy way out of the dilemma. It insured the government a monopoly of agricultural produce. When the peasants pooled their land and their implements and their work animals, and did their work jointly, they could not easily deceive the government officials. There would be too many of them to carry out a conspiracy successfully. Certainly it would be impossible for them to deceive the government as successfully as when they exercised individual control of their land. Besides they would have to keep accounts of everything they produced, and such accounts they could neither hide nor falsify. Best of all, Soviet officials and party workers and *agronoms* and party members of the collectives would be on watch and see that the government was not cheated of its share of the produce.

And so collectivization was launched as the one sure method of pushing Russian agriculture out of ancient backwardness, and of laying out the path for the ultimate consummation of the social program of the Revolution in the villages, and, best of all, of enabling the government to obtain the food it needed so desperately for its fast-growing armies of industrial workers.

But to the peasant it was a new thing, a bold, unheard of scheme of farming, contrary to all his experience and all his wishes. He listened intently to explanations of the advantages and promises collectivization held forth. But he was slow to take action. He would deliberate long and minutely before making a decision in so momentous a matter as a change in life. He would discuss it pro and con with wife and neighbors. He would wait until some one else had tried it in some other village and he could observe what had happened. But the Communists were impatient. Every day was precious. The Five Year Plan had to be pushed. Industrialization had to press on. The Revolution had to march forward, and the Communists would tolerate no obstruction from peasants. And so when persuasion failed to lure the *muzhik* into the new scheme of farming, pressure was applied with a fierceness that roused the peasant rancor. If he could not remain on his individual allotment of land, neither would he of his own volition aid the new movement. And so he struck back at the Soviets—he proceeded to sell implements and slaughter livestock. Cows, sheep, horses, pigs, goats, by hundreds of thousands were killed. Only after drastic ordinances were issued against the slaughter of livestock, and assurances were given the peasant that he need not join a collective if he did not wish to, and that when he did he might keep his own cow and his own pig and his own chickens and cultivate his own garden, and that everything he turned over to the collective, whether it was ready cash or implements or livestock, would be regarded as an investment which would yield him a dividend—only then did the peasant stop the slaughter of his livestock.

The more well-to-do peasants continued to resist the movement, and, to dispose of their opposition, the Soviets proceeded to liquidate them. They dealt with them as mercilessly as they had with the trader in the city. Only those who visited Russian villages in those stormy days can appreciate the human tragedy that liquidation brought in its train. *Koolacks* had their property unceremoniously taken from them, and were cast out of their homes on to some barren or swampy piece of land outside their own, or in some other village, to wrest a living from a niggardly soil as best they could. Or, with their families, they were packed into overcrowded freight cars, sometimes with scanty food supplies, and exiled to some northern region—to start life all over again on virgin land, in a lumber-camp, or in some new construction project. Russia trembled with the cries and the curses of these benighted folk. But there was no abatement in the punishment visited on them. They were in the way of the Revolution and they had to be swept aside at all costs and hazards.

Of course one must remember the immense difficulties attendant on such a grandiose scheme of land reforms as collectivization, whereby the individual farmers merge their landholdings, their implements, and their animal power, and work the fields jointly, dividing the produce according to the amount and quality of the work each performs. There have not been enough competent organizers to manage the new farms efficiently. There have not been enough agricultural experts to guide the work properly. I have seen collective farms build huge piggeries with cement floors without tiles underneath; thereby causing high-priced sows, brought all the way from England, Germany, or Poland, to get chilled, develop pneumonia, and die. I have seen them operating massive incubators and failing to obtain a decent return of hatchings, or, having obtained it, leaving the chickens to the mercy of bad feeding and bad housing and thus losing them in large numbers. I have seen them sow Indian corn with grain-drills, as they would oats or wheat, thereby making it impossible for the stalks to attain proper growth and to mature. Endless are the blunders they have made.

But these blunders are not inherent in collectivization. In 1930, the collectives were on the way to triumph. The crop was the best Russia had had since the Revolution. The youth of the land was bubbling with hope. Not only a new method of farming was sweeping the land, but a new way of living was coming into being. Nurseries, schools, clubhouses, shock brigading—these were bringing fun, adventure, hope. Hardly a village one went to but young people and leaders could point with enthusiasm to some visible gain already achieved. The word *kolhoz* had become a symbol of a new day and a new reward. In the press and in conversation the word peasant was being used with less frequency. The peasant was not a peasant any more, that is, not after he had joined a collective farm. He was a *kolhoznik*—a new man with a new conviction and a new aim, driving vigorously on to a new destiny. In the hotels and restaurants, they stopped writing the item "peasant soup" on the menu. It was *kolhozny* soup now, and in proof of the success of the *kolhoz*, the chef in a peasant home in the Ukraine added to its ingredients so as to enhance the flavor and the quality of the dish.

At the Communist Congress in 1930, speaker after speaker pointed to collectivization as the signal achievement of the Revolution—the one phase of the Five Year Plan that had already exceeded expectations. Now at last the government had solved the perplexing grain problem. It had enough grain not only for home use but for export. Yakovlev, the Commissary of Agriculture, in a speech bristling with figures and boastfulness, sought to prove that in district after district the peasant who had joined a collective farm reaped a richer monetary reward even in his first year than he ever had as an individualist farmer. Here are Yakovlev's own words: "We find that the income of the middle-peasant family in the collective exceeds that of last year, while that of the poor peasant exceeds the former income of the middle peasant." And again: "What does it show? This—that the advantages of large-scale farming already make it possible in the first spring for the income of poor peasants in the collective farms to attain the level of former middle peasants, while the income of these rises still higher."

On the strength of his figures and the general outlook of the movement, Yakovlev promised the Congress and the Russian people that at the end of the Five Year Plan they would have, in spite of the prodigious slaughter of livestock, twice as much meat and milk in the country as there was at the beginning. All over the country the newspapers caught the spirit of the convention and printed columns of figures and names of peasants, showing that the advantages of collectivization were already amply manifest in the increased incomes its members were enjoying. In 1930, helped by the richest crop Russia had had since the Revolution, collectivization loomed as a most promising boon. Had the Communists nurtured the movement with tact and understanding, and, above all, with appreciation of peasant needs and sympathy for irrepressible peasant longings, they might have weathered the hard year that followed without serious reverses. But they did not. They were bent on fulfilling an immediate task, and bothered little with the effect on future development. Everything that happened during 1931-32 seemed to conspire to give the collective movement a shattering jolt, and nowhere was it felt as keenly as in the Ukraine.

There was the war scare with Japan. Russia could not take chances, so the Soviets began to mobilize themselves for the worst, which meant increasing the military food reserves of the country. There was the bad weather in 1931 which had ruined the crops in five grain regions. There was the need of increasing the export of grain to obtain much-needed *valuta* with which to meet foreign obligations. There was the fatal falsification of figures on acreage and yield, on the part of officials in the Ukraine, which caused the authorities in Moscow to impose heavier collections of grain than the crop warranted. There was the surge of political zeal in the rank and file of Communists, who grew impatient with the slow advance of Socialism in the villages and decided to give it a push. They proceeded to socialize livestock by compelling members of collectives to turn theirs over to the community herds, despite the fact that in 1930 assurance had been given the peasants that the stock which they kept for themselves was exempt from socialization. The peasants reminded these over-zealous officials of this promise. But the latter only pooh-poohed it. In retaliation, the peasants proceeded once more to slaughter livestock. Higher authorities then interceded and put an end to compulsory socialization, but that did not bring back to life the cows and pigs and sheep that had been killed.

There was further the interference of local officials with the peasant's right to sell his produce in the open market. Collectives, as such, were forbidden by national law to do so, but individualist peasants and members of collectives who had a surplus to dispose of had been in the habit of taking it to the bazaars. Now local officials began to confiscate produce taken to the market-place and to fine their carriers.

To make matters worse, there was also the stern system of meat collections. Let the reader recall the incident of the old couple whose cow was taken in fulfilment of the meat collections and the resultant strike by the neighbors, who stopped raising cows. Collections of vegetables, milk products, and fodder were likewise heavy, and there were instances in which individualist peasants and collectives ran short of potatoes, beet, and cabbage for themselves, and fodder for their stock during the winter months. Worst of all was the excessive collection of grain. This was carried out in the Ukraine with especial vigor. From the previous chapter the reader has learned that peasants implored grain collectors to pause and consider what they were doing, how they were with their own hands ruining the movement they were supposed to succor. But soldiers of the most highly disciplined civilian force in the world—the Communist Party—wouldn't be bothered. They knew that peasants always wailed, and they were ever conscious of party discipline—of the fact that they must not fail in the achievement of the mission on which they were sent. Even though their lives might be in danger, they could not afford to waver. They knew the wrath and scorn that would be leveled at them if they faltered or fumbled in their tasks.

And there was no time to lose. The dates for the fulfilment of the grain collection were set in advance, and it would be, so they imagined, a confession of defeat and weakness to pause in order to make investigations and lodge complaints with higher authorities. Every day counted. So they steeled themselves against all appeals and all laments. At times, of their own volition, they gathered more grain than their instructions called for. They were brave and faithful and they wished to demonstrate their devotion to their superiors by proving that in spite of difficulties they could more than fulfill their program. They did not count the cost in consequences. Nor did anybody bother to remind them of this cost.

When February, March, April (1931) came, the peasants in the Ukraine were short of food for themselves and their stock. Grain was available in other regions in the north Caucasus, in the upper Volga, but instead of the party, or the Soviets or somebody, mobilizing transportation and trade facilities to ship this grain to the distressed districts, they left the collectives to shift for themselves as best they could. The lack of mobility to cope with a critical condition is one of the worst features in Soviet organization.

Later, when the full facts of the situation came to the surface, hundreds of these officials all over the Ukraine were dismissed, disciplined, tried, jailed, or expelled from the party. Recently in Dnepropetrovsk, in the

Ukraine, three officials were shot for falsifying grain figures.

But summary punishment of blundering officials brought little solace to the distressed peasant. His grain was gone and it was not returned. He saw himself face to face with a ghastly situation, and so on his own initiative he started out in search of bread. Often he packed up his belongings and fled from the collectives. Thousands came to Moscow, because they knew that in Moscow there was an abundance of food. Young people rushed to the factories. They knew that in factories there was no shortage of food. The Ukraine, with its lovely lands and its lovely skies and its lovely white villages, was seized with panic and gloom. The mortality of livestock from starvation during this time was enormous. I have never seen an accurate statement of the figures, but they must have constituted a substantial percentage of all peasant stock. Pigs and horses were special victims of the famine. On one collective farm which I visited, 50 pigs had died; on another, 10; on still another, 100; on still another, 22 horses and 10 cows fell. Everywhere the cause was the same—lack of fodder. Naturally enough, the peasants grew disheartened. Not only were they made to give to the government quantities of grain which they needed for themselves, but when want overtook them the government bureaucracy failed to hurry to their aid. They had to squirm out of their difficulties by their own effort, and they did. They found rye and corn in other parts of the country, and brought it home to their families and neighbors. But that did not abate their rancor. The government finally rushed grain for seed, to make sure that the prescribed acreage would be planted in the spring, and often enough the peasant ate up all or a part of the seed. He had ceased to care about the future. He felt he had been imposed upon, and he lost interest in the collective farm.

Again and again he indulged in sabotage. He deliberately ploughed the land poorly, sowed thinly, disked badly. He had reached a point where he actually did not want a good crop, partly out of revenge and partly out of apathy. This, of course, was not universal even in the Ukraine, but it was widespread. In all my visits to Russia I never had seen such an abundance of weeds in the fields as there were in the summer of 1932. Sugar-beet in the Kiev area were literally submerged in weeds.

"In a number of places," said Kaganovitch, in his speech to the village shock brigadiers in February, 1933, "we have many weeds. We are pulling them out and burning them. But why did they come up? Because of poor tillage of the land." This is an official admission of the breakdown of peasant morale.

At the same conference, Yakovlev, the Commissary of Agriculture, narrated his experiences on a collective farm, named *Peremojhetz*, in the Odessa region in the Ukraine. Here, he said, was as choice a farm as there was in that part of the country–rich soil, superb climate with 9 hectares of grain land alone per family. Yet in 1932 it failed to fulfill the grain obligation to the government, even though the amount was reduced to one-fourth of what it had been the year before, and many a family had on hand only scanty supplies of bread. Of its 153 horses, only 53 were left. The other 100 died of starvation. Yakovlev hints that the man in charge of the horses, an old-time gendarme, might have deliberately starved them, though he admits that the only food available for the horses was straw and a little hay. There were chaos, disorder, and thievery on this farm, and, with the exception of a few brave shock brigadiers, the peasants took no interest in the work and loafed on the job. In other words, paralysis of the will to work had brought this most fertile collective farm to ruin.

Such a condition though not universal could not but have its sad political repercussions. The recalcitrant element on the collective farms had a new weapon in their hands. Peasants who had been opposed to collectivization, but had gone into a collective to save themselves from exile and other punishment, had something with which to stir up opposition, and they lost no time in doing so. Some of them had worked themselves into positions of command as chairmen or managers of collectives. With disappointment in the affected areas widespread, among the *bedniaks* (poor peasants) as much and sometimes more than among the others, these oppositionists had a fertile field in which to operate. Hence the rising resistance in such sections as the North Caucasus, where the Cossacks, though subdued, never had been reconciled to collectivization and to the abandonment of private enterprise which the Revolution had imposed on them. Hence the deportation to the north of several Cossack settlements, more perhaps as a lesson to the remaining Cossack population than as punishment to the people in those settlements.

Clearly, collectivization, in the Ukraine especially, needed immediate bolstering. In other parts of the country, complaints were also loud. It could not be otherwise in the midst of a shortage of manufactured goods and under a system of heavy grain collections and exorbitant meat collections.

I have the feeling that the greatest failing of the Communist organization, in spite of its oneness of purpose and rigorous discipline, is its callous insensitiveness to evils and errors at their inception. Whether it is sheer bureaucracy or hardness, or preoccupation with so many weighty tasks, or all of these, the results are no less calamitous. This was the case with the slaughter of livestock in the winter of 1929-30, with the policy of education, with the attitude toward the arts. In every instance the evil of error had attained the proportions of a catastrophe before the official searchlight was turned on it and measures were rushed through to avert a breakdown. For nearly a year the ferment in the Ukraine continued to brew before much was done to stop it. In other parts of the land, notably in the North Caucasus and in Siberia, dissatisfaction was also widespread with the peasantry crying for attention and demanding action but in vain. Finally the ban that had been imposed on *kolhoz* trading in the open market was lifted and a campaign was launched to speed up the manufacture of consumption goods.

But these concessions, though they eased the tension in the villages, failed to bring the reassurances that the peasants needed to sustain their faith in collectivization. During the *plenum* of the Communist Party in October, 1932, the whole country waited breathlessly for action but nothing much happened. Not until the Communist Conference in January of 1933 were decisive measures rushed through to repair the damage that the collectives had suffered. If only this were done a year earlier!

Now the Communists are pushing these measures with all the energy and all the resources at their disposal. They have abolished grain collections and have substituted in their place a grain and produce tax. They have turned Communist high schools and academies into agricultural schools and colleges so as to develop capable leaders. They have further intensified the manufacture of consumption goods. They have launched a campaign for army and factory units to raise ever-increasing amounts of their own food in order to ease up in the demands on the peasant. They have expanded the network of tractor stations so as to embrace a larger area of land with modern machines. There are nearly 3,000 such stations in the country. They have poured a huge army of seasoned Communists into the villages to exterminate opposition and to aid in the rehabilitation of order, discipline, morale, and confidence. It is as though they had mobilized the whole country, from the trade unions, Soviet factories, and party organization to the Pioneers, to heal up the wounds that mismanagement and mistreatment from above and from below have inflicted on the collectives, especially in the Ukraine and in the North Caucasus. On the face of it an agricultural crisis in Russia on the conclusion of the first Plan, seems an absurd anomaly. Compare the condition of the country in 1923 and at the present time. In 1923 Russia had just emerged from the worst famine she had had in her history. Nearly all the land had been dribbled up into narrow strips. There were no tractors in the country, no combines, and the implements that the peasants used were mostly primitive and worn. There were few experiment stations and few *agronoms* in the country. Yet the land literally flowed with food. Down the Volga, in the Ukraine, in White Russia, wherever I traveled, even in the Tartar country which was most severely hit by the famine, there was an abundance of food, of breads, dairy products and vegetables especially. Now with 80 per cent of the land taken out of the strip system, with over 100,000 tractors in use, with thousands of grain drills and combines and disk harrows and other machines available, with thousands of *agronoms* flitting about with advice and help, with the objective conditions more favorable to good crops than ever before in all Russian history there is this serious food crisis! The soil is the same, the climate has not changed, science and the machine have been lifted to unheard of heights. What has happened? The reader knows the answer. The human element has failed to lend nature and science proper coöperation, and without such coöperation nature and science can do little. The leadership or management of the collectives has been faulty, and what is equally ruinous or even more so, the rank and file of peasant workers, with some happy exceptions, have sunk into apathy.

What Moscow needs most is to develop a sensitiveness to peasant needs and peasant complaints. Clearly the Commissary of Agriculture has failed egregiously in this task. It has shown an incapacity to understand or to respond to mass sentiment of the peasantry. Fighting *koolacks* will not revive the peasant's morale. Moscow has had enough experience with the *muzhik* to realize that, when he thinks himself wronged, he strikes out with weapons which administrative procedure cannot counter. When he is confused and distressed, he sinks into apathy and lets things take care of themselves, and he will not shuffle out of this apathy if one year he is told that he may keep a cow and a pig and chickens for himself, and the next, that he is a *koolack* and counter-revolutionary if he does not turn his livestock over to the collective farm. Nor will it help him or the supply of foods for the country when, with all his land gone, he does not obtain enough fodder and grain from the collective for his own cow and pig. Local officials may be chiefly responsible for this particular condition, but that is of no comfort to the peasant and of no aid to agriculture. "The peasant joined the collective farm," said Kaganovitch in his speech in which he severely upbraided the whole Ukrainian Communist Party for its mistreatment of the Ukrainian peasantry in 1931, "to obtain the advantages of large-scale farming, and if he does not obtain them he will feel badly and will seek improvement for himself elsewhere," which is precisely what he has so often sought to do to the detriment of the whole country.

That is why the formation of the newly formed *politotdely*, or political committees on the tractor stations which supply machines to the collectives, loom so important, indeed transcend in importance any other measure the Soviets have as yet promulgated to lift the collectives out of their slump. These committees have been vested with extraordinary powers, and, if rightly used, they can retrieve the peasants' morale. Of course they cannot hope to do so by administrative procedure. A purely military or dictatorial approach to the peasant and his burden of perplexities and grievances will not rouse enthusiasm, and is foredoomed to failure. One must assume that these political organs will fight ruthlessly political opposition. That is one reason for their existence, but their chief task is to encourage the peasant to bring out of the land, with the aid of science and the machine, all that it can yield, and this they can attain only through a sympathetic understanding of peasant complaints and the satisfaction of peasant needs, above all through a reassurance, not in words but in acts, of suitable immediate rewards for his labors. Vested with power to make decisions without recourse to higher authorities, they can also prevent local and central officials from perpetrating further blunders, and can clear the atmosphere of the uncertainty and confusion which have permeated the collectives and contributed so much to the impairment of peasant morale. There is no task in the whole of Russia which demands so much tact, wisdom, and sympathy as the one that these political committees are now facing.

Yet of one thing we may be assured: as long as the Soviets endure there will be no return to individual farming. I have the feeling that, even if the Soviets were to collapse, Russian agriculture would remain collectivized with control more perhaps in the hands of the peasants than of the government. The advantages of collectivization as a method of farming are indisputable. There are even now scores of highly successful collective farms in the black earth region and the Ukraine. Collectivization has within it the power to convert Russia from a backward to a progressive agricultural nation, as individual landholding with its in-evitable small acreages never can. The individual farmer in Russia never can have land enough to warrant the purchase of binders, tractors, mammoth grain-drills, disk-harrows, hay-loaders, and even potato-diggers, unless of course Russia swings back to a system of free sale of land. Then the more powerful and the shrewder of the peasants would crowd the less energetic and less capable ones off the land, and come into possession of large acreages, at least large enough to justify the investment in new machines. But that would mean a return to landlordism and to chronic and widespread landlessness—the very condition that gave such violent impetus to the overthrow of the old régime. . . .

The salvation of Russian agriculture lies in the application of science and the machine to the land, and under Russian conditions this is only possible under some form of coöperative farming. If collectivization were to lean more on peasant coöperation and less on government control, particularly in the division of the crops, the shortages in meat and dairy products would soon disappear. Meanwhile the whole of Russian industry—steel shops, tractor plants, chemical works, machine-building factories—has been attuned to large-scale farming. Theoretically and practically, the army and the land have profited most from the advance of science and the machine which the first Five Year Plan has made possible, and the first Plan is only a beginning, in truth a first step in this advance. The machine and science, once they conquer a region, never abandon it, whether in city or village. They become a part of the very landscape and of the very elements which they have come to combat or succor.

The whole of education, in the villages especially, has likewise been bent to collectivization more than to any other utilitarian purpose, and all of agricultural education has been shaped to fit into its all-embracing mold. A glance at the figures on agricultural education in the old days and now will indicate what prodigious progress in this direction Russia had made since the Revolution. In 1915 there were 5 agricultural universities in the country with a student body of 3,300, 16 agricultural *technicums* or colleges with a student body of 1,600; and in 1932 there were 152 agricultural universities with a student body of 84,000, 967 *technicums* with a student body of 207,800, and 321 agricultural *rebfacs*, or workers' high schools, of which there were none in the old days, with a student body of 207,000. The increase in experimental stations is especially significant. Before the Revolution there were 200 of them, and in 1932 the number, including all branches, had increased to 1,587!

Given proper management and fit recognition of the human element on the collectives, the movement can become the crowning achievement of the Soviets.

PART II

FOR A NEW HUMAN PERSONALITY

VIII
RELIGION

THE LAST STAND

NOTHING so clearly shows the rapidity with which the old world is disappearing in Soviet Russia as the state of religion. On my first visit in 1923 I found atheism already rampant, especially among the young. Yet it was still possible to make out a case for religion and even for maintaining its vitality. In town and village alike the church was still a conspicuous object, and the Greek Orthodox priest, with his flowing locks and his dangling cloak, was a conspicuous figure in the social scene. Attendance at services had, it is true, fallen off woefully, but there were still multitudes of congregations, and few churches—less than two per cent of the whole number—had closed. Country girls were seldom willing to be married except by the priest, and, although large numbers of peasants had given up going to church, they continued to have their babies christened, and they always sent for the priest when there was a funeral. New religious sects were even springing up. Protestantism especially seemed to be in for a new lease of life. In spite of the Revolution, religion was, on the surface, then still flourishing.

How utterly different is the scene today! In the towns the church is no longer a landmark. As you approach Moscow by train or on the highway, no longer does the golden dome of the Temple of the Savior beckon to you from the distance. It is gone. The entire structure has been pried and blasted apart to give way to the much-planned and much-heralded Palace of the Soviets. No new churches have been built, and many, very many, of the old ones have either been put to new uses or pulled down to make room for other buildings. The ones that still function as houses of worship present a desolate sight—faded, rusty, actually cracking. Look in any direction you like, and you will find nothing but decay in the Greek Orthodox Church. All the old religions, indeed, are succumbing to the onslaught of the Revolution.

To this universal *débâcle* I came across only one exception—the so-called sects. I am speaking not of the mystical but of the rationalistic sects. They consist of common people, chiefly peasants and laborers, who, dissatisfied with the shortcomings of the old Church, had, sometimes with the aid of some outside preacher, sometimes wholly on their personal initiative, set up religions of their own. Two outstanding examples are the Baptists and the Evangelical Christians, who between them have had several millions of followers. They form the backbone of Russian Protestantism, and they have contributed a stirring page—indeed, a chapter—to the religious history of their country; even, one might add, to the history of the Revolution itself.

The career of Protestantism in the time of the Czars was checkered enough. It had its birth and its growth in martyrdom. No sooner had it made its appearance and shown itself capable of attracting converts than the Greek Church began to look upon it as an enemy and a rival, and to try its best, with the help of the old government, to suppress it. But Protestantism would not be suppressed. It throve in spite of persecution. The Protestant flocks were primitive folk, just as Russia herself was a primitive land. Their faith had retained much of the character of early Christianity. Its survival was in no sense due to organization, or to the union of the different groups, but simply to the devotion of the individual. It saw in religion not merely a ceremonial but a way of life, a body of principles to guide man in his relations with his fellow men and with the outside world. The Protestants read the Bible omnivorously, read, pondered, and absorbed it. They taught each other to read so that they should all be able to study Holy Writ. Those who could not read had it read and expounded to them. Unlike the Greek Church, Russian Protestantism paid more attention to the meaning of religion than to its form. In fact it had no form save baptism and music, and the choirs, wherever there were any, were among the best in the country. Puritan to the core, it banned the use of tobacco, spirits, violence, abusive language, dancing, the theater, and other indulgences of the flesh. Yet its votaries were no ascetics. They did not shrink from what they regarded as legitimate earthly pleasures; and from their foreign brethren, chiefly Germans, they had learned modern methods of agriculture and the virtues of thrift, cleanliness, and sobriety. They became, indeed, the most progressive farmers in Russia. "Sectarians" (the reference was to the Protestants), writes a well-known Bolshevik atheist in a pamphlet attacking all religions alike, "value highly literature on natural science, and especially on modern agriculture." Coming from an enemy, these words are especially significant. In the course of my travels I found the land of the Baptists and Evangelical Christians better worked than that of their Orthodox neighbors. They also lived a cleaner, more wholesome life and were better educated. They always loved to talk and to shower a stranger with hospitality.

Then came the Revolution, and with it freedom for the sects. Because their members were mainly peasants and proletarians, who had been persecuted in the old days, they were regarded by the Communists as wards of the Revolution and accorded rights and privileges such as they had never before enjoyed. The Bolsheviks were at that time trying to break the power of the Orthodox Church, and, following their usual tactics of dividing the enemy's forces, they were only too eager to enlist the help of the Protestants in discrediting Orthodoxy with the masses. In 1924 I found, in city after city and village after village, the Protestants out in the open. Everywhere in the bazaars Evangelical and Baptist preachers were holding forth on the meaning of their faith, unmolested either by Soviets or Communists. Sometimes they were heckled fiercely. But that neither dismayed nor disturbed them. If they were challenged to public debates, unlike Orthodox clergymen who often refused to meet revolutionaries in open discussion, they joyously accepted such challenges. Russia at that time teemed with talk of religion, and public debates on the subject were more common than motion pictures, were indeed one of the chief intellectual diversions and indoor sports of the masses.

In their local and national conferences both Baptists and Evangelicals passed resolutions thanking the Soviets for the consideration shown for their rights. In Moscow, Seventh Day Adventists were allowed to hold a convention in the Third House of the Soviets. In Tzaritzin, now Stalingrad, the great industrial city on the Volga and one of the revolutionary centers of southern Russia, a Baptist minister told me that the local Soviet was allowing him the free use of the city theater on Sunday afternoons. He invited me to his home to meet his family and some of his flock, and as we sat around eating cakes and jam and drinking countless glasses of tea, his friends and he spoke with glowing satisfaction of the new hope that had come to their people in Russia. At last there was nothing to interfere with the free exercise of their religion; Orthodox priests no longer spied on them, gendarmes no longer hounded them, and Cossacks no longer dragged them to jail as in the days of the Czar. Baptists and Evangelicals were both quick to use their new-found liberty to emphasize the social side of their faith, which, on the surface at all events, was in harmony with some of the social objects of the Revolution. They formed clubs, coöperatives, and mutual-aid societies; they encouraged music and sociability; and they immediately began to attract people. What they offered seemed to be something quite new in religion—philosophy, good-fellowship, kindness, practical help, a new social purpose, which, as already suggested, was in some ways akin to that of the Revolution; at least it appeared so at the time. Even the young, with all their distractions, found it worth their while to listen to the new word and to enjoy the new friendship, and the Protestants did their best to win their ear. The law did not allow them to hold religious classes for pupils under eighteen, but it did not interfere with the organization of clubs, picnics, festivals, musical gatherings, lectures, and athletics. Their young people formed their own organizations—the Baptomol for Baptist youth, and the Christomol for Christian youth; names with an obvious family likeness to that of the Communist youth organization, the Komsomol, an instance of the open way in which the Protestants copied the social technique of the Revolution. In their dealings with the young they always laid stress on the importance of cultivating good habits—self-control, politeness, industry, chivalry to women, respect for elders, and friendliness towards strangers. So much so, indeed, that the Soviet press would now and then chide the Young Communists for lagging behind the Protestants in this respect.

And so there came about this remarkable phenomenon: while all the other religions in Russia were losing ground with the new generation, the Protestants were not only holding their own but attracting converts. They were offering a purpose and immediate benefits. No wonder that Bukharin, at a conference some years ago, warned Young Communists that, unless they got busy, the Protestants would have more influence on Russian youth than they had.

But when the Bolsheviks began to realize how influential Protestantism was becoming they became alarmed. From one end of the country to the other one began to hear talk about the new enemy within the gates, an enemy which seemed, like the phœnix, to have sprung out of the ashes of the old religions. A new campaign was at once set on foot. What the policy of the Bolsheviks would have been if the New Economic Policy had been continued it is hard to say. But with the coming of the Five Year Plan and the leftward swing of the Revolution, their hostility to Protestantism was bound to grow, for, from their standpoint, it had now become one of the chief counter-revolutionary forces in the country. Said Yaroslavsky, perhaps the most noted atheist in Russia: "Whichever front of our struggle you take, whether for a new manner of living or anything else, everywhere we clash with the *sectants* [Protestants]. Not only are they against anti-religious but against non-religious training of children, against Pioneer groups, against Young Communists, against the party, against reading-rooms which carry anti-religious literature."

Nothing, indeed, so eloquently gives the lie to the plea, often put forward by sentimental liberals, that Russian atheism is merely a reaction from the degraded condition of the old Church, as this new attitude toward the Protestants which has changed from one of benevolent tolerance to unmitigated enmity. In cartoons and pamphlets the Protestant now figures alongside the other active enemies of the Revolution, the "damager," the priest, the *koolack*, the bootlegger, and the rest.

What, then, has caused this change? To find the answer we must examine the fundamental and irreconcilable principles to which the clash between Bolshevik and Protestant in their approach to the problems of life is traceable. Certain features in the community life of the Russian Protestants would at first glance suggest that, both in their theology and in their social views, they are modern and progressive. Yet nowhere in the world could one find a more primitively fundamentalist type of Protestantism. The Bible is its sole source of inspiration, its guide in thought and action; and anything which seems to be subversive of Bible teaching it rejects as untrue and unworthy. This of itself was sufficient to bring down upon it the wrath of the Bolshevik. Russian Protestantism has no more use for modern theories of evolution than has American fundamentalism. To the Bolshevik, on the other hand, science is the law of life, and evolution its chief glory. Nor could the Bolshevik remain indifferent to the uncompromising puritanism of Russian Protestantism, which forbids divorce, abortion, and birth control, regards the theater as something degrading, and, in certain spheres, even encourages the segregation of the sexes. Fundamentalism *versus* science was the first issue over which Bolshevism and Protestantism crossed swords—an issue which allowed for no quarter.

Dogmatism *versus* flexibility was a second. The Bolshevik charge against religion, especially a religion of so fundamentalist a nature as Russian Protestantism, is that it is rooted in dogma. The fixity of purpose which such dogmatism implies, they consider to be incompatible with both the principles and the practices of the Revolution. To them it means standing still in the years of social growth. It is useless to tell them that Marxism and Leninism have, in their hands, become just as rigid as anything to be found in fundamentalism. Their reply is that this is not so. Change, on the contrary, is, they say, the very essence of Marxism, which at best is itself merely a way of approach, an instrument of guidance. They love to quote Karl Marx's answer, when some one once asked him what was his chief diversion: "To subject everything to doubt." Lenin himself spoke of Marxism as a "guide to action." For the Bolshevik it is dynamic, something like a river which never stands still, which may ebb and swell and wind backward and forward, but which never ceases to flow on. Communism itself, they affirm, though a coming stage in human development, is by no means the final stage. What will follow they do not presume to say. But something will follow it. They consider that this attitude is at the opposite pole from the dogmatism of Protestantism as they see it.

Nor could the Bolshevik countenance with equanimity the Protestant reverence for authority. It is true that the authority to which the Protestant looks is not an earthly authority. But for the Bolshevik it is enough that it affects life and conduct. For him the very act of worship implies a recognition of this authority and is a confession of man's weakness in its presence. Besides, the authority itself is derived from a self-contained arbitrary and exclusive power which is represented upon earth by a group of its own—clergy and prophets. In the eyes of the Bolshevik this group itself constitutes an aristocracy and expresses a will which is not that of the masses. The masses, indeed, have themselves to honor and obey this aristocracy. They cannot criticize it. They cannot overrule it. They cannot even compromise with it. The system is thus a duplication of the very one which obtains under a capitalist régime; it represents rule from above instead of rule from below, mastery on the one side and subordination on the other.

If you say to the Bolshevik that his own dictatorship is the most hidebound authority on earth, he will reply with no small show of vehemence that it is only a temporary phase. He will argue that his dictatorship, though indispensable, is only incidental to the transition from an individualist to a collectivist state of society, and destined like the state itself, the instrument through which the dictatorship exercises its will, to disappear in due course. Eventually there will be no ruling class—indeed, no classes at all. There will be a classless society. Humanity will then consist only of producers, and the real power will be vested in the masses, or producers, with nothing above them—neither God, angels, nor Church—to keep them in a state of subjection. All authority, initiative, and creative energy will derive from them. And so it comes about that the fight against Protestant reverence for authority is, in Bolshevik eyes, a fight against the very evil which lies at the root of the civilization that they are determined to destroy. It is a fight against the principle of social and spiritual superiority and mastery.

Most inexcusable to the Bolshevik is the Christian doctrine of toleration, a dead letter in the Greek Orthodox Church, but dear to the heart of Russian

Protestantism. Under this doctrine man, and not class, comes first. Man's social origin, economic pursuits, and political allegiance are of secondary or no consequence. Whatever his circumstances in life and whatever his sins and misdeeds, he remains an object deserving of pity and forgiveness and the respect of his fellow men. Such a doctrine is a direct negation of the theory of the class war, and to the Bolshevik, immersed in his Great Offensive and his struggle to reconstruct society on a non-class basis, it is naturally anathema. For it demands respect for the *koolack*, the *nepman*, the counter-revolutionary, the "damager," and others whose extermination he deems essential. The sworn enemy of individual accumulation, and bent on its destruction, he has nothing but contempt for a religion which extends a welcome to the wealthy and the needy alike. The time for toleration will come, he says, when his new system of society is established, and man has attained a classless society; but today, while the battle is still on to ensure its realization, Christian toleration seems to him to be tantamount to social and political suicide.

Nor does he regard with favor or approval the clannish tendencies of Russian Protestantism. Evangelical Christians and Baptists, in spite of their overflowing hospitality to strangers, speak of members of their own folds as believers and of others as unbelievers. Though bent on making converts, they nevertheless keep very much to themselves in their social and charitable work —indeed, in most of their activities. They address one another as "brother" and "sister." Even more than their co-religionists in foreign countries, they look upon themselves as a brotherhood complete in itself, open to others for admission on acceptance of their faith but not otherwise.

To the Bolshevik, with his exaggerated suspicion of customs that differ from his own, this close religious brotherhood means separatism, detachment from the masses, an attempt to disrupt the unity of his new society. Nor does it give him pleasure to see his own trade unions break up into smaller units and turn aside to pursue what he regards as extraneous aims. He remembers how certain groups of miners in the Don basin, and of textile workers in Ivanovo, and of builders in Moscow, became converts to the Protestant faith, and how this faith drained their revolutionary ardor.

He is afraid, too, of the Protestant Church becoming a city of refuge for the counter-revolution, and this keeps the edge of his hostility especially sharp. The church was and is the only organization allowed to hold meetings of a non-revolutionary nature. It is true that there is nothing in its form of worship which in itself constitutes a threat to the Revolution; but—so the Bolshevik reasons—political plots might be hatched under the cloak of religion, and if Protestantism were to go on spreading, it might in time attract counter-revolutionary elements, who would thus find a place ready to hand where they could meet and coördinate their efforts. Foreign help, too, might be forthcoming in the guise of religious contributions, and the Church organization would make it easy to get into touch with foreign conspirators. To the outsider, these fears may seem exaggerated and absurd; but to the out-and-out revolutionary they are as natural as his faith in Marx and Lenin.

Equally hostile is the Bolshevik to the pacifism of Russian Protestants. Of course, neither the Baptists nor the Evangelical Christians have formally adopted pacifism. They would have had they dared, for their faith is in a way rooted in pacifism. They are averse to violence, particularly when it involves the taking of human life. They accept literally the command, "Thou shalt not kill." They had in fact begun an extensive campaign against war, and they thought that, inasmuch as the Bolsheviks continually denounced war as a nefarious scheme of capitalists to win profit for themselves out of human slaughter, they would be encouraged in their anti-war crusade. But they sadly misconstrued the Bolshevik attitude toward war. True enough, the Bolshevik flamingly condemns national and capitalist wars. But he is no pacifist. He never was. He believes in battle when it is necessary to promote the interests of the proletarian class. He is the world's most eloquent champion of class war as the sole means of emancipating workers from subjection. He eschews terrorization of individual capitalists or officials. He denounces uprisings just for the sake of trouble-making. But he would welcome nothing more than a battle to the finish against the bourgeoisie as a class, and would fight at a moment's notice for the promotion of workers to a position of mastery. He believes in violent overthrow of existing governments wherever conditions warrant it. Besides, he is war panicky. He imagines that the whole outside world is constantly plotting to overthrow his system of society. Under these circumstances it is in-evitable that a movement like pacifism, even though not officially encouraged by Russian Protestantism, should rouse his rancor. He regards it as inimical to his very security as the ruler of Russia.

Lastly, there is the economic situation, and here again the Bolshevik and the Protestant are at loggerheads. Bolshevism spells death to private property; the Bolshevik is determined to wipe it out. He regards it as the chief source and cause of all forms of exploitation. The Protestant's view is different. He may not believe in piling up riches, but neither Baptist nor Evangelical Christian condemns the institution of private property in itself. Their cartels and coöperative establishments were among the most successful in Russia. In Moscow the Evangelicals used to operate a number of vegetarian restaurants which were among the best eating-places in the city; but, being outside state control, they might, from the Communist standpoint, just as well have been private concerns owned by a private individual. Protestant peasants, too, were among the thriftiest in Russia, a result of their personal habits and their higher cultural standing. But it is a truism to say that the more prosperous the farmer, the more hostile his attitude is likely to be toward the collectivization of the land. The Protestant is no exception. Besides, the Protestant knows well enough that on the collective farm he would find a tense revolutionary atmosphere. The principles of the Revolution with regard to family, religion, and the relationship of man to man and of man to woman—principles which he could never accept, which in his heart of hearts he abhors—would be assiduously propagated. He would not be kept from practicing his religion in his own manner, but in the course of his everyday life he would always be coming up against the Revolution and its requirements. His children would have to attend the nurseries, the kindergartens, and the schools, and would soon slip away from their parents' influence. He would lose them beyond recall. He has seen what has happened to children in the case of other religions in Russia. If allowed to form his own collective farms, he might have acquiesced in the new movement, but that was out of the question. The Bolshevik was intent on supervising all collective farms. This issue in itself was bound to bring on a clash, and a bitter one, between Bolshevik and Protestant.

With such divergent views on questions of principle and practice, both in the social and the economic way of living, it was only natural that Protestantism, as soon as its exceptional capacity for rapid growth had become manifest, should stir the active hostility of the Bolsheviks. Here was a new influence in their midst, spreading through farm and factory alike—the very citadels of their power—an influence quite unlike that of the old Orthodox Church. For this was no mere cloak of antique formalism, sure to rip from top to bottom before the first gust of modern ideas, but a new spirit, a body of new ideas which had sunk deep into the hearts of those involved. No wonder that Lenin's widow pronounced the Russian Protestant a greater menace to the Revolution than Orthodoxy, and Bolsheviks all over the country echoed and re-echoed her sentiments.

In their attack, propaganda has as usual had its part. But a still more deadly blow was the law of April,

1929, a law which applies to all religious bodies alike, but which hits the Protestants harder than any of the others. For although the law reasserts the principle that religious confession is free and the individual has the right to worship in whatever way he chooses, it does not, as the old law did, permit religious and anti-religious propaganda alike; it permits anti-religious propaganda only. This, of course, has put an end to missionary work and to preaching in bazaars and places other than officially recognized houses of worship. There is a further provision which bars clergymen from ministering to more than one congregation at a time, and of course stops Baptist and Evangelical pastors from visiting other congregations than their own. From the point of view of the Protestant, the unkindest cut of all was the revival and amplification of an old law which prohibited a religious body from exercising so-called "administrative functions." In the early years of the Revolution, for reasons already explained, the Soviets refrained from applying this law to the Protestants. Had they done so, Protestant social work would have been impossible, for an organization which has no right to exercise administrative functions obviously cannot take part in social work. But the new law does more than put a ban on such functions. It specifically prohibits religious bodies from pursuing any activities except worship. It permits freedom of worship and nothing else. This puts an end to coöperatives, clubhouses, mutual aid societies—the very things that have helped the Protestants to gain their hold upon their followers. At the same time the spread of nurseries and kindergartens and the introduction of universal education are subjecting Protestant children to a thorough process of Sovietization, which by the very definition of the word implies, among other things, atheism.

Russian revolutionaries are now no longer disturbed about religion, not because they have had a change of heart, but because they regard the issue as settled. Never before in any public demonstration in the streets were there so few anti-religious banners and posters as in the celebration of the fifteenth anniversary of the Revolution. Anti-religious societies, which even two years ago were flamingly and boisterously in evidence all over the country, are hardly heard from nowadays. The Russian revolutionaries regard their battle against religion finished, with all religions, Christian, Jewish, Mohammedan, Buddhist, stripped of power and appeal and in a state of utter collapse.

IX
RELIGION

IS THERE A NEW RELIGION IN RUSSIA?

IT HAS often been said that Bolshevism itself is a religion; that this is one reason it has been successful in its attack on existing religions. It has, it is avowed, merely transmuted an old emotion and an old longing into a new form. The Bolsheviks, of course, shake with fury whenever they hear Communism spoken of as a religion. So deep is their hatred of the institution that they loathe to be classed or even mentioned in the same category. Yet outward similarities between the two are not wanting.

Bolshevism has a faith, a ceremonial, a morality, even a theology—partly doctrine. It has, in a way, martyrs and priests and prophets, and, like churchmen of old or of today, in time of disagreement, or conflict with each other, or adversaries, their chief reliance for support and justification is authority. In their case, authority means Marx and Lenin. In the memorable battle between Stalin and Trotsky, both leaders sought to annihilate each other by volleys of quotations from these men. Indeed, Marx and Lenin are respectively the Old and New Testaments of Bolshevik Russia.

Since the rise of Stalin to supremacy in the party, the Bolsheviks have even championed recantations in the manner of the mediæval church. Not that they have copied it from the church. But that does not make the similarity the less striking. Whenever a party member of importance strays from the so-called general line—the policy pursued by the party—one way he can restore himself to its graces is to disavow the error of his beliefs in public, usually in print, and to promise conformity in the future. Trotsky, Bukharin, Kamenev, Rykov, and many other Bolshevik leaders have had to pen such disavowals. Discerning people do not for a moment believe the sincerity of these recantations. In private conversations I have heard them lampooned and ridiculed. Men like Bukharin or Rykov or Trotsky do not change convictions as readily as they do their garments. But it humbles them before the mass, and commits them to an end of their opposition. This in turn increases the prestige and power of the party and of the persons at its helm, and enables them to push ahead, unopposed, with their plans and policies.

There is also a likeness between the church confessional and the so-called cleansings to which party members and Soviet officials are periodically subjected. Of course, unlike church confessionals, there is nothing secret about these cleansings. They are always held in the open, and anyone, even a clergyman, a former merchant, a *koolack*, or any other disfranchised individual, may come and listen to party men or Soviet officials give a detailed account of themselves, of their deeds and transgressions, from their earliest years to the last day of their lives. They are enjoined to omit nothing important. They must swallow pride and dignity and lay their very souls bare for everyone to see and to appraise. The audience may participate in these cleansings by pointing out falsifications or omissions, or bestowing eulogies on the confessor. Always it is the audience or the mass, and not a specially delegated functionary as in the church, before whom the confession is recited.

But, unlike the church, the party does not easily forgive misdeeds. If these are serious, neither the audience nor the presiding committee will show mercy toward the transgressor. They examine not only actions but motives. At a cleansing at which I was present, discussion raged vehemently over a Communist who was suspected of having married a girl because her mother with whom she lived had a house of her own. It was a small house, but it was a comfortable place to live in, and Communists are not supposed to marry people for reasons of material gain. At every cleansing of the party a telling percentage of members is ruthlessly expelled from its ranks.

In spite of these differences, the fact remains that a cleansing is a confession, affording the individual more or less emotional release, and intended to test and, if need be, to retrieve his rectitude.

Like the churchman, the Communist loves to crusade. He is so overcome with a sense of righteousness of his cause that he can keep neither his feelings nor his convictions to himself. Together with two young Englishmen I was once riding in a trolley in Moscow. With us was a peasant youth, a soldier in the Red Army, and, as soon as he learned we were not Communists, he proceeded to talk to us of the glories of Communism. He spoke at length and with earnestness, and when we parted he expressed the hope that some day we might awaken to the truth and embrace Communism, precisely as a religious evangelist might say to a stubborn infidel, that some day he would see the light and embrace the faith. At home, in school, in factory, the Bolshevik is always crusading.

He also has a sense of sin. He does not use the word excepting in jest, but the feeling he has of wrong-doing partakes of the nature of a religious man's feeling of sin. Always there is the consciousness of offending an external force. In the case of the Bolshevik this force is not God but the Revolution or the party and the new society. There is nothing, for example, that the Bolshevik regards as so gross a sin as the pursuit of private enterprise. His *don'ts* are as emphatic as those of any church or any religion, and are even more rigorously enforced. Let the reader recall the incident of the Russian girl who was so shocked, on learning that the father of an American girl employed thousands of men, that she exclaimed, "Aren't you ashamed of having a father like that?" Certainly the spirit and the feeling that went into her words partake of a consciousness of sin.

If one views religion as a passion for a cause or as a way of life, then, regardless of Bolshevik protest, one discovers no end of similarities between Bolshevism and religion. In the form in which it exists in Russia, Bolshevism is one of the most dynamic social forces in the world today. It permeates every nook and corner of human life. It has its own ethic and prescribes definite forms of behavior in a multitude—aye, in all social relationships. It offers solutions to a host of vexing problems, and enforces discipline more rigorously than any existing religious body. It exacts self-sacrifice and devotion as no present-day religion or church does.

Yet even those social thinkers who speak of Bolshevism as a religion must remember that it accords not the slightest recognition to the supernatural. It will have no Christian, Mohammedan, Jewish, or any other God. It is completely intolerant of any conception of deity and of faith in any divine or superhuman power. One often hears that the worship of Lenin is akin to the worship of Christ. Nothing of the sort. One may as well say that the American worship of Lincoln, or the French of Bonaparte, is like the worship of a religious prophet. There is nothing of the supernatural in the worship of Lenin, and no man has so volcanically condemned the supernatural as he did. "It is not true," he once wrote to Gorky, "that God is a complex of the ideas which arouse and organize the social emotions. God is (historically and socially) first of all a complex of ideas engendered by the ignorance of mankind and by its subjection, firstly, to the forces of nature and, secondly, to a certain class. These ideas perpetuate ignorance and dampen the class struggle. Every defense of justification of the idea of God, even the most refined and well intentioned, is a justification of reaction. The idea of God has always lulled and blunted 'social emotions' and substituted concern in the dead for interest in the living. The idea of God has never 'united the individual with society.' By faith in the divinity it has always placed the oppressed classes at the mercy of their oppressors."

Let those who speak of Bolshevism as a new religion ponder over the meaning of these words. Nowhere likewise does Bolshevism offer anything in the nature of prayer. Even atheists must admit that prayer, to the sincere man, brings relief and consolation. He feels that he is in communion with some one wiser and more powerful than himself who is in some mysterious way assuming protection over him and guiding him to some well-chosen destiny. Certainly the man in mourning or in travail, if he be a true believer, obtains from such communion no small amount of surcease. But to the Bolshevik there can be no communion with any external force. In one of the offices in the department of agriculture of a large city I read in the wall newspaper a letter which one of the functionaries had received from a friend who was sent on a revolutionary mission to some far-away village. The writer was complaining that from day to day he was sinking deeper and deeper into despair. The people in the village were ignorant, stupid, dirty. There was nobody with whom he could share his thoughts or his feelings—nobody who would offer him comfort in the midst of constant heart-ache. The headline which preceded the letter read: "The Voice of a Defeatist." To the editor of this paper a man who yields to despair while on duty in a village is a weakling and a renegade. Confessions of gloom and despair are confessions of impotence and futility, and these are always anathema to the Bolshevik.

There are, of course, advanced thinkers who dissociate the supernatural from religion. They are small in number and represent a new movement. But theirs is not the brand of religion that people ordinarily accept, and, even if it were, there still would be irreconcilable differences in belief and in practice. Even in most advanced religious thought there is a modicum of mysticism. But Bolshevism rejects all forms of mysticism. The one thing that the Russian censorship—whether of the printed word or the motion-picture or the theater—bars ruthlessly is the least allusion to the mystical. There is the repudiation by Bolshevism of most of the Ten Commandments and of the Golden Rule. Above all there is the Bolshevik ethic and the new set of loyalties. Man as such evokes neither respect nor sympathy. Emphasis always is on social origin, not on what man is but on what his father was and what he does. "I have given twenty years of my life to the working class," I heard Gronsky, the editor of the Moscow *Izvestia*, exclaim. Not to humanity but to the working class. And what religion has ever received its initial impetus and all its superstructure of belief and practice from economics and the natural sciences? And yet economics and the natural sciences form the basis of Bolshevik ideology and Bolshevik attitude toward society, men, women, children, art—everything in fact! What religion has ever approached the relations of the sexes in the manner in which the Bolsheviks have approached it—with a clean sweep of the *mores* which prevailed in the Western world and with utter disregard of the injunctions and precepts of religious teachers and prophets? And what modern religion has professed the precept that the end justifies the means?

If there are certain similarities between the two it

is because in spirit, in appeal, in emotional response there always are similarities between man's movements, however divergent they may be in aims and methods. In this case the divergencies are so flagrant that the similarities on reflection lapse into insignificance.

Thus the new man in Russia has lost all faith in God and all fear of God. The very idea or concept of God has no place in his consciousness.

X

MORALITY

WHEN the Soviets first swept into power in Russia the world was witness to a series of innovations which shocked its ideas, its temper, and its taste. I mean, of course, the world which had come to accept its own way of living as the one best suited to civilized society everywhere.

Not the least shocking of these innovations was the new morality which the Soviets had proclaimed. With one stroke of the pen they brushed aside taboos, usages, and laws which had governed man's sexual behavior in the modern world. They placed man, in his sex life, on his good behavior in a manner which no other modern state would contemplate and no religion would countenance. Excepting for the provision that an act of the individual must in no case do damage to the new society, in his sex life man was left to his own taste and judgment. It may indeed be said that the Soviets allowed the principle of free love full sway. By free love I do not mean what so many expectant visitors to Russia hope to find and soon discover does not exist—freedom of the male to satiate at will his erotic appetites. Rather do I mean freedom of sexual selection for man and woman on a basis of equality.

In deference to this freedom, marriage and divorce in Russia were stripped of external compulsions. The emphasis now is not on marriage but on mating. A man and woman may live in a free union and for as long a period as they find satisfying. Neither public opinion nor the state will offer interference or disapprobation. The very word adultery does not exist in the Russian legal code. The only time the law steps in to impose discipline on a person is in the event of so-called "sex exploitation"—or a violation by one sex of the wishes of the other. Seduction constitutes a major crime in the Russian code. In the early years of the Revolution certain large cities were witness to a most atrocious kind of seduction—mass seduction. A group of youths, usually workers, overpowered with alcohol, would capture a girl and violate her. Invariably the offenders were seized, and put on trial, as soon as their deed became known. On several occasions the press and workers in mass meetings vehemently denounced this form of what they called "hooliganism" and called on courts to impose on its perpetrators the highest penalty that the law prescribed. Nor did such demands go unheeded. In one instance in Leningrad eight youths, including several Young Communists, charged with the mass seduction of a girl were sentenced to be shot, and after final appeals for commutation were denied the sentence was executed. The Soviets punish any forced sex relationship, whatever the circumstances or the motives of the aggressor.

A man and woman who wish to give their union

official validity may visit a *zags*—marriage and divorce bureau—and have it registered. The procedure is simple and informal. Witnesses are never required to testify to anything. There is no oath to subscribe to—oaths everywhere have been abolished—no promise to make either by the man to the woman or the woman to the man, and no ceremony to consummate. Registration does not of course bar a ceremony, not even a religious ceremony. If a couple wish to be married in a church the law offers no interference. Usually friends of the betrothed solemnize the event by a dinner with all the accessories, including songs and speeches.

Recently a young American couple in Moscow, wishing to be married legally, went to one of the registration bureaus. They were invited to sit down at a desk at which a young lady was presiding. On learning the purpose of the visit the young lady offered them for perusal a printed statement mounted on a piece of cardboard. This statement was a reprint of the Soviet laws pertaining to marriage. There was Article 4 of the legal code which provides that applicants must enter the marriage pact by mutual agreement, that they must be at least eighteen years of age and have proper documents of identification. Another provision in this Article forbids registry in marriage to a person already registered in another bureau—that is, registered and not divorced, and forbids the marriage of feebleminded and of close relations, even step-brother and step-sister. There was also a reprint of Article 88 which stated that evasion of the above requirements may bring a penalty of one year in jail or 1,000 roubles fine, and of Article 150, which reminded applicants that infecting a mate with venereal disease is punishable with one year in jail.

The registration clerk invariably offers the above statements for examination to all applicants for marriage and never asks them to subscribe to them in writing. She assumes that they are willing to bear full responsibility for their actions. In the case of the Americans she did not even bother to ask the interpreter whether or not he had translated the statement to his friends. Without the least delay she proceeded to her task. She asked both bride and groom a number of simple questions—their name, their age, their social condition, whether or not they had ever been married or divorced or had any children, their nationality, their occupation, and whether or not the bride wished to bear her own or her husband's name. She wrote down the answers in her book, put a stamp on her *questionnaire*, and pronounced the applicants married. The charge was one dollar in American money.

The groom was so overcome with surprise at the swiftness with which this important event in his life had been consummated that in jest more than in sober thought he asked the young lady if divorce could be as quickly negotiated?

"Indeed it can," replied the young lady. "I can divorce you right now, but I do not advise it—divorce is bad." And in the same breath, as if to give emphasis to her admonition, she asked the Americans if, before leaving the bureau, they would care to hold a consultation with a physician?

A physician? This was something new. Even the interpreter, who had spent much time in Moscow, had never heard of the presence of a physician in a *zags*. On inquiry the young lady explained that the *zags* of which she had charge happened to be the model one in Moscow, and the presence of a physician was a new feature in its service to the community. Only a few of the registration bureaus in Moscow, she continued, had adopted this feature, but in time, when finances permitted and there were enough physicians in the country, every regular *zags* would have a physician on duty. In this bureau applicants for marriage as well as for divorce are advised to consult the physician. In neither case is the consultation obligatory, and if applicants for marriage or divorce refuse to avail themselves of it they obtain their certificates anyway.

Never loath to partake of a new adventure the newly married Americans told the young lady they would be more than happy to talk to the physician. Thereupon she sent the bride in first, and when the bride came out she asked the groom to follow. Both in absolute privacy, accompanied only by their interpreter, went through a novel experience. The physician was a middle-aged woman with a soft voice and kindly manner. She was no Communist, but she had been a medical practitioner since the days before the Revolution and was associated with a number of clinics and hospitals. She assured her foreign visitors that they need answer no question which might seem too intimate or too embarrassing or too elementary. But if they wished the best advice she could offer them, if they needed any at all, it was essential that they answer her questions in full. One of the questions she asked both of them was whether or not they wished to have children. She then proceeded to explain that she always put this question to a newly married couple, and, in the event of their wishing to postpone the rearing of a family or lack of interest in children, she invited the bride to come to her clinic for instructions in birth control. Such instruction is legal everywhere in Russia.

When the Americans left the court they carried away with them the blessings of the entire staff, and the young lady who married them expressed the hope to the interpreter that neither of them would ever be in need of further ministrations from her or officials like her in the Soviet Union–implying of course that she hoped they would never be divorced.

Divorce, however, is always granted to people who ask for it. Now and then I have encountered instances in villages where Soviet officials advise an applicant, whether a man or a woman, to wait ten days, in the hope that the excitement or grievance would wear off and they would continue living together. Such Soviet officials act wholly on their own account. The law makes no provision for such procedure or any delay in the granting of divorce. Either the husband or the wife, with or without each other's consent, may secure it merely on application. They need no lawyer, no witnesses, no cause for the action. The questions which they have to answer to the clerk of the bureau differ but little from those asked on application for marriage. These relate to age, nationality, occupation, social origin, place at which marriage was registered, children, and terms of the agreement, if any, made between husband and wife as to their disposition and support. The cause of the divorce is never included in the *questionnaire*. If a man or a woman who has obtained a divorce has not the desire or the courage to inform the former mate of the action, the clerk on request will send him or her a printed postal card conveying briefly and succinctly the necessary information.

The law does not interfere with the right of an individual to obtain a divorce. It does, however, step in to settle disputes over the disposition of property and the protection of the weaker party, especially of children. If a divorced woman is unable to support herself because of illness, she commands one-third of her husband's earnings as long as she is ill or until a year after her divorce. If the divorced husband is incapacitated for labor he may command one-third of his former wife's salary, but likewise for no more than a year. Under the Russian law, especially now with the government in virtual control of all economic life, it is impossible to dodge the payment of alimony. If the individual fails to meet it of his own accord the government will attach his wages or salary for the amount necessary and send it to the person who is supposed to receive it.

The law is especially vigilant in enforcing the payment of alimony for the support of children. Invariably the mother is awarded their custody. The Russian courts hold that no father, however kindly and devoted, can offer children the care that they need as amply as can a mother. Only when the father can prove that the mother is a drunkard or a moral reprobate is he allowed the custody of a child. Divorced Communists have again and again sought to obtain control of children by the plea that they are more competent than their former wives to give them the proper political upbringing. Invariably the courts have refused to heed such a plea.

A woman judge in one of the courts in Moscow told me of the case of a close friend of hers, a Communist of parts, who sought to win the award of the children through such a plea. He argued that his wife was of a bourgeois origin and lived in a circle in which not Soviet but bourgeois ideas and sentiments prevailed, and on that account there was danger of the children growing up in a spirit of hostility to the Revolution. The judge told me that she knew that her friend was speaking the truth and yet she declined to grant his petition. He was so heart-broken over the verdict that he almost became her enemy and appealed to a higher court. But the higher court upheld the original decision. In disgust and despair the man left Moscow for a long vacation.

The most troublesome alimony cases, particularly those dealing with the support of children, are those in which the marriage is not registered and the man, while admitting that he has cohabited with the woman, will deny that he is the father of the child. In proof of his contention he may bring other men to testify that they too have cohabited with the woman. In the early years of the Revolution when the courts were at a loss to ascertain who was the real father of the child, they made all the men jointly responsible for its support and thereby imposed on the child a multiple fatherhood.

Now invariably the courts fix responsibility on one man. The very conception of a multiple fatherhood they hold incompatible with Soviet justice. In cases where the evidence is uncertain they follow their intuition or the recommendation of the special investigators of the case. They select the one man they think most likely to have been the father. If the man can prove that he has been misjudged he is assured of a reversal of the verdict. But I have never heard of a single instance in which such a man has been able to convince a court of error in judgment.

With sex freed from ancient usage and taboos, and with divorce and marriage more easy and simple, and with birth control and abortions legalized, what is the state of sex morality in Russia?

The whole world, on first learning of the Soviet sex and marriage code, wondered what would happen, and many were the prophecies that eventually Russia would sink to a condition of barbaric indecency. It is because of this code that the story of nationalization of women gained at one time such universal credence. A group of Russian novels which had found their way into foreign translation gave added cogency to these beliefs. Outside of Russia people talked and still talk of such novels as Romanov's *Three Pairs of Silk Stockings* and his incomparable short story, *Without Flowers*, or another novel under the title *Dog's Lane* or a play like *Squaring the Circle*, which is still being played with astonishing success in Moscow and other cities, as living proof of the collapse of ordinary sex decency in Russia.

Yet actual conditions fail to corroborate this assumption. The important thing to remember in an appraisal of any Russian event is the swiftness and the violence with which changes transpire—not so much in principle and in law as in behavior and social adjustment. A year is an epoch in that country. Life flows on in swells and ebbs, and a condition which may dominate the scene at one time may completely disappear and be forgotten a year later. Following the trial and error method in the application of principle, the Bolsheviks are never loath to start an innovation whether in industry, art, or everyday life, or to stop it when they are convinced of its damage or futility. In the early years of the Revolution there was a period when young and excited revolutionaries, chiefly intellectuals, male intellectuals, had confused liberty with licentiousness and plunged into sexual orgies. That was the period of *Three Pairs of Silk Stockings* and *Squaring the Circle* and similar literary creations. Then the press and the party and the trade unions launched a vehement campaign against sex laxity. The country, and particularly the youth organizations, in an effort to achieve emotional stability, roared with debates, lectures, resolutions, mock trials, and mass meetings at which the subject of sex was violently discussed from every conceivable angle. Lenin himself gave an interview to Clara Zetkin in which he denounced laxity and promiscuity as bestial and detrimental to the individual and to society.

And then the orgies subsided. Now they are even forgotten. So much has happened in the country since then that the period of Russia's "flaming youth" seems like a bygone age. It is so remote from present-day actuality, even in literature, that people no longer speak of it, and the press never even alludes to it. When Russians read the novels of that day they pause to ask themselves if the conditions they portray did actually exist or were within the realm of probability.

Not that no incidents of laxity occur now. They do,

but rarely to a degree which makes them a conspicuous social phenomenon. When sexual conduct in any group becomes lax, either the press starts a crusade against it or the group with which the guilty personages are associated takes the matter in hand—issues a sharp reprimand or institutes a social trial or in some other manner brings pressure to halt misconduct.

I came once to a collective farm that had just witnessed a social trial of such a nature. The peasants still talked of nothing else, for it was something new and memorable and diverting. A young couple from some far-away village had come there the spring previous and applied for membership. Their documents showed them to be of the proper social origin, that is as coming from families that had not had the stigma of "exploiters" fixed on them, and they were gladly admitted. The man was in his late twenties, and after a stay of three weeks on the farm he divorced his wife and married a milkmaid, and shortly afterwards he was found in a hay-loft with the wife of another member of the farm. The Communist group immediately decided to bring him to trial, a so-called demonstration of social trial, in which the evils of promiscuity were to be dramatically presented not only before the members of the farm but before the population of the entire countryside. The trial lasted into the morning hours, and when it was over the man was expelled from the collective farm and given only twenty-four hours in which to effect his departure. The decision did not affect his wife. She was given the privilege to remain, and so exasperated was she with her husband for his misbehavior that she divorced him and remained on the collective farm. The pressure of public opinion against promiscuity is ever present. There have been instances when men who flitted from marriage to marriage or affair to affair were brought to court on the charge of seduction.

The one institution where one would expect to find a manifestation of abuse of liberty would be the universities. Here lives the advanced youth of the country, and though in social origin and in political attitude the student of today bears hardly any likeness to the student of yesterday, he is nevertheless the most emancipated and the most adventurous person in the land. Besides, in universities the sexes mingle more readily and more intimately than anywhere else. Men and women not only eat in the same dining-rooms and study in the same classes, but live in the same dormitories, though in separate rooms. They have no proctors, no chaperons, no housekeepers, no guardians. Freely and at all hours of day or evening they go back and forth to each other's rooms, study, drink tea, eat black bread and sausage, go on walks, to the theater, to parties, to meetings. And yet the universities are surprisingly free from sex scandals. Students of the opposite sexes form close friendships, fall in love, mate and sometimes marry, and live in about the same manner as do people on the outside. Student sentiment frowns not on friendship or love or sex association but on a light-hearted attitude toward sex or on casual relationships. If a couple decide to unite, whether in registered marriage or in a free union, their fellow-students will congratulate them, perhaps arrange a little supper, and, what is even more important, will rearrange themselves in their rooms so as to offer the bridal couple a room to themselves. If a child is born to them there may be another celebration of their fellow-students. But the life of the father and mother flows on as before. The woman leaves the child in the university nursery and continues her studies. If, on the other hand, the woman on first learning of her pregnancy wishes to have an abortion, she may go to a clinic and have it performed, though the tendency nowadays is to dissuade women from such operations.

In like manner if a girl student should give birth to a child as a result of a casual relationship, whether with a fellow-student or some one on the outside, her standing is not impaired. Neither students nor faculty will reprimand her. In their estimation she has committed no moral wrong. Besides, they will regard it as her personal affair. She too will leave the child in the nursery during the day and continue her studies as though nothing unusual had happened. Of course the father of the child, whether a student or not, will have to shoulder his share of the responsibility in supporting it, and if he be a student and has not the reputation for being irresponsible in his sex life, he too will suffer no opprobrium. Only when a student, a man or a woman, is found to be making a practice of casual sex relationships will the student body seek to discipline him, for students, like party leaders, regard promiscuity as a vice and never so much as now. In fact the Five Year Plan, with all the distresses it has brought in its wake, has effected a balance and stability in emotional relationships which make the new morality with all its freedom and lack of convention seem like an old and entrenched institution.

Certainly visitors to Russia are impressed with the absence of sex suggestiveness or sex stimulation in the outward appearance of things. At a parade of physical culture enthusiasts thousands of men will march with no more attire than a pair of trunks and thousands of women will march beside them with no other garb than a scanty bathing suit. They will parade through the main avenues and the Red Square with no sense of embarrassment or impropriety and yet no manifestation of erotic excitement. Along the banks of any river on a bright day in summer one can see thousands of men and women basking in the sun with no clothes at all or in scanty bathing suits—which incidentally are always required at the official bathing pavilions. All over the country in summer are groups and crowds of men and women out on long walks in scanty clothes, and again without the slightest consciousness of impropriety. At parties of young people in Moscow or any other city, if festivities last deep into the night and if guests who live far away cannot conveniently go home, they will spend the night with their host, sleeping on benches, tables, floor, men and women side by side, and again without a trace of self-consciousness. On trains, whether in the open hard coaches or the closed sleeping-car compartments, men and women likewise travel together by day and by night. All over the country, at work or at play, the sexes mingle with one another more freely than in any land in the world.

Nowhere in the motion pictures does sex serve as a subject of excitement. Nor does it in the theater or the ballet. True enough in two of the leading hotels in Moscow, where chiefly foreigners stop, there are American bars with comely and well-dressed hostesses who are ready to wait on customers, dance with them, eat and drink with them. But their presence is a concession to foreigners. If they are known to trade with their sex they are discharged. And there are many Communists in the city who grumble fiercely against this concession to bourgeois commercialism. They think it worse than loathsome. But nowhere else in the country, not in a single resort where Russians get together, is there commercial exploitation of sex. I can no more conceive of a Russian cabaret featuring nude posturings as a means of enticing customers than I can of a Communist in good standing offering a contribution to a church. Either is regarded as a deadly sin.

Russian morality is a striking mixture or balance between liberty and discipline, personal enjoyment and social responsibility, utter frankness and utter disdain of abuses. Further light on the subject we shall gain from an examination of the manner in which they have dealt with prostitution.

Thus the new man in Russia has lost all fear of sex. He is taught to preserve an attitude of earnestness toward the function and purpose of sex. But he cherishes none of the taboos and fetishes which in the western world so often make sex a problem and a torment. If he is ever disturbed by a sex problem the cause invariably is physiological and not social or emotional.

XI
PROSTITUTION

SOME ten years ago, on my first visit to Russia after the Revolution, I happened to be sauntering along the bazaar of a large city in the south. Of a sudden I saw people leaving their wagons and carts and running down a near-by street. I followed them and came in sight of an extraordinary procession. About two hundred women, surrounded by police, were marching down the avenue, and they were among the best dressed women I had seen in the town.

They wore good shoes and stockings and well-made clothes, some of bright-colored silks, and, even more surprising, some of them actually wore hats and had make-up on their faces.

Some one in the crowd of onlookers ventured the suggestion that they might be members of the old bourgeoisie who had been rounded up in some anti-Soviet conspiracy and were being taken to the train to be sent north into exile. But an inquiry addressed to one of the policemen elicited the information that they were prostitutes.

Prostitutes—and the best dressed women in the community! It seemed an anomaly and yet it wasn't—not when one considered their past. Some of them doubtless had been inmates of brothels in the old days, or mistresses of rich men. In the wreck of the Revolution they had managed to salvage at least parts of their wardrobes. Others, novices in the profession, had come from the well-to-do classes ruined by the Revolution. They had been left without money, without property, without incomes; in many cases even without homes, their fathers or mothers, or often both, exiled, jailed, or dead. What was worse they never had done any work. They never had been taught to work and had no chance of learning it now. Even if they had, there was no work for them. In those days of stress and chaos, with the wounds of the civil war unhealed, work was scarce and the government, unless it needed their services, bluntly refused to give any of it to members of the former bourgeoisie. And so to earn a living many women who had formerly lived in idleness and luxury now took to practising the most ancient profession in the world.

That was the situation not only in this town but all over the country. Prostitutes everywhere came from the same groups and they were everywhere in evidence. In Moscow, in Leningrad, in Kiev, in Kazan, in Odessa, no sooner would dusk descend than, like creatures who came to life in the dark, they would troop down the streets and swarm into restaurants, wine-cellars, hostelries, sometimes even bath-houses, and openly solicit patronage. Even in Siberia, in city after city, all the way from the Urals to the Chinese border, they were a conspicuous part of the social scene. And always they were among the best dressed women in the community.

Yet now, ten years later, with the completion of the first Five Year Plan, no country in Europe is so free from prostitutes as Russia. Indeed, one has to hunt with a searchlight to find a survival of prostitution. The Five Year Plan has failed to bring to the Russian people the higher standard of living it promised them. In fact it has chipped it down to a level lower than at the beginning of the Plan. Certainly the shortage of meats, eggs, butter, cheese, and sugar has not been so acute in ten years. But it has rooted up prostitution. Though stray remnants still linger here and there they are always under cover.

This achievement is more noteworthy when one remembers how sodden with prostitution Russia was in the old days. The law not only recognized but pampered it. In one of the museums in Moscow, in a glass case, is a collection of yellow booklets which tell a stirring tale. These are the so-called "yellow tickets" which the police under the Czar issued to inmates of brothels. They were a badge of trade and of privilege. Jewish girls, for example, who had no residence rights in cities outside of the pale, immediately won these rights if they acquired yellow tickets. They could not, of course, hold these tickets without fulfilling the function that was required of them. The moment they ceased to be prostitutes their special privileges were revoked and they had to return to the pale.

There wasn't a town in Russia which did not boast of its coterie of brothels. Only the villages were free from the scourge. Peasants, unless they lived close to a city and became inoculated with city ideas, for the most part never had even heard of the existence of such institutions. But in cities they flourished. They were under the immediate control of the police, and medical officers made periodic examination of their inmates.

No sooner was the old government overthrown and the Soviets in power than a decree was issued outlawing brothels and all other forms of commercial vice. Keepers of brothels who failed to comply with the decree were haled before a court, tried, and given severe sentences. I remember the trial in a Moscow court of a man and his wife who were accused of moving a brothel to a near-by suburb. The prosecuting attorney, in fierce denunciation of them, demanded "the highest measure of social defense," which is death by shooting.

The new code of morals which the Soviets promulgated also struck a heavy blow at prostitution, for through it sex was freed from historic taboos and disciplines. Marriage became easy and simple and so did divorce, and divorced people in Russia always re-marry, sometimes one another.

This, of course, cut deep into the patronage of prostitution. And so did the new fashion of early marriages which in the city was also a result of the Revolution. Young people no longer had reason to postpone marriage. They ceased to bother about acquiring a competence. It wasn't the thing to do, it was difficult of achievement, and besides, one never knew when under some pretext the government would step in and seize it. It is significant that the two social groups which comprised the chief patronage of the organized prostitution in the old days, soldiers and university students, became under the new order its bitterest foes.

But at first prostitution persisted even after the brothels were closed. And though the demand had fallen the supply continued to swell. It could not be otherwise as long as there were thousands of women without jobs, without income, and with no other way of gaining a livelihood. The police would raid the restaurants and other places where they might assemble, or pick them off the streets and haul them to headquarters. But they didn't know what next to do with them. Nobody did. So the women would be held for a few days, a few weeks, or a few months, and then released. Naturally enough, the released prostitutes returned to their old profession. Sometimes the police would order them to leave the city. That was no special hardship. They would pack up and move to another city. There always was another city to go to.

Only with the coming of the Five Year Plan did the situation change. With its advent the war on prostitution took on the character of a campaign for national safety and the Soviets had a number of fresh weapons at hand. They had acquired control of all eating and drinking resorts, all hostelries and lodging-houses, and all other places in which prostitutes gathered to seek customers. In all these places solicitation was firmly forbidden. In the streets the police, both uniformed and plain-clothes men, likewise became more vigilant. But these destructive measures, no matter how thorough, probably would have failed of their purpose, as they had in so many countries, had they not been followed up by a series of far-reaching constructive remedies.

First of all, work was provided for everybody who

wanted it. The Five Year Plan had started Russia on an ambitious program of national development. Hundreds of new factories, as large as any in the world, were to be built, more than a score of new cities were planned, thousands of new schools were to be opened. Millions of people were needed to execute these colossal projects. By the time the third year of the Plan was reached, all idle hands were absorbed and there was an acute shortage, particularly of skilled labor. Women, especially, were urged to go to work, and they did. More than three millions of them entered Russian industry in one capacity or another.

The opportunity to find work at once shut off the source of fresh recruits to prostitution. For women who had never practiced it, a position in a factory or in an office was more lucrative. Likewise it was easier to find a good room to live in and to obtain a permit to trade in government stores where things could be purchased at the lowest prices in the country.

But there were still the confirmed prostitutes who would not abandon their profession. It had become too strong a habit with them. Their time was their own; they could sleep late, and they had no discipline of any kind to endure. Besides, there was always the chance that they might meet a foreigner and obtain from him a precious gift of stockings, cosmetics, or European clothes. To eliminate these prostitutes was the big problem. In Moscow alone there were in 1928 over five thousand of them. To deal with them the government had established special institutions known as prophylactoriums. But it wasn't until the coming of the Five Year Plan and the surge of energy and action it whipped up that these prophylactoriums became firmly and beneficently established. Now they are among the most remarkable institutions in Russia.

On one of the side streets in Moscow is a long three-story house built of solid brick, with large windows and a spacious yard. In the old days it was the home of an ancient and wealthy Muscovite merchant who had a large family and many servants and who was noted for his lavish dinners and parties. Like other privately owned houses in the cities all over Russia, this one was taken over by the Soviets.

As you go into this house now you are greeted by a man who offers to check your coat, hat, rubbers, umbrella, and any packages you may be carrying. In fact he will not let you proceed unless you first check your outer wraps. This gives you the feeling that the place has a dignity all its own, like a theater, an opera house, a club house, where no one is allowed to enter the rooms or auditorium without first leaving hat and overcoat in the check-room. A place of no small consequence then.

This feeling heightens as you mount the spacious, freshly painted stairway and enter the office. A sizable office it is, with a mahogany desk, soft chairs, elaborately framed pictures on the wall, all no doubt relics of the old days when the merchant lived in the house. A young man of about thirty is at the desk. His appearance is so different from that of the usual Soviet official that you almost gasp in astonishment. He is clean shaven. He wears, not the usual Russian blouse or worker's jacket which so many leaders, including Stalin, love to affect, but a modern suit of clothes, complete with collar and tie, and, what is even more astonishing, spats! He is well-mannered, polite, soft-spoken, and obviously well educated.

Communist though he is, he deems it essential to keep up as presentable an appearance as the scanty supplies in Moscow haberdashery shops permit. Perhaps he does it for the sake of the dignity of his position, perhaps only because of personal taste, or perhaps because the organization over which he presides ministers to hundreds of women, for this institution is a prophylactorium and it occupies the whole house and all the grounds. On first sight this man seems too young to have charge of an institution which guides the destinies of so many maladjusted women. But then you remember that in Russia it is youth that runs the national show. Youth dominates and governs the country.

This young man will gladly show you through the building, and it is worth seeing, for it is unlike so many of the houses in Moscow in that there are no cracks in the ceiling, no spots on the walls, no peeling paint and no holes in the floors. It is well kept. As you pass through room after room you observe that beds, furniture, windows, walls, floor, are bright and clean. If it is daytime nearly all of the four hundred girls who live there are off to work, but a few linger about, sewing, reading books, writing letters. They are well dressed. They make no objection if you stop and watch them work or talk to them. They are glad to engage in conversation. Some of them, in true Russian fashion, do not hesitate to speak of their old life and of their hopes and plans for the future.

The prophylactorium is in reality a house of detention. The inmates are brought there by the police or by some social agency and they have to stay there. Yet nowhere in the building or in the processes of administration is there evidence of rigor, compulsion, or discomfort. Nowhere are there heavy locks or bars. Nowhere is there a guard—armed or unarmed. The place looks more like a university dormitory than a house of detention.

In the basement there is a restaurant which is one of the best in Moscow. In spite of shortages of animal products in the city and all over the country, this restaurant serves meat three times a week. Cereals and sugar also are never lacking, and occasionally it even serves milk. Knowing the general shortage of food in Moscow, you ask the director how he manages to provide such fine meals for the girls. In reply he smiles and says: "It takes a little extra time and effort, but I get what I want." You realize that he must spend more than just a little time and effort to obtain the foods he needs. The prophylactorium must offer its inmates a superior living in food and lodging or it would fail in its purpose, he explains.

When a girl first reaches the institution she is given a painstaking medical examination. If she is infected with disease, as she usually is, the physician maps out a course of treatment for her. If her condition requires isolation, she is isolated. If she needs rest, she rests. Whatever the physician prescribes is law, and there are trained nurses about to help the girls observe this law.

But medical treatment is only a beginning in the girl's process of redemption. The most important factor in her treatment is work. As soon as her physical condition permits she is assigned some occupation for which she is especially suited and put to work at it. The prophylactorium maintains its own sewing shops and knitting mills. In these shops there is nothing to remind a girl that she is an inmate of an institution. She is treated like any factory employee. She works from six to eight hours a day, depending on her age and physical condition, and under strict observance of trade union regulations as to hygiene, wages, social insurance, and vacations.

The director, in describing his policy, emphasizes this particular feature in all the ministrations of the prophylactorium. From the first day the girl comes to the place she is made to feel that she is a person of worth and responsibility, capable of taking care of herself and of making her contribution to the life and welfare of the Soviet community. Never is she patronized or pitied. Never is she made to feel that she needs to be reformed or that she is an object of charity or benevolence.

In point of fact she is not an object of charity. Unless she is too ill to work she becomes self-supporting from the day she enters the institution. She is paid for her work as is any other woman who works in a shop. She earns, on the average, seventy-five roubles a month, of which she pays forty to the prophylactorium for board, room, medical treatment, and the other comforts that she enjoys. The balance she may dispose of as she pleases. She may save it, buy clothes, spend it for tickets to the theater, the movies, the circus, or send it home to her mother or some other relative in need. No one has a right to tell her what to do with her surplus earnings.

Since the prophylactorium makes much of play, social life, and hobbies, "cultural interests" as the Soviets term them, a girl during her stay there is encouraged to play games, read, or cultivate some particular talent in her leisure hours. Does she wish to learn to play the guitar or the balalaika? Has she ambition to become a writer, an actress? Does she want to learn to dance, paint, design clothes? Classes in all of these subjects are provided. Is she interested in following a political career, in making a place for herself in a Soviet, a trade union, a collective farm? There are lectures and books and group studies in all of these subjects. Always the girl is made to feel that the great world of Russia—within the limits, of course, of the Soviet dictatorship—offers her the chance to realize whatever ambition she may cherish, that it places her on a basis of equality with other women and with men, that it stands ready to help her achieve a successful life, forgetting the past.

In some respects these former social outcasts find themselves more favored than other women. Even daughters of the former bourgeoisie, whom the Revolution has disgraced and suppressed, unless they show open hostility to the Soviet, find the doors of advancement and promotion open to them.

Throughout her stay in the prophylactorium there are few *dont's* that a girl has to observe, and she herself sponsors and modifies these as need arises. There are no guards to watch her, no housekeepers to discipline her, no officials except the director and the nurses and physicians who are there to minister to her. She is there on her honor and on her good behavior. If she becomes unruly or annoying, her room-mates take her to task precisely as do students in a university dormitory. But she is never made to feel socially inferior, whatever her behavior may be. If there are any celebrations in the city which she wishes to attend, she is free to do so. If there is a parade, as on the first of May or on the anniversary of the Revolution, and she wishes to join in the procession, she may. The one requirement she must fulfill is at least one year's residence in the institution and as much longer as the director may deem necessary. For in any shorter period it would be most difficult to acclimate her to the new conditions of living and prepare her for a normal life afterwards. If she escapes, which happens seldom, the police invariably bring her back.

On the completion of her course of training—it is always "training" and never "service" or "sentence"—the prophylactorium finds an outside position for her, but she does not leave until arrangements have been made not only for work, but for good living quarters as well. After her discharge from the prophylactorium there is nothing to remind her of the past. She has no yellow ticket to hide, to destroy, or to forget. The documents which she carries with her bear no reference to her former life. Her record remains only on the books of the institution, where no one except police officials has access to them, and then only if for some reason it becomes necessary to make an investigation of her past.

In her new work and play associations she is treated by everyone as an equal and is judged on the basis of achievement and character. Nobody even knows her past unless she herself discloses it. Anyone who discovered it and tried to taunt her with it would be severely condemned and punished. She is encouraged to join the trade union, which in Russia is a signal social honor and carries with it no small amount of prestige and privilege. She is even invited to join that most exclusive of all Russian societies, the Communist Party. Often she joins both. Twelve per cent of the graduates of the Moscow prophylactoriums have risen to membership in the party, some of them to positions of eminence. In new surroundings these former prostitutes rapidly revert to normal living. Often they get married, bear children, and live as do other women. Significant of the success of the Soviet rehabilitation system is the fact that very rarely does one of these women slide back into her old life. This is true not only in Moscow but throughout the country.

The results of the work of these prophylactoriums are epoch-making. In Moscow at the beginning of the Five Year Plan there were five such institutions with a total of 4,000 inmates. The original plan was to bring this number down to 1,200 by the end of the Five Year Plan. Instead, it has been reduced to 575! Four of the original prophylactoriums have had to close for lack of inmates. Now there is only one—the one which I have just described.

What is true of Moscow is true of other cities. The campaign has been nation-wide, and everywhere the results have been salutary. Prostitutes, even as the hordes of homeless children who used to darken the highways and byways of the country, have practically disappeared from the scene. Those who are still about ply their trade well under cover, for the eye of the law is sharp and ever present, and the arm of the law is ever ready to reach out and put them in an institution. The prostitutes that are still abroad are usually girls of low mentality from the villages, who have come to the city to work and have found the strain of city life too much for them. They do not react to treatment in the prophylactorium as readily as do normal girls. They require stricter supervision and discipline, and plans are now in process of elaboration to open a special type of institution for them.

Meanwhile, the authorities are considering legislation which will penalize the man who patronizes them. In the cities of Kiev and Tashkent the local press devised its own scheme for punishing such men. Reporters circulated about the city keeping their eyes open for such cases. Whenever they found the man involved they would photograph him and print his picture on the front page of the newspaper along with his name, address, and a full account of his misconduct. In Moscow there was discussion of the advisability of adopting this method of public censure. But it was thought that it might cause persons thus publicized to commit suicide, and the proposal was dropped. But the idea of working out some system for penalizing the men who patronize prostitutes has not been abandoned.

One wonders though what will happen in times of unemployment? Offices and factories are highly overstaffed and a widespread weeding process has already been begun. If dismissed women should find work elsewhere, even if out of town, or if in the event of loss of a job they should be receiving sufficient allowances from the social insurance funds to provide them with a living, there is in my judgment no danger of their becoming prostitutes, certainly not on a large scale. But should the time come when large groups of women are again facing economic insecurity—there is no assurance that prostitution will not again become a problem in Soviet Russia.

XII
FAMILY

WHEN the Chinese National Government severed relations with the Soviets in 1929 the son of Chiang-Kai-Sheck was a student in a Moscow university. On hearing of the break he issued a public statement in which in spite of his Chinese upbringing with its tradition of parental fealty, he said: "Chiang-Kai-Sheck was my friend and father. He still is my father but he is no longer my friend."

In 1928, during the so-called Shakhta trial, in which a group of engineers was tried for sabotage, the son of one of them, a young Communist, printed a statement in the press in which he denounced his father as a traitor and demanded for him the highest measure of social defense, or death by shooting.

Recently, in a village in the Urals, two peasant youths, one aged nine and the other thirteen, denounced their father, who was chairman of the local Soviet, as a friend and abettor of *koolacks*. The person to whom they made the denunciation was a district official who had come to investigate the man's poor record in office. Subsequently the man was sent off into exile, and his two sons, shortly afterward, were found in a wood literally cut to pieces.

Incidents like these are not of everyday occurrence, but they accentuate and dramatize the sharp cleavage between parents and children when there is lack of accord in their political allegiances. In time of crisis this cleavage leads not only to estrangement but to battle to the end. Appeals do not matter. Blood becomes thinner than water. For there is something in the Revolution that overpowers the mind and the heart of the child and blots out all sense of loyalty to father, mother, friend, to any person. He is loyal only to the Revolution.

Of course the child gets the best of everything—in food, clothes, shelter, play, fun. But it is more than that. The child is made to feel that he is a personality of importance with a share of responsibility in the everyday affairs of the community. His voice is not merely tolerated in big and little things; it is heeded and sometimes obeyed. Never is it scorned. The child is sent on errands, excursions, missions which he is made to feel are as pressing and worthy of effort as anything grown-up persons are doing. Now it is a campaign to gather old sacks for grain, on the Volga or in Siberia. Now it is a movement to exterminate insects, and heaven only knows how desperately Russia needs such a movement. Now it is a search for scraps of metal, rags, paper, and anything else that could be used as raw materials in the factories. Now it is a flying visit to a restaurant, a shop, an office, to ascertain the causes of poor service. Now it is a trip for a day, a week, a month, to a state or collective farm, to weed cucumbers, set up sheaves of wheat, or dig sugar-beets. Now it is an excursion to a museum, a forest, a river, a park. Always there is something new—a fresh interest, a fresh task, a fresh adventure. I do not know of any country in the world where the child is treated with such an absence of condescension as in Russia, or is vested with so much responsibility. And the child responds with eagerness and fervor. He becomes not only a disciple but a crusader of the Revolution.

I am talking of the child that belongs, whose parents have not had the curse of disfranchisement visited on them. The child of the latter, though admitted to the elementary schools and allowed to engage in certain social activities, is barred from playgrounds and Pioneer organizations. Once in a town outside of Moscow I saw several boys of about seven or eight peering enviously through a rail fence into a park where a crowd of children were merrily at play under guidance of an instructor.

"Why don't you go in and join them?" I asked.

"They won't let us," replied one of them.

"Why not?" I asked again.

"Because," replied another, "our parents are disfranchised."

Disfranchised! What a withering word. How much shame and desolation it conveys. Children sometimes feel its hurt more poignantly than do their elders. Why they should be made to feel it at all passes my understanding. Is it to nurture an irrepressible urge for revenge? I can think of no other reason. With all their hearts these boys, and thousands upon thousands like them all over the land, long to be inside the rail fence.

But the bars are so thick and high that they can neither crawl through them nor vault over them. These boys, as I viewed them, were as much children of the Revolution as any child born in a hovel of a poverty-stricken *muzhik* or proletarian. In spite of constant communion with parents who might harbor only hate for the new order of things, they accept the Revolution as their own, replete with promise and virtue. They care for nothing so much as to make themselves a part of the excitement and adventure of the Revolution. There are few children in Russia who are different. In body and spirit they are Soviet children. They feel they belong nowhere else. All the more reprehensible is the discrimination levelled against them. In spite of all the supposedly rigid home discipline that they are subject to, neither the Jews nor the Mohammedans nor the Protestants nor the Roman Catholics have been able to keep alive in their children an allegiance to the ways of their fathers. They just cannot offset the lure of the Soviet adventure even when its enjoyment is made difficult!

To parents with the old conception of the family this attitude of their children is a tragedy and a torment. Because of the sense of sin and defeat that the Soviet outside world visits on such parents, their craving for the sympathy and cheer and good fellowship of their own children may become a desperate need—as the one thing to sustain what little self-respect and dignity they may have left. But their children are lost to them and they are helpless. They cannot compete with the state and the outside society in the appeal to the child's imagination and its spirit of adventure.

Since the state or the outside society absorbs so much of the devotion of the child, what joy, it may be asked, or satisfaction, have parents, mothers especially, in bringing children into the world and rearing them? I heard an American woman of prominence exclaim once that if she were in Russia she would refuse to have children. "Why," she exclaimed, "have them at all if in the end you only lose them?"

To those mothers who have been accustomed to watch constantly over their children and guide them in all their discoveries and adventures, all their conflicts and triumphs, it would seem that the over-powering hold of the outside society on the child is tantamount to its loss by the parents.

But the new Russian mother does not think so, and it is she who is the symbol of motherhood in Russia and to whom the future belongs. She has an utterly new conception of the nature and function of the family and of the relations between parents and children.

Once I went with a group of American newspapermen to the dormitory of a Moscow university in which lived more than one hundred girls who came from various parts of the country. They were all medical students. Though it was late in the evening we entered the dormitory without knocking at any door or ringing a bell, and without any previous announcement. All this is proper enough in Russia, and the girls showed not the least sign of resentment or embarrassment. Most of them were busy with homework, but the arrival of a group of foreigners, especially writers, was a rare treat to them. They flocked around us eager to ask and to answer questions. They were as frank in speech as only Russian girls can be. Whatever subject we touched upon they discussed it without the slightest show of reserve. Marriage, divorce, career, birth control, abortions, prospective summer trips to villages to do medical work on collective and state farms—they talked of everything. They informed us that legal marriage meant nothing to them. But they would all be married some day, at least they hoped to be. Some of them were already married. A few had been married and divorced but they would be married again. And of course they would have children. The very mention of marriage without children seemed absurd to them. Such a marriage might be well enough for a *bourzhui* woman who had her mind centered on her own immediate self and who refused to bear children for fear they would spoil her figure or interfere with her pleasures. But they were different. They would not deny themselves the fulfillment of a biological function which both nature and the new society demanded of them.

But of what use, we asked, was it to have children when in the end the state would win their complete allegiance and they would lose them? Their unanimous reply was a howl of surprise that we should even ask the question. The state could not win their children from them. That was not the way they looked at it. They helped their children to develop a whole-hearted devotion to the state and to the new society. They themselves lived for the fulfillment of the aims of their new society and they could see no conflict between the allegiance of their children to them and to the new society. On the contrary, there would be conflict if their children were not engrossed with the new order.

To these girls, and their number in Russia is legion, the family has lost many of its old functions and purposes. It is no longer an economic or spiritual entity. It is no longer a world in and of itself to build, to entrench, to exalt. It has no meaning as an independent body. It is indissolubly linked to the outside society and all its purposes. "My home is my castle," is an anachronism to them—an absurd and unworthy concept. They never think in terms of family tradition, family prestige, family glory, family exclusiveness. They deny that a family has a right to make its own tradition or perpetuate its own purposes. There is no such a thing as "an old family," "an honored family," "a great family," in their vocabulary. The family to them is like a river that feeds the sea—something bigger and more all-embracing than itself. All talk of family pride has vanished from their consciousness. There is pride in social origin. But social origin means not the name or the fame but the *occupation* of your father or your grandfather, and how these new people in Russia dread and detest the very notion of having had a father or a grandfather who bought cows, sold dry goods, imported tea, ran a grocery store, or engaged in any form of private enterprise, which they call exploitation!

Considering the social implications of the Revolution it is only natural that Russia should develop this concept of the family. Always the new society is exalted as the most pressing interest of the hour—as the one and only source from which all material and cultural gifts and blessings flow. Then a host of forces have come into play which have shattered the multitude of bonds which held together the old family. The Five Year Plan has been an especially powerful force in this. It has brought religion to a state of utter collapse and has wiped out income-yielding private property—two stalwart supports of the old family. It has crystallized and stabilized the marriage and divorce laws, which are intended not so much to protect the unity of the family as to free the individual from a too close family bond which he may find irksome. In addition there is the socialization of the numerous functions of the old home which this Five Year Plan has pushed into a new magnitude. A nursery and a social dining-hall are as much a part of the plant for a new industrial enterprise as are engines and motors and belts and gears. Nearly ten million children are now embraced by nurseries and other pre-school institutions. In the villages alone six million children are thus affected, and the plan is to extend the network of these institutions so that by the end of the second Five Year Plan all children will be drawn into them.

The growth of social dining-halls is likewise significant. More than fourteen million adults including three-fourths of the industrial population of the country are now fed in community dining-halls from one to three meals a day. During the coming Five Year Plan there will be a further and vast expansion of the system of social feeding. True enough the quality of the food and the service in these places need correction. But that too is a matter of future planning. The important fact is that the idea of community feeding is gaining ever increasing momentum.

And so is the tendency of women to enter into the active life of the outside world. Here again the Five Year Plan has played a momentous part. It has created numberless jobs for them, and even though married they are continually being called upon to take these jobs. Over three million of them have been drawn into industry alone during the first Five Year Plan, and now every effort is being made to draw every woman of work age, married or unmarried, into some pursuit outside of the home. Indeed, when a woman fails to respond to this call her refusal is spoken of as an imposition and an outrage. Constantly the notion is being propagated that not only does she owe it to the new society to make herself useful outside of the home but that she never can gain the self-realization that the Revolution has promised her if she fails to do so. If she allows personal emotion to interfere with this usefulness she need expect no sympathy or even toleration.

A few years ago I happened to be visiting the city of Ivanovo at a time when they were holding "cleansings" of members in the Communist Party. A cleansing is an ordeal which no Communist, however pure and righteous, enjoys. It involves a full and frank unfolding of one's past, one's origin, one's sins, one's deeds and one's hopes, one's ambitions. The confession is followed by a rigid cross-examination not only by the presiding council but by the people at the meeting, which is thrown open to everyone who cares to come. It is the one place and only time at which the individual Communist, however puffed up with self-importance, becomes humble and anxious. If he has a guilty conscience he trembles with fear lest some one in the audience, foe or friend, rise to hurl accusations of misdeeds at him.

One of the Communists to be cleansed at the meeting which I attended was a dark-haired girl of twenty-two. She spoke with an ease, a fluency, a simplicity, a charm, that roused everyone's admiration. She told of her early life as the daughter of a small-town butcher who was brutal and illiterate and who beat his wife and made life a torment for everyone in the household. At an early age she went to work as a nurse for one of the families in the town. Only after the Revolution came had she learned to read and to write. She was one of the first girls in her town to join the Pioneers and later the Young Communists, and from there she entered the party. Though holding a responsible position in one of the textile mills she was giving much of her leisure to social work, helping in various campaigns, teaching a class of illiterates and attending an advanced class in Marxism. She told a straightforward dramatic story and the audience was pleased and sympathetic. Then the chairman of the presiding council put several questions to her and called for criticisms from the audience. "Does anyone know of any sins she has committed?"

Thereupon a young man with a shaved head and an unshaved face and with his shirt collar unbuttoned stood up and in vigorous language denounced the girl as unworthy of remaining a member of the party. He charged that she had grown indifferent to all her social duties. Giving dates and places, he cited instances when she failed to attend meetings and fulfill obligations imposed on her.

The chairman asked her if the charges were true, and to everyone's amazement she said that they were, but excused herself on the ground that the meetings were of no importance.

"That's not for you to say," shouted her accuser. "Every meeting that the party calls is important."

"Why did you do it?" asked the chairman, a mild-mannered man who was editor of the local newspaper. "You seem so intelligent, so understanding; and you have been through a secondary school and have studied Lenin and Marx and graduated from the Pioneers and the Young Communists."

The girl did not answer.

"Perhaps you have not been in good health?" asked one of the examiners.

Again she was silent.

"Speak up," suggested the chairman, "it is a serious sin you have committed, and we must know the reason."

"I know the reason," exclaimed her accuser, "she is in love, and she is spending all her leisure with him—Come, admit it, Marusya."

"Is that true?" asked the chairman.

She did not answer.

"Of course it is," continued her accuser. "There are comrades right here who have seen her in the parks and clubhouse and they can testify."

The chairman interrupted him.

He turned to the girl and asked her if she had anything to say in her defense. But she seemed so overcome with embarrassment and grief that she remained tongue-tied. Finally, amidst a strenuous effort to keep back a welling sob, she said: "I guess I have done wrong. I have no defense other than that none of us are saints, and when we have worked as hard as I have it is natural now and then to lapse into error. I plead guilty before the party, and promise never again to ignore its orders."

There was a motion to expel her, but the chairman reminded the maker of the motion that the comrade in question had done notable work in the past and promised to submit to discipline in the future and did not deserve such severe punishment. She was not expelled, but she was severely reprimanded.

Other Communist organizations might have been more severe with her. None of them would have spared her a sharp reprimand. Not that any of them as a body or as individuals would deny the right of a man or woman to love and to indulge this love.

But they would not tolerate the interference of any personal enjoyment, even love, with party orders and party assignments. The party always comes first!

From her earliest days the Russian girl is educated to the idea that the main objective in the world is not a personal love-life but service to the Revolution and to the new society which it is building. Many a foreign observer, learning of this objective, concludes that the Russian revolutionaries deny the power and the need—indeed the very reality—of romantic love.

Of course if he were to search into the pronouncements of responsible leaders and theoreticians he would find not a word in support of his assumption. On the contrary he would be astonished to learn that one of the chief objectives of the Revolution is to emancipate love from the external compulsions with which they hold it is now weighed down in an individualistic society. He would discover that they mean to rid love from the intrusions of wealth, parents, mother-in-law, religion, conventions, and other social and historic forces that may now beset it. Indeed, they say that eventually only in their society can love attain its highest fruition.

Of course the outside visitor has his impressions of the external scene to reckon with. Powerful impressions these are. In his travels about the country he observes that the Russian girl is shabbily dressed. She seldom uses make-up and when she does the result is often preposterous. Nor is she possessed of any of the mannerisms and affectations which to him are inseparable from femininity and from the ability to excite and experience romantic love. Her environment likewise seems to him as barren of sensuous stimulation as the very cobbles of the old Moscow streets.

In the window displays of the leading shops, in the news and advertising columns of the press, in the theaters and motion pictures, he may look in vain for any suggestion of erotic feeling which might serve to stimulate her sex-consciousness. On the other hand he sees her exposed to very powerful emotional excitement in which love has no part. In the schools and playgrounds, in the trade unions and factories, there are always campaigns on behalf of some new idea or new project, and forces are perpetually at work to arouse her enthusiasm for the new government and the policies which it is so strenuously promulgating. Naturally enough he concludes either that the Russian girl is deficient in sex feeling or that all her emotions of this nature have been sublimated into a purely social enthusiasm. Foreigners, especially Americans, have frequently asked me whether the Russian girl is really capable of emotional response. Such a question shows that the observer has failed to understand the Russian girl's background and training and is judging her in terms of his own environment, in which sex is constantly emphasized in almost every phase of life and in the outward behavior of women themselves. Thus for him visible sex excitement becomes the basis of romantic love. This, of course, never was true in Russia and is less so now than at any other time. Turgenev has created a gallery of highly romantic women, perhaps the most romantic in Russian literature, yet how much visible sex excitement is there in their outward manner or the external appearance of the world they live in? The Russian girl may subordinate love to a social purpose; but that does not imply that she regards it as something unimportant or casual. This, at least, is her attitude today, notwithstanding the lurid pictures drawn in the recent crop of Russian sex novels which were based on the hectic life that marked the early days of the Revolution, when everything was in a state of dissolution. Physically and emotionally Russia is becoming stabilized, and the neurotic behavior of former times has little place now. The Russian girl of today takes her love seriously as is the nature of the women of her country. Again I must emphasize that the day of *Three Pairs of Silk Stockings* is as remote as the day of Rasputin.

This is not to say that the Russian girl is difficult to

approach, for she plays about with men more freely perhaps than the girls of any other nation. But love is to her a precious emotion, not to be squandered lightly. When her love has been aroused she responds with an intensity unrestrained by inhibitions and conventions, and the law of her land does not interfere with her love-life. Marriage may not mean much to her, but love most assuredly does, as one quickly discovers when he comes to know any group of young Russians. Be they college students or factory hands there will be found among them the same turmoil over love affairs that besets youth everywhere—indeed perhaps even more, since in Russia everyone involved, especially the girl, takes these affairs so much more seriously.

This does not mean that because of her emotional earnestness and her freedom the Russian woman is enjoying an ideal or even a satisfying love-life. A host of external conditions work against it in these days of revolutionary fervor and reconstruction. In most cities the housing is so wretched that families and newly mated couples are obliged to live in meagerly furnished one-room apartments. Food conditions also are difficult, and always, above all, there is work, work, work! When husband and wife are devoted revolutionaries there are not many free evenings which they can spend together. Meetings and social work keep them out late into the night. This may be a temporary condition, but while it lasts it is bound to be a disturbing feature in the love-life of men and women.

Thus while accepting and even exalting love and parenthood, though never above duty to society, the revolutionary-minded Russian regards the family not as a sanctuary or an ideal, but as a geographic and social convenience.

The new man in Russia has lost all fear of parental authority, of family opinion, of family position and of all the other fears with which in the old days the institution of the family was surrounded. He accepts the biological and emotional functions of the family as natural and indispensable to human happiness. He welcomes love. He welcomes children. But he is conscious of none of the compulsions and fears of the old family life.

XIII
SCHOOLS

THERE was a dignity and luster about the old Russian gymnasium—high school—which made it a place of distinction in any community. I recall the one in the town in which as a boy I attended school. It was one of the very few fine buildings in the community—a three-story brick structure with large windows and many of them, and always freshly painted and clean inside and outside. Class-rooms and offices were decorated with portraits of the Czar and Czarina mounted in gilded frames and with pictures of noted men of letters and scientists, both Russian and foreign, and reproductions of famous paintings likewise mounted in fitting frames.

The teachers accentuated in manner and appearance the dignity and formality of the institution. There was nothing slouchy or negligent about them. They looked and acted important, and they were important—mingling in the best society and treated everywhere with deference. Like soldiers and officials they wore handsome uniforms of blue or black cloth with golden epaulets and with a double row of gilded buttons. If they cultivated beards they kept them well-trimmed, and if they shaved they did not allow their faces to become overgrown with hair. They made much of personal appearance and they were competent men. They knew their subjects and they knew how to teach. They were rigid disciplinarians and were exacting in their demands upon their pupils. Sometimes they might spy on students, but they never neglected scholarship. That was why the old Russian gymnasium enjoyed such high repute even among people who were sworn enemies of the old government. Academically it ranked with the best of its kind anywhere in Europe.

The students heightened its luster. They came from the best families, the most affluent and the most prominent, and they too wore handsome uniforms—black blouses with shiny leather belts, light gray coats with shiny silver buttons, and stiff military caps to match. They were the young aristocracy of the community, the envy of the boys who could not enter the gymnasium.

Indeed there was style, dignity, order, about the old Russian gymnasium.

Nowadays the scene is very different. The gymnasium as such has disappeared. The Soviet nine- and ten-year school has taken its place. But gone is the old glitter and the old formalism. Gone are the uniforms for teachers and students. Gone, above all, is the official gulf between the two.

On a recent visit to the city of Saratov, a seat of culture in Russia, with more universities and high schools of various kinds than any local citizen can count offhand, I went around the schools. One of them, regarded as the best in town, was located in the same building which in the old days a gymnasium had occupied. It was a large three-story structure, stretching over a whole block, with large windows and with the tin roof and the rain-pipes rusty with age. Recess was on when I entered, and the place reverberated with a multitude of noises—human and mechanical. Boys and girls were running around in all manner of attire—with nowhere a suggestion of style, distinction, or uniformity save among the Pioneers, all of whom wore red neckties. I asked a little girl to take me to the principal. She piloted me through a tumultuous corridor to a porch in a yard, and introduced me to a man of about thirty. "Here he is," she remarked, and dashed off to join her playmates. Never in the world would I have taken him to be principal of a school. But then for the moment I had forgotten I was in Soviet Russia. There was nothing even remotely to suggest a likeness to an old time gymnasium director. He was tall and haggard with shaved head and an unshaved face, and with a Tartar skull-cap pushed over the back of his head. He wore sandals and a shiny blouse and corduroy-like trousers which had evidently never been pressed. He looked more like a workman in a factory than principal of the finest school in one of the most cultured cities in the country. He was polite and talkative and excessively frank. A worker—a locksmith by trade—his trade union had commissioned him to give up factory work and enter the teaching profession, and here he was. He had only graduated from a workers' high school, but in the near future he would go to the university and prepare himself adequately for his task. He did no teaching.

He admitted that he didn't know enough. All his teachers were university graduates, and his job was merely to administer the school and to see that there was no perversion in the so-called party line. He was in reality the eye of the party in this school, or its political supervisor.

He showed me around the class-rooms, and particularly interesting were the manual training-shops—as much for their superb equipment as for the personality of the instructors. The one who taught carpentry was a carpenter by profession, with little education. He spoke Russian ungrammatically, but he made the students build splendid book-racks and desks and tables and benches and other pieces of furniture. The man who taught locksmithing was likewise a worker from the factory. He too had no high-school education, but he was a good locksmith. Such teachers, men directly from the factory, the principal informed us, got their appointments as a matter not of choice but of necessity. There just were no men with high education in the country who could teach manual-training subjects. There would be in time. But until that time came they would have to employ ordinary workers as teachers.

The contrast in the external appearance between the old gymnasium and this school in Saratov was symbolic of the contrast between the respective worlds which they were supposed to represent—one with rigid emphasis on formalism, discipline, external sparkle, social glamor, the other as yet without the time and the means to emphasize external appearances, and with small regard for formalism or social prestige and with no sign of officialdom in the relations between teachers and pupils.

These, however, are only a few of the contrasts one observes everywhere between the old and the new schools. There are many, very many others.

In 1914-15 there were slightly over 7,000,000 pupils in the Russian elementary schools, and slightly over 500,000 in the secondary schools. Excepting the parochial schools, they were of high standing academically. Especially was this true of the *zemstvo* schools.

In 1932 there were 19,000,000 pupils in the Russian elementary schools and 4,550,000 in the secondary schools.

In 1914-15 there were 125,000 students in the Russian universities and 267,000 in the trade and technical schools.

In 1932 there were 500,000 students in the Russian universities; 850,000 in the technical schools, and 1,100,000 in the so-called factory schools.

In 1920, 60 per cent of the male population of the country and 70 per cent of the female—or 68 per cent of the entire population—were illiterate.

In 1932, only 9 per cent of the population was illiterate.

In 1914-15, compulsory universal education was a far-off dream of liberals and intellectuals.

In 1931-32, free, universal, compulsory education for children between eight and eleven had become a fact. By 1933-34 it will become a fact for children between eight and twelve. In the cities and industrial centers, compulsory education for children between eight and fifteen has already been established, and in two years the age limit for compulsory education in the cities will be lifted to seventeen. In the villages this goal will be slower of attainment, primarily because of lack of physical facilities and competent teachers. But even there eventually all children between eight and seventeen will be compelled to attend school. The original program of the party calls for compulsory education of youths between these ages.

In the old days religion was a required subject in all schools, and there were numerous schools in which religion was the most important subject in the curriculum. Now no religious schools for youths under eighteen are allowed, and all government schools are vigorously anti-religious.

In the old days secular education was conducted chiefly in the official language of the country. Foreign languages, modern and ancient, were studied. But the dominant language was Russian. Only religious schools were allowed to be conducted in the native language of the people, and Jews and Mohammedans, for example, had extensive religious schools in which their native tongues were used.

Nowadays education may be conducted in the language of any people living in Russia. In fact, the Soviets encourage subject nationalities to have their own schools, and such schools are now being conducted in seventy languages. Some of these languages, like that of the gypsies or Buryats, had no script and no printed alphabet of their own. Now they have both. They have grammars, dictionaries, text-books, newspapers, and even theaters in which the lines are spoken in their native tongues.

In the old days there was little pre-school education in Russia. In 1914, in Moscow, a certain Alexander Zelenko, who had spent some time in America, in association with a Mrs. Schloger, opened a kindergarten in a settlement house. It was the only one in Moscow. The few other pre-school institutions that existed catered to the very rich or the very poor.

In 1932, 10,000,000 children were cared for in the nurseries, kindergartens, playgrounds, and other pre-school institutions. By the end of the second Five Year Plan the Soviets hope to include all children in such institutions.

In the old days co-education was on the rise in the lower more than in the secondary schools, and also in some of the colleges. Now there isn't a single school, from kindergarten to university, that is not co-educational.

In the old days, with the exception of the elementary public schools and church schools, and certain teachers' institutes, students had to pay for tuition. In the secondary schools and the universities the fees were high. Students in these schools, in addition, had to wear costly uniforms.

Now all education in the elementary and middle schools, excepting for children of high-salaried engineers and other Soviet specialists, is free. In the technical schools, the universities, and the various institutes, about three-fifths of the students are not only taught free, but receive monthly stipends to cover living expenses. Only if they fail in their studies are the stipends withdrawn from them.

In the old days, free meals in elementary or secondary

schools were limited to small groups of students. Now there is not, to my knowledge, a single elementary or secondary school in Russia which hasn't a dining-room that provides, at least during a part of the year, one hot meal a day to the students. In the villages the meal is free. In the cities it is free for children of the lower-paid workers and officials. Others pay from 12 to 25 copecks—that is from about five cents to fifteen cents a meal.

The school is the one institution in Soviet Russia which has enjoyed steady and galloping growth. The Bolsheviks who in many ways have inherited the ideas and passions of the old Russian revolutionary movements have absorbed their ardor for the education of the masses. Lenin, who was himself a child of the old revolutionary movement, had warned his followers in 1921 that "as long as we have such a calamity as illiteracy in our country, it is impossible to talk of political enlightenment. The illiterate person is an outsider to political thought. He must be taught the ABC. Without literacy, there can be no politics; there are only rumors, gossip, prejudices, fairy-tales—anything but political class-consciousness."

In subsequent years the Bolsheviks were to forget many a wise counsel of their highly revered teacher, as, for example, that it is natural for children to humanize animals, that roosters would not be real to them if they did not talk. Only now, after years of costly blundering, are they discovering this and many another wise suggestion of Lenin, and they are beginning to embrace them as though they were a newly discovered life-saving balm. But they never for a moment forgot his warning that the bringing of a knowledge of reading and writing to every living person in the land was the most urgent task of the Revolution. Trotzkyites or Stalinites, followers of the Right or the Left dispensation, they all agreed that there could be no waiting in the building of schools. Wherever there was a Soviet, or wherever Soviet influence penetrated, whether in the sunny Caucasus or the snowbound tundras of Siberia, one of the first things the revolutionists brought to the people, like the gift from a parent to the child, was a school. The building might have been a splendid brick structure or only an old barn or a hastily constructed shack, but it was a school.

Not only has the number of schools multiplied rapidly, but the social composition of the students has changed beyond recognition from what it was in the old days.

In the old days, even in the secondary schools, the dominant group of students was made up of children of the nobility, officials, clergymen, the merchant classes. There was a small sprinkling of well-to-do peasants, and now and then of more highly paid factory-workers. I remember, when I was a boy, a playmate of mine who passed his examination for the gymnasium. His parents were overjoyed, but soon their joy gave way to anxiety lest they fail to pass the so-called residence test. To avoid failure in the test, they borrowed from obliging friends expensive furniture and made their apartment a picture of affluence and respectability. The visiting inspector was duly impressed and gave them a high rating.

Whether such a test was universal I do not know. It

was enforced in the town in question, and some people behaved like peasants in the villages who sought to marry their daughters to much-wanted young men from other villages. To impress the youths with their wealth they would stock up their barns with cows, horses, sheep, hogs, and fill their grain-bins with grain, all borrowed for the occasion from obliging neighbors.

It required wealth and social position to gain admittance to the secondary school. Exceptions were made for children of the poor nobility, who were often given allowances for their maintenance.

How different is the picture now! In the universities, peasants make up a good third of the student body, and factory-workers almost one-half. Children of the former nobility and merchant classes, however, are barred as rigorously and as brutally as children of the poor peasants and the factory-workers were in the old days. Until June, 1931, even children of the intelligentsia—engineers, physicians, college professors, school-teachers—though their parents were in the employ of the government and enjoyed citizenship rights, were admitted to the university only after the quotas of peasant and factory-workers were filled. Since June, 1931, children of the intelligentsia have been placed on a level of equality with workers. But children of the former ruling groups may find their way to a higher institution of learning only after they literally sweat themselves into social fitness. After they have done at least two years' hard labor in a lumber camp, a freight yard, construction job, or a farm, they may be regarded as humble and hardened and chastened enough to grace a seat in a university!

The numerical growth of the schools in Russia, remarkable as it has been, tells only one side of the story of Russian education. There is another, even more exciting, which relates to purposes and quality.

On my first visit to Russia in 1923 I happened to stray into a class on literature in a high school in Moscow. The work under discussion was Pushkin's well-known poetic romance, *Eugene Onegin*. The class was discussing the character of Tatyana, the heroine of the romance. Now in the old days Tatyana was the dream and the idol of Russian high-school girls, in fact of all women who read books. There were few of them who did not learn by heart Tatyana's touching letters to her lover—learned them and brooded and wept and suffered over them. They form some of the most famous sentimental poetry in the Russian language. But in this particular class the students cherished an altogether new approach to Tatyana.

"She was as much a slave of her class," said a youth of about sixteen, "as were Onegin and Lensky [the other two leading characters in the romance]. They didn't any of them know anything about the mass. They were content to wallow in luxury while their serfs sweated and starved and died for them. If Tatyana were alive today we'd have to remake her, exile her, and compel her to become one of the mass of workers."

The teacher called on another student, and her speech was as censorious as that of the student who preceded her. "What does this woman live for?" she asked. "Just herself, her pretty sentiments, her tears, her loneliness, her men. Tatyana was a dismal failure because she never learned to work and never lived for the mass, or even thought of the mass."

Several other students expressed themselves in an equally denunciatory manner. Then another girl was called upon—a dark-haired girl with a flushed face and shifting black eyes and wearing a gray dress and a frayed gray sweater. She seemed timid, and spoke haltingly and quietly.

"This is what I want to say, *tovarishchi*; it is not for us to condemn Tatyana. We are the product of an era of which Tatyana hadn't heard. Marx was unknown. Nobody had ever thought that there ever would be a Lenin. There was no Communist Party in existence. The masses of our people were serfs. There were hardly any factories and scarcely any workers. And so I say there is no use condemning Tatyana. She was not to blame for her ideology. She meant well and she was noble, and even though you may think me stupid and perverted I do want to tell you that I like her, and I cried when I read of her misfortunes."

The girl sat down, and there was a commotion in the class. The teacher in a condescending manner, as though striving hard not to give offense to anybody, attempted to bring the students to order. He was a man of about forty-five with sparse gray hair, an unshaved face, and protruding eyes that illumined his face like searchlights. But the students would not calm down. They were not taking sides; they were all on one side—against Guryeva! One proletarian lad expressed no doubt the sentiments of the whole class when he said, "Tovarishchi Guryeva is a clear example of how impossible it is for some persons to slough off their bourgeois heritage," and he launched into a long and bitter harangue against people like Tatyana, no matter where and when they lived, and also against Soviet youths like Guryeva, who might have sympathy for a character like Tatyana.

When the class was over I went for a walk with the teacher. He had taught literature in the old Russian gymnasium, and in spite of political repression in the old days teachers not only were allowed, they were required to analyze literary values, character, plots, style. Literature was literature and not an excuse for a political sermon. But now he was helpless. So were his colleagues, who felt as he did that a generation was growing up which would know neither the joy nor the inspiration of literature. In the early days of the Revolution, he continued, they attempted to assert themselves, but soon enough they were made to feel that their lot was not to lead, but to follow, and woe to the teacher who failed to bow in submission. The students had neither respect nor tolerance for him, and often enough denounced him to the authorities and subjected him to investigations. Also in those days there was the chance of losing the job, with no new one in sight. And so, when a Pushkin's Tatyana was denounced as a nefarious *bourzhuika*, and when a student who was courageous enough to express sympathy for this *bourzhuika* was treated to a scorching denunciation, the teacher, however resentful of such perversion of literary values, had to smile and nod in assent and refrain from taking sides.

In October, 1932, nine years later, I visited another high school in Moscow—one of the best not only in Moscow but in the country. The newspaper *Izvestia* has assumed guardianship over it, and, being a prosperous enterprise, it has spent large sums of money for equipment, some of it of foreign make, for the shops and laboratories—which are among the best I have seen in Russia. There is a gymnasium there, a dining-room, a printing press, and all manner of manual-training departments.

I visited the laboratories and then walked into a class in literature. The teacher, a woman of about forty-five with her shiny brown hair combed straight back and with one of those melodious voices for which Russian women are noted, and with a diction which any actor might envy, was in complete control of the class. One felt her presence, her personality, her dignity, her authority. She showed none of the timidity which one observed among teachers nine years earlier. The students were between fifteen and sixteen years of age, and they were discussing Griboyedov's famous comedy *Grief from Intelligence*. The teacher had told them to prepare talks on the personality of the two leading characters, Chatsky and Famousov.

She called on a dark-haired girl to make her talk. The girl arose, stepped forward, and, facing the class, began to speak; and as I listened to her I could hardly believe that Soviet education had become so changed within so brief a period as nine years. Fluently, and in excellent Russian, interspersing her remarks with telling phrases, the girl proceeded to give an analysis of the very things she had been commissioned to do. She spoke of Chatsky's rebellion against the ideas of the good and wise people of the time. She stressed his recourse to hyperbole and antithesis as a means of sharpening his thrusts at the things and people he disliked. She traced the influence of his sojourn abroad on his beliefs and on his very speech. She dwelt at length on his inner conflicts and on the tragedy of his personal life. Though he was a *bourzhui* like Tatyana in Pushkin's *Onegin*, she spoke of him with sympathy and understanding, and there was not the least trace of an effort to pigeonhole and label him as a friend or an enemy of the masses or to denounce him because of his social origin.

In her analysis of Famousov, this bright girl did the same thing. She gave a portrait of the physical appearance of the man, and then spoke of his conservatism in politics, in home life, his belief that the things which mattered chiefly in life were riches, rank, comfort, his tendency to be verbose, to philosophize at length and to lecture to his friends, his exasperation with people who did not share his beliefs, his utter inability to appreciate the break of new ideas over the Russian land, and his contempt for anything foreign. Above all, she emphasized the simplicity, lightness, and colorfulness of his speech, and of his imagery.

When this girl finished, the teacher asked for criticism of her speech. Student after student arose and made additions and amplifications. They were all remarkably fluent of speech, some of them accompanying their words with emphatic gestures, and they too concerned themselves with the literary values of the comedy—of style, character, plot, imagery. Not one of them approached his analysis in terms of political convictions. Not once did any of the students indulge in political rhetoric in denunciation and castigation. One student spoke of the high-born social origin of Chatsky and

Famousov, but did not proceed to deluge them with contumely as did the students in the discussion of Pushkin's heroine. Here scholarship was superseding politics.

Not that politics is left out: it cannot be in a Soviet system where devotion to the system itself is the main purpose of education. But politics is no longer a matter of catchwords and slogans. Politics is the mantle of life and the important thing is not the mantle, but life, and the problems that a Soviet citizen and the Soviet State encounter in their everyday existence.

The shift of emphasis from politics to scholarship, or rather the subordination of the first to the second, is an epochal event in the Revolution and would have been much slower in coming had it not been for the Five Year Plan. The Plan awakened Russian leaders to a new wisdom in education, as it had in so many other national problems. It hurled forth a host of difficulties which the Russian leaders had not foreseen and which demanded instant and effective attention.

In the early years of the Revolution the thing that mattered most was political conformity. The school was supposed to develop "citizens for the communist society," and in those days, with memories, passion, hurts of the civil war still rife, the one thing that such citizens were supposed to possess was political fealty. Of course the powers that were quoted Lenin in justification of their attitude. Had not Lenin said that "while students are in school they are to be made participants of the struggle for freedom from exploitation?" and again, that "our task in the school is likewise to struggle for the overthrow of the bourgeoisie and we openly proclaim that education outside of life and outside of politics is a fraud and a deception?" Lenin had also said other things about education. For example: "You can become a Communist only when you enrich your mind with all the intellectual treasures which humanity has attained." And again, students in school must gain a command of "the accumulated knowledge of mankind." Both these pronouncements sound very much like Matthew Arnold's definition of culture as "the best that has been said and thought by man." Marx had also said, "The only goal worthy of humanity is the greatest possible enlargement of all human capacities."

Moreover, Marx and Engels, in the resolution which they had drafted for the Congress of the First International, laid down definite principles of Communist education. They emphasized three things: all-round intellectual development; physical education, such as physical culture and military drill, for the maintenance of the health of students; and polytechnical education which was to acquaint students with science and with the productive processes of industry and enable them to acquire habits of work and an ability to handle with facility instruments and tools in factories.

But these principles of education enunciated by the three fathers of modern Communism, the Russian Bolsheviks misunderstood and misapplied. They emphasized above everything political conviction and also music. They always made much of music. I visited schools in 1923 and 1924 which had hardly any books and papers but where the students knew by heart the political phraseology of the moment and could sing with vigor and emotion the latest revolutionary songs.

In those days there were leaders who even sponsored the idea that the school "must die," that is, eventually be converted into a sort of apprenticeship to the factory and the farm.

The purely intellectual development of the students the Bolsheviks hoped to attain through the so-called complex method of education. Communists all over the country were seized with a passion for this method. Instead of studying geography, history, literature separately, they studied them together in an inter-related manner. In villages teacher and pupils together would build a complex lesson about some familiar subject. The seasons of the year—autumn, winter, spring, summer were used extensively as starting-points. In the course of these lessons the students would be considering the climatic conditions of the given season, the work that the peasants were obliged to do—ploughing or harvesting, cutting wood or weeding gardens, also the life they were living individually and collectively. Then they would discuss the methods the peasants pursued in working their land, and the methods they should pursue to increase productivity, the sanitary conditions of the village, its cultural backwardness, and how to overcome them. Always they sought to synthesize and unify the conditions in their environment with their own and the community's everyday experience. In those days books were scarce. The state could not print them fast enough to supply the needs of the ever-growing schools; but under the complex system of education few books were needed. Sometimes none at all were used. Side by side with these studies there was the practical work of the students in shops and fields. In theory all education was supposed to be activist, calculated to develop the capacity to act decisively and to do things with one's hands; carpentry, blacksmithing, the handling of machines, electrical apparatus, radio, and other mechanical devices. Education was also supposed to be collectivist, calculated to develop collective habits of thought and work. Individual effort and individual study were frowned upon as likely to intensify individualistic traits. In time, Communist educators developed a so-called brigade method of study whereby students formed into units of six or eight and studied jointly under the leadership of an elected schoolmate. There were no examinations, no marks. The brigade was responsible for the work of the individual student. The students also had an important, sometimes a decisive, voice in the administration of the school, the disciplining of the students, above all in the preparation of the complex lessons. The teacher was supposed to supervise student activities, but often enough, for reasons of political expediency, he was a silent onlooker. Of course students were interested in politics and were continually holding political meetings, and were called upon to engage in all manner of social work. Teachers also were constantly drawn into outside activities—drafting political resolutions, writing political documents, helping in Soviet bookkeeping, or in any other task for which they might qualify. The salary of a teacher was low, and often months passed before he received it. Because he was an intellectual, he was not quite the social equal of a peasant or a worker, and his children, as already stated, were admitted to high school and university only after the quota of workers and peasants had been filled.

And so, while schools were rapidly multiplying, the quality of education, save in matters of political faith, was either at a standstill or actually deteriorating—this in spite of constant experimentation with new methods and almost annual changes of text-books. Then came the Five Year Plan. Russia needed mechanics, engineers, chemists, agriculturists, organizers, managers. She needed tens, hundreds of thousands of them on the numerous mammoth enterprises she had begun to build. But to the amazement and consternation of leaders, Soviet college graduates, multitudes of them, failed to qualify for the posts to which they had been appointed. Their preparation was so meager they could not meet responsibilities imposed on them.

In the resolution of the Central Committee of the Communist Party of September, 1931, it is specifically stated: "Our children graduate from school insufficiently educated, without the high level of knowledge necessary to pursue successfully their studies in the technical schools and universities, and they are unable to gain command of the technical processes which are of such decisive importance in our Socialist construction." Another resolution by the same Central Committee in August of 1932 reiterates these charges, only more vigorously. The chief defect of the school system, according to this resolution, is that the curriculum is too diffuse; too many subjects are studied, with little unity between them, with inadequate preparation in mathematics, chemistry, geography, history, rhetoric—all of which any Soviet youth, and particularly a Communist, must know if he would be a leader in industry or in government. What is even more remarkable, the resolution complains there is "too little perspective in the study of history." This subject had been slighted by the Soviet curriculum and now there is a demand that it be accorded a proper place in all education. The resolution further complains that too heavy a burden of social work has been imposed on the teacher and too much authority has been vested in the students, and that they manifest too little respect for the teacher. It reminds party workers in education of Lenin's pronouncement that the "public school teacher must be placed on a height which he never has attained and which he never can attain in a bourgeois society." It condemns vehemently the brigade method of study as deadening individual initiative and individual responsibility. One writer, in commenting on the resolution, excoriates both the complex and the brigade methods of study, and holds that if continued they would ruin the whole system of education.

The two resolutions of September, 1931, and August, 1932, marked a revolutionary turning-point in Soviet education. The Central Committee is very decisive in its pronouncements. It enjoins boards of education completely to overhaul their theories and practices; "knowledge of science and art must be real." Students may continue to study in brigades, but only when it will liven up and not deaden knowledge of a subject. They must get a thorough grounding in rhetoric, mathematics, geography, chemistry, physics; shops and laboratories must be well equipped so that students can apply theory to practice and learn how to work and build and plan industrial projects. They must, in short, prepare themselves to be not only agitators but workers and leaders. They cannot squeeze themselves out of responsibility by pointing to a certain situation as being bourgeois or contra-revolutionary or non-proletarian. Above all they must submit to discipline. They must respect the work of the teacher and they must pass examinations. If they fail to comply with regulations or offend the teacher, no amount of political zeal is to save them from expulsion without the right to enter other schools for from one to three years. The teacher likewise must be treated with deference and he must be obeyed. He must receive his salary on time and he must get his quota of foods and manufactured goods. Above all, he must not be burdened with extra-curricular jobs which keep him from advancing himself in his studies.

The basic purpose of education remains the same as it was in the early years of the Revolution—the preparation of a new citizen for a new society. But this preparation must proceed with full regard for the actual everyday tasks and obligations of the new citizen. He must know his subjects, and know them well. He is to enrich his mind, as Lenin urged, with the intellectual treasures of man. He is to apply political principles to the study of the arts, but he must also cultivate an understanding of art values. His education is to be purposeful. He is not to pursue a so-called liberal arts course that leads to no specific goal. He is to prepare himself for a definite position in the new society—teaching, medicine, engineering, or anything that he may choose. The school is to prepare him for his life-work, and must always be linked with Soviet life: industry, commerce, agriculture, and everything else that makes up this life. Always of course the school is to make him a loyal soldier of the Revolution.

The result is that now when one enters a Russian school one finds a discipline and an earnestness that did not exist in the early years of the Revolution. Some students have been irked by the changes, and have protested against the loss of what they call their rights. But the protests have remained unheeded. In fact, Russia is drifting toward increased formalism in education and an increased curtailment of so-called student rights. Her years of experiment with the complex and the brigade methods of study have convinced her that there is no easy road to education. Unless students apply themselves individually and with diligence to their studies they will be in no position to further the tasks and aims of the Revolution. They may indeed thwart this progress, and that the leaders are resolved, in no circumstances, to allow.

XIV
ART

GORKY'S new play, *Yegor Bulitchev*, has excited Moscow as no literary event since the Revolution; and in it there is a scene which gives insight into the kind of mentality that a Soviet artist has to reckon with if he wants to have his work appreciated or even accepted.

The hero of this play, a merchant in the pre-revolutionary days, is on the point of death. He is a cynic and an infidel; but his wife and her sister, being profoundly religious, cannot bear the thought of his dying without receiving the last sacrament, and so they send for a priest. Followed by the wife and her sister and several other members of the family with lighted candles in their hands, the priest and the deacon, garbed in gorgeous vestments and swinging incense and intoning solemnly, "*Hospodi Pomilui*" ("Lord, have mercy"), proceed to the dying man's chamber.

It is a moving scene, and in the old days a Russian audience would have been stirred to tears. The incense, the candles, the chanting, would have aroused in it a sense of awe of death and life. But on the evening when

I saw the play the audience (which jammed every available seat in the theater) burst into a laugh. And this behavior was not exceptional. Every time the play is given the audience, at this particular scene, behaves in a similar manner. It simply laughs! To the present-day Russian audience, religion—even the ministration of the last rites to a dying man—suggests something not only incongruous, but comic!

Now let the reader ponder over the importance and universality of religion as a subject in the arts. For generations it has been an endless source of inspiration to painter, composer, playwright, novelist, poet. Some of the most stirring music Russia has given to the world is religious in theme. But now religion is discarded from Russia, and the artist who would deal with it seriously will find no friend and no buyer for his creations.

The family likewise is no longer a theme that excites Russian audiences. As a social institution it continues, but it has, so to speak, lost its flesh and blood. It is only a skeleton of its former self, and no artist can press out of it the drama that it furnished in the old days or that it may still furnish to the artist outside of Russia. Were Dostoyevski now alive, he could not have written a *Brothers Karamazov* in the manner in which he did. He could not have built his story around the Karamazov family. Were Shakespeare alive at present in Russia, he could not have created a *King Lear*. Nor could a Balzac have given the world a *Père Goriot*, or Galsworthy a *Forsyte Saga*. Family conflicts and tragedies are not impossible in Soviet Russia, but they provide nowhere nearly as weighty an experience or as exciting an adventure as the relationship of the individual to the new community. This relationship has superseded or swallowed all other social relationships. Indeed, religion, business, the individualistic family—the three institutions which artists in the Western world and in old Russia have invested with exciting and heroic qualities—are in present-day Russia the three chief villains or clowns.

What, then, are the subjects that occupy the attention of the Russian artist?

For a long time—roughly up to 1926—the Bolshevik civil war, and the famine and suffering that followed in its wake, preoccupied the Russian artist. The best literature that has come out of Soviet Russia deals with these two epochal periods. Bulgakov's *Days of the Turbines*, a civil war play, is still the best piece of dramatic writing that any Russian author has produced. The finest Soviet motion pictures likewise relate to the civil war. Pudovkin's *The Fall of St. Petersburg*, and Eisenstein's *Potemkin*, are still the high lights in Russian cinema production. Though Eisenstein bases his story on the revolt of the Black Sea fleet in 1905, in spirit the picture includes so many elements of the Bolshevik civil war of 1917 that it can safely be spoken of as a Bolshevik civil war picture.

The new period which followed so-called military Communism provided a fresh range of subjects for the artist. Private enterprise was legalized, and this stirred up excitements, ambitions, abuses, inner conflicts, which stimulated the artist's imagination. The government had no intention of allowing *Nep* free rein. On the contrary, it held its sword over what one writer called "this political monster" which it had not ceased to hate but which it had to endure. But *Nep* whetted appetites for accumulation and for carnal self-indulgence. Some Communists became first-rate rascals and some first-rate rascals became Communists.

Groups of youths plunged into orgies of drinking and sex indulgence. This was the period of *The Embezzlers*, *Moon on the Right*, *Dog Lane*, *Squaring the Circle*, and Romanov's incomparable story, *Without Flowers*, and his novels, *Three Pairs of Silk Stockings* and *The New Table of Commandments*. It was the period of endless debates in the press and on the platform on religion, the family, sex morality, and the array of other personal problems which the individual was facing. It was a period of taverns, shady restaurants, prostitutes, outbursts of hooliganism, and a period of earnest heart-searching on the part of intellectuals who grieved over the cruelties of the Revolution, and on the part of Communists who grieved over its compromise with bourgeois practices—a period, in other words, of uncertainty, maladjustment, and endless perplexity. It was the gap between *Nep* and the Five Year Plan and offered challenge and stimulus to the creative mind.

With the advance of the Revolution into its so-called reconstruction period and the arrival of the Five Year Plan, the civil war and, to a somewhat lesser extent, *Nep*, ceased to occupy the Russian artist, in part because he and his audience had tired of it, and in part because the government was beginning to demand his helping hand in the realization of the big tasks on which it has embarked. Henceforth the artist is to shift emphasis from human experience to social enterprise. He is to center his attention on the aims and tasks of the state and the new community. In other words, he is to deal pre-eminently with the factory, the collective farm, and the new communal order which they presuppose.

To the artist reared in the old traditions and conventions, the transition from one set of subjects to another has involved a readjustment which was not easy to achieve. Neither the young nor the older artist had lived with the new subjects long enough to be able to re-create them into living symbols. Especially difficult, of course, was the subordination of character and human drama to the political formulas of the moment. Yet the censorship looked askance at the treatment of any contemporary theme that did not contribute to this very purpose—that is to say, to the triumph of the immediate policies and the ultimate principles of the Revolution. What further embarrassed the artist who believed in creativeness and not in mere propaganda was the rise to power of the so-called *Rapp*, or Proletarian Writers' Society, which, with the growing interest of the Soviets in political achievement, received increasing support, until it became the sole arbiter of all art in the country.

Certain functions that the *Rapp* performed were commendable. It encouraged factory laborers to take up writing and to record on paper their own experiences and those of their friends. It did the same with the peasant. In a country as predominantly illiterate as Russia, this stimulus to self-expression was productive of a new literary interest and appreciation. Even when the resulting compositions were badly written they meant something culturally. It was the idea, the cause, the political purpose that mattered, and nothing else.

I was invited to a meeting of proletarian writers in the city of Ivanovo and heard some of their compositions read. They were young men and young women of limited education, and their compositions were interesting not as literary achievements but as documents revealing their personalities and their attitude toward the work about them. Constantly they sought to emphasize the thing that *Rapp* had been clamorously demanding—faith and fulfillment of the Revolution. But in their own crude way they fused idea with experience and the everyday actualities in their factories and homes, and presented a picture of life which had a semblance of reality. If the *Rapp* had confined itself to developing writers out of factory-workers and peasants it would have performed a most useful service. But it reached out for a more ambitious goal. It sought to control all art and to press it into a definite political mold. Painting, sculpture, music, literature, theater, cinema, all were to serve only one purpose—the promotion of the program of the Revolution.

Painting and sculpture suffered least from this encroachment on the free creativeness of the artist. Portrait painting is either good or bad, regardless of whether the subject is a business man, a king, a madonna, or a factory-worker. The factory and the collective farm (which means the land) offered a variety of subjects to excite the man with the brush or the chisel.

On November 7, 1932, one of the features of the celebration of the fifteenth anniversary of the Revolution was a display of flowers in the eating-places of

Moscow, and exhibits of paintings in the windows of the leading shops on the main streets of the city. For the time being every important shop had been converted into an art gallery. The subjects concerned themselves pre-eminently with the factory and the *kolhoz.* There were paintings of blast furnaces and workers tending them; of machine shops with men bent over their tools; of forges with men stalking round molten metal; of new construction projects with men singly, in groups, in multitudes, heaving brick, lumber, and other materials. There were paintings of cattle and horses grazing in rich pastures, and of fields, forests, brooks, buildings, on collective farms; of men doing the work in the fields. Crowds of pedestrians stopped and looked and discussed these exhibits. Whatever their shortcomings as works of art, the subjects were decidedly arresting.

They were not only in tune with the Revolution; they made one feel that there was beauty in steel and iron, coal and lumber, and in the men who were performing the irksome tasks of industry. The new subjects allow the painter, by the very nature of his art, sufficient sweep of imagination to make his work striking and appealing. The same is true of the sculptor. Besides, painting and sculpture are not arts in which the Russians have excelled. They have produced a Vereshtshagin, a Repin, an Antkolsky. But they have not the array of great names in these arts as have the French, for example.

The effect of the *Rapp* dictatorship on music, literature, the theater, and the cinema—arts in which the Russians have shown themselves to be masters—was lamentable. It just about ruined the Russian cinema. In the past half-dozen years very few Soviet pictures have commanded the attention of the outside world or aroused excitement in Russia—simply because of the dullness which has resulted from an excess of political sermonizing. The scenarios are of a stereotyped pattern: A hero who is a worker, or an engineer, or an official, and who strives for the success of some governmental enterprise: a villain who is a *koolack*, a business man, a clergyman, a spy, and who strives for its failure. A conflict ensues, with the hero in the end winning the battle; the picture usually ends with a triumphant speech on the glories of building Socialism and sometimes with a revolutionary song and the waving of the Red flag!

The theater has suffered less than the motion pictures, and then only in the literary quality of the new plays it has had to produce. In all other respects it has made noteworthy advances. A revolution means action and conflict of the most impassioned kind, and these had a powerful repercussion on the stage. The Revolution has indeed infused a new vehemence and majesty into the theater—the vehemence and majesty of mass action. Such plays as *The Armored Train*, *Bread*, *The Rails Hum*, and *Temp*, with their masses of workers and peasants in a tempestuous mood and in a spirit of righteous self-assertiveness and triumphant achievement, unheard-of for such people in Russian history, have called out new powers and new talents in Russian actors and producers. One reads in the Russian newspapers of "production meetings" in factories, when workers rise and speak their minds of failings and of measures to overcome them; one reads also of so-called "counter-plans," when workers meet with their management to discuss the plans that have been drafted for them by the Planning Commission of Moscow and ways of exceeding their numerical requirements. One reads of such gatherings in the daily press, in short stories, and in novels, but somehow they never excite, never attain the magnitude of drama. They seem mere matters of routine without a gleam of exaltation. But when one sees such a meeting in a play like *Tempo*, with men and women in overalls, in boots, in *lapti*, spattered with lime and clay, and scattered over the ground and the manifold scaffoldings of the factory they are building; when one watches them jump around and gesture with their arms, and hears them laugh and harangue, acclaim and denounce, one feels that he is in the presence of terror and majesty, and, above all, of indomitable will and power. One forgets playwright and political purpose and is only conscious of a mass of human beings caught in a torrent of passion and turmoil.

The outstanding playwright in point of popularity is a certain Kirshon, an eminent member of *Rapp*. He is an unprepossessing young man of little culture and with no feeling for the reality of character and personality, but with an excellent knowledge of the stage and of his political catechism. He has written the most popular plays of the Revolution, the most notable of which is *Bread*, a play on peasant life. So false is the picture it gives of the peasantry that even Communists with a trace of literary taste speak of it with contempt. The characters are all complete heroes or complete villains, with hardly a living person among them, puppets all, who speak and act in accordance with the political need of the moment. And yet in the hands of the Stanislavsky Art Theater this inferior play becomes a superb spectacle. The directors and actors have blown into it a soul which the author never intended it to have. They have lifted it to a height of dramatic beauty which makes it an overwhelming theatrical triumph.

The Revolution has fostered a number of new schools of the theater with a philosophy and a technique of their own, and has given a fresh impetus to a number of the old theaters. The Vachtangov players even as early as 1923 were housed in a small auditorium. Now they occupy a new theater, one of the largest in Moscow, and are no doubt the most exciting though not the most artistic theatrical group in Russia. The various Tram theaters, particularly the ones of Leningrad and Moscow, started out as amateur companies, interested in problems affecting the life of factory-workers, and have now become established professional theaters that can be counted on to liven up the theatrical season with spectacular productions. The "Blue Blouse," the "Satire" Theaters, the numerous children's theaters of which there are sixty-seven in the country now, are likewise firmly established, and now and then do something that rouses exciting comment.

Yet the literary quality of the new plays is lamentably low. With the exception of *The Days of the Turbines*, *Yegor Bulitchev*, and *Fear*, they are, like the motion pictures, undisguised and outdrawn political sermons, relieved now and then by striking episodes and clever dialogue. Had it not been for the genius of Russian directors and actors, the Russian theater would have sunk to the level of mediocrity to which the cinema has fallen. It is these directors and actors and scenic designers who make the Russian theater—in spite of the dreary plays it has had to produce—the most artistic and spectacular theater in the world.

Of course, the old Russian plays, especially those of Chekhov and Ostrovsky, are constantly being given. Maeterlinck's *Blue Bird*, and Tolstoi's *Resurrection* and *Fruits of Enlightenment*, and Gogol's *Inspector General*, and Griboyedov's *Grief from Intelligence*, and a host of other literary plays of Russian and foreign authors are likewise frequently staged. Eugene O'Neill's *Desire Under the Elms* and *All God's Chillun Got Wings*, are given year after year by the Kamerny Theater.

Meanwhile *Rapp* was becoming more and more aggressive, with the result that it terrorized or paralyzed some of the leading Russian writers and artists. The poet Volozhin could not get any of his work printed. The two leading literary magazines, *Novy Mir* (*The New World*) and *Krasnaya Nov* (*The Red Beginning*), became mere propagandist journals. A man like Alexei Tolstoi, finding it impossible to write of the passing scene, turned to historical subjects. Other writers did the same, and for a while the historical novel became almost a literary fashion. Babel, whose superb short stories of the civil war have won him international fame, remained silent. Others likewise ceased to write, or kept their manuscripts in their drawers or passed them around among friends. Seifulina, the most gifted woman novelist in Russia, tried to do something new and gave up. Still others, among them Pilnyak, whose *Naked Year* has won him high praise and wide popularity, plunged into the propaganda novel, and with disastrous results. Even Leonov, the most talented of Russian writers of fiction, when he sought to write a novel around the building of a paper factory, failed to produce anything more momentous than a beautifully written and dull book. Composers called upon to create sonatas, symphonies, songs, and operas in the new spirit—that is, in the spirit of so-called Marxian dialectics and in praise of Socialist construction—turned out reams of musical compositions which with very few exceptions even the workers did not enjoy. The ballet responded with its contribution, *The Football Player*, extolling the glories of physical culture and bringing to the stage oil dances, coal dances, other industrial dances, and leaving the audience, even the proletarians, after a long evening's performance, cold and bored. Only the music saves it from complete inanity. Now it is rarely shown. The other revolutionary ballet, *The Red Poppy*, is infinitely more appealing in its music and its dancing, and is still often given in Moscow and in other cities. It has vitality, suspense, and a certain beauty, but no real Russian critic I have heard of would class it with the old Russian Ballets. All forms of art, save acting and painting, had ceased to become creative, and the talented artist was patiently waiting for better days when *Rapp*, whip in hand, would no longer stand over him.

Soon, however, the protests against *Rapp* became so loud and so sharp that they could no longer be ignored. Even workers were displeased and began to complain. They were having all the sermonizing they wanted in their factories, in the daily press, at their mass-meetings. When they went to an entertainment they wanted to forget their everyday problems and conflicts. When they read a book they wanted something more than mere political palaver. They had, in fact, been reading the good literature of Europe and America and found it diverting and instructive. They welcomed Bolshevik morality in Russian literature and in the other arts, but they wanted more—story, character, excitement, diversion. The Russian audience in its artistic tastes had pushed beyond the political formalism which *Rapp* had been foisting on them. Under these circumstances Stalin and his associates could no longer ignore the art activities of the country.

Earlier Stalin had occasion to intercede in behalf of certain artists. *The Days of the Turbines*, for example, the most stirring play written since the Revolution, was, after a run of several years, ordered to be put away. There was much discussion, at the time it was in process of rehearsal, as to whether it should be allowed. To a pious Communist it has one unpardonable fault—it pictures the Whites in the play not as dyed-in-the-wool villains, but as sympathetic human beings. After much discussion and certain changes it was allowed, and it won instant acclaim. But with the coming of the Socialist offensive it was ordered off the stage. Over a year ago, due to Stalin's influence, it was put back and is once more in the repertoire of the Art Theater. More recently, when Afinogenov had his *Fear* ready for production, there was a loud murmur against it. Afinogenov is himself a Communist, and the play ends with a triumph for the proletarian and his cause, and in as important intellectual a sanctuary as a famous university laboratory. But Afinogenov has dared to picture Russian intellectuals as men who have a real and deep-seated grievance against the discriminations that had until recently been visited on them. His professors speak freely, vehemently, and touchingly. For the first time since the Revolution intellectuals are permitted to give expression to their pent-up complaints, and what more natural than that pious Communists should find it blasphemous? But Stalin and his close associates over-ruled them, and now the play is one of the outstanding successes in Russia.

The tyranny of *Rapp* grew so invidious that action against it became a revolutionary duty as much as an act of grace to Russian artists. In consequence, on April 23, 1932, by special decree *Rapp* was dissolved and the control of the arts was instantly taken out of its hands. When I arrived in Russia last summer I found the art atmosphere as fresh and clear as is the air after a storm. Never had I known painters, musicians, writers, editors, so buoyed up with hope and courage as they were last summer. The censorship still prevails, and while it is still rigorous it no longer is as petty and formalistic as it had been. There is no longer the savage insistence of former days that everything must be a political sermon. Rachmaninov, for example, was under ban. His music was regarded as counter-revolutionary. As long as *Rapp* dominated the artistic scene in Russia there was no hope of having the ban lifted on this gifted composer. Now, however, Rachmaninov has been restored to good-fellowship on the concert stage. Gypsy music, which likewise had been under ban for two years, has been readmitted to legitimacy. Old pictures of Harold Lloyd which had been stored away in the warehouses have been dug up and put on the screen again. True, they teach no political lesson, but they afford extraordinary amusement. And how the Russians jam the theaters in which his pictures are shown. In fact any old American pictures, whether comedies or melodramas, if they are at all entertaining, draw immense audiences, which shows how truly hungry the Russians are for mere entertainment. Russians may actually again arrange and attend literary evenings consisting entirely of lyric poetry, whereas under *Rapp* the very word lyric was anathema. I asked Eisenstein recently what he was working on now, and his reply was, "A slapstick comedy." A year ago neither he nor anyone else would have dared even think of turning out a picture which was not a political sermon. The dissolution of *Rapp* has removed the most stultifying force in all fields of Russian art.

Of course, the new subjects that the Russian artist, if he would be true to life, has to deal with impose certain limitations on him. The individual in Russia lives in a setting the like of which the world has never known, and to portray him as he is, with all his problems and conflicts, his defeats and triumphs, is no easy task, especially as the Revolution is still in a fluid state and subjects him to a constantly changing scene. But the artist can think and create character and story as he could not before. He can return to the old subjects of love and life and death and the whole gamut of human experiences and emotion in a new way and in a new spirit. He cannot exalt ideas that are inimical to the Revolution. But he can portray human beings that *Rapp* never would tolerate. If he writes juvenile stories he may even interpolate the improbable, provided of course it is not definitely anti-Soviet. Lenin's widow has come out boldly for the return of the fairy-tale—not the fairy-tales of angels and mermaids and witches and house goblins, but the fairy-tale of miraculous achievements in the new society. As already mentioned, someone has even discovered that Lenin had once said that it is natural for children "to humanize animals, and to a child a rooster that didn't talk wouldn't be real," and so in juvenile stories it may soon become again legitimate to endow cats and dogs and ponies and doves and nightingales with human speech. No wonder that Moscow was so elated with the production of Gorky's new play *Yegor Bulitchev*. Here is a play in which the hero is a capitalist of the pre-revolutionary days. True he is a symbol of the decadence of capitalist society, also he is an atheist and has no use for magicians and miracle-workers, though they amuse him immensely. But he is an "exploiter" and knows it, and is not ashamed of it. He never mouths proletarian slogans. He never once mentions Karl Marx or the class struggle or the triumph of the masses. He lives in luxury and opulence, and so do his children, who, like so many children of the former bourgeoisie, have no serious purpose in life and no social consciences. They eat sumptuous meals and drink good wine, and the women parade in silks and glitter with jewels; they do all the things that proletarian etiquette disdains. And yet they are portrayed as human beings almost loved by author and audience.

As a play *Yegor Bulitchev*, in this writer's opinion, does not compare with any of the other plays Gorky has written. Had it not been for the superb performance of the Vachtangov players it would not even have been a theatrical success. But it is a vivid slice of life such as the Russian theater-goer has not seen in any of the new plays since the Revolution, excepting of course Bulgakov's *Days of the Turbines*. It deals with the age-old subjects of love and life and death and intrigue and ambition without a trace of political palaver or proletarian sermonizing! Above all, it makes the Russian language live again on the stage. The dialogue is free from the new cant and the new shibboleths. It is Russian at its best—simple, luscious, and noble.

If the Russian artist during the period of *Rapp's* dominance found himself cramped in his creativeness, and even if now he must still face a censorship, he never has had reason for serious complaint of the treatment accorded him personally as an employee of the Soviets. Since the coming of the Five Year Plan life has been hard, and never so much so as now at the finish of the Five Year Plan. There is a shortage of everything, from meat and butter to paper and safety pins. But life has been less hard for the artist whose work has been accepted than even for workers, the special favorites of the Soviets. The artist and the engineer are perhaps the most privileged individuals in Russia, and get the best that there is in salary, in food, in entertainment, in clothes, in living quarters—the artist sometimes more than the engineer. I have never known a worker, even a high-salaried one, to set such inviting foods and drinks before guests as do artists. Nor have

I ever known workers to patronize the expensive restaurants in Moscow as do so many artists.

What is most important, the Soviet artist need never worry about a customer for his works, provided of course they are politically acceptable. The Revolution has developed an immense audience for the appreciation of all arts including painting and sculpture. I have a feeling that, barring an economic collapse, Russia in time will become the most extensive art market in the world. The socialization of everyday life has opened up a vast number of institutions which clamor for the ministrations of the artist. Every new factory, for example, has a clubhouse, a restaurant, a library, a reading-room, a nursery, usually a theater, and all of these have to be decorated and furnished and supplied with books and musical instruments and stage paraphernalia. The same is true of the collective farms. At present owing to Bolshevik blunders they are in a bad economic slump. But sooner or later they will rise to greater affluence, and when that time comes they too will be wanting to decorate their clubhouses and libraries and little theaters and schools and nurseries and social dining-halls, and provide themselves with all the things and partake of the enjoyments that the artist has to offer. All of which means more and more work for painters, sculptors, publishers, theatrical and motion picture producers, musicians.

Even now authors or playwrights whose writings get published or produced are among the richest people in Russia. True, there is a high income-tax, and if they are members of the Communist Party they have to pay a double income-tax, one to the government and one to the party. But even then they enjoy a higher degree of prosperity than perhaps anyone else in the country, including high-salaried engineers. The reason is that they are paid on a basis of royalties. A successful play like Afinogenov's *Fear*, or Kirshon's *Bread*, may be given simultaneously in over one hundred theaters all over the country, and each theater pays the author a definite percentage of its receipts. A successful book goes through numerous large editions. Leonid Leonov's new novel, *Skutarevsky*, which is just off the press, came out in a first edition of forty thousand copies, in spite of the fact that only the more cultivated people read him.

Russia is so hungry for reading-matter, that any book which is published finds a ready public. Russian publishers never have to worry about remainders. They do not even have to advertise their books. If they do, and the books are by known authors, the stores are instantly mobbed with purchasers who are ready to throw money at the clerks for the privilege of possessing the books. Nor does a Russian theatrical manager have to worry about filling his auditorium. He seldom has vacant seats. Workers alone have got so much into the habit of attending theaters that they buy out whole performances. Over three hundred factories, for example, have sent in orders to the Vachtangov Theater for huge blocks of seats for the performance of Gorky's *Yegor Bulitchev*. The Revolution has cultivated in the Russian masses a hunger for intellectual and artistic diversions which the present resources of the country, however extensive, are insufficient to satisfy.

So, whatever the grievances and disabilities of the artist, if his work is acceptable he lives as abundantly as is possible under existing Soviet conditions, and he need never worry about a market for his work or an appreciative audience.

XV
THE ARMY

UNDER the Czar military service was compulsory, and under the Soviet military service is compulsory.

Under the Czar soldiers wore uniforms, and under the Soviet soldiers wear uniforms.

Under the Czar soldiers when on march sang lustily, with a soloist starting each verse and the company joining in the chorus. Under the Soviet soldiers when on march sing lustily, with a soloist starting every verse and the company joining in the chorus.

These are about the only likenesses I can think of between the old and the new Russian army. In all other respects they are worlds and ages apart.

Once I happened to be spending a few days in a Ukrainian village. In the course of my stay there an army officer arrived and called together the young men of the village. Most of these youths were scheduled to enter military service that year, and the army officer had come to give them preliminary preparation. He began with a lecture on the aims and purposes of the Red Army, emphasizing the fact that in time of peace it was a school for citizenship, and in time of war, a fighting machine to repel invasions of capitalist enemies.

When, after his lecture, he asked if any one had any questions to ask, youth after youth plied him with queries. How many hours a day would they have to be on duty? How often would they be allowed to go home for vacations? What privileges would their folks at home enjoy during the period of service? What occupations would they have opportunity to learn? And one wanted to know whether he would be permitted to learn to play the cornet. Every question was answered in detail by the officer, and in a spirit of intimacy and good fellowship.

This lecture furnished a good example of the difference between the old régime and the new in their approach to the military recruit. Under the Czar there was no pre-service campaign of education and preparation. The old government made no effort to inculcate in the future soldier, before he was called for his physical examination, sympathetic understanding of the aims and purposes of army service and the advantages to be derived from it. The recruit was left to his own imaginings. Every young peasant in the villages knew that he would have to serve in the army. He knew that if his health was good, and his father was able-bodied and he was not an only child, and if the quota for his district was not filled before his number was called, he would have to go into the army and serve from three to seven years, depending on which branch of service he entered. He knew also that he would be subjected to hardships, humiliations, and to severe discipline. He had heard returned soldiers speak of these things. Consequently, on the day set for his departure from home he was sad of heart. And not only he. His whole family would be in mourning, its women weeping and bewailing the fate that had befallen him and them. Going into the army was regarded as an ordeal and a calamity.

And no wonder. In the old days the very word *soldat* had an unpleasant ring. It implied a man of low manners, and was generally employed as an epithet of reproach and contempt. In the market-place the expression *soldatskaya morda* (soldier's jowl) was freely bandied about by traders and customers in the bargaining and altercations that so often accompanied the consummation of a deal.

For the young soldier, usually a peasant fresh from the village, often illiterate, with no knowledge of the outside world, was sure to be confused and intimidated by the new surroundings and new faces and especially ill at ease in the presence of a uniform. He knew no manners, no habits, no ambitions other than those he had observed or acquired in his native village. Never having been away from home except possibly for brief periods of winter work in lumber camps or near-by towns, he felt alone and homesick in the military camp —a feeling intensified during his first days there by the fact that he was made continually aware of his lowly position, his inferiority, and his duty always to submit.

If in a moment of peasant forgetfulness he addressed a superior in the familiar *ty* (thou) instead of the formal *vy* (you), he was sure to receive a severe tongue-lashing. His superiors, of course, never deigned to address him other than by the inferior pronoun *ty*. On duty, off duty, in camp, in town, in street, on highway, always he had to be conscious of his inferiority. If he ever traveled in a street-car he stood on the platform, because an officer might be inside. He couldn't even smoke a cigarette in a railroad station, if an officer chanced to be there, without first asking the officer's permission; and if by chance he had the price of box or orchestra seats for the theater, he never bought tickets for these preferred places because an officer might be seated there. He was fed well, clothed well, drilled strenuously, but always he had to know his place, and dared never in any way appear to regard himself as the equal of an officer. If he ever forgot his obligation, he was reminded of it in a manner which he never failed to remember. Punishment was severe. Though by law officers were forbidden to resort to corporal punishment, there were always those who, on provocation, did not hesitate to slap a soldier in the face.

Because of the rigors, pain, and humiliations of army life, youths in the old days sometimes sought to escape it. If they were well-to-do, they attempted to bribe their way out. If they were poor, they often went without food for long periods or stayed up nights until they appeared properly emaciated. Others employed drugs to induce irregular heart action. There were even special practitioners who would inflict sufficient injury to render a youth physically unfit for military service. For this purpose, damaging the index finger of the right hand was one of the most common devices.

I am speaking here of the common people—peasants, factory workers, members of subject nationalities.

There were, of course, other classes in Russian society who regarded army service as an honor and a glory. This attitude was general among members of the nobility, the merchant classes, and other groups socially superior to the so-called "masses." For these social *élite*, service in the army was a career which carried with it prestige, power, position, a comfortable salary, and, in addition, a life of excitement and adventure. They constituted a caste of their own. Now and then individual peasants could filter into their ranks. In the last years of the Czar's rule more and more peasants who had been educated embarked on army service as a career. Chiefly, however, peasants and workers served as ordinary soldiers, and official position in the army was beyond their reach.

Now hardly a vestige of the old army system remains. The position of officer and soldier and their relations toward one another have changed beyond recognition. Now it is the private who gets the glory. He is the public's hero, everywhere acclaimed as a defender, a builder, even as a spiritual symbol of the Revolution. Even the nomenclature applied to him is changed. He is no longer called *soldat*, with its implication of rowdiness, but *krasnoarmeyetz*, Red Army man, a term that carries with it as much honor and prestige as the proud word proletarian. The populace has been taught that the Soviet soldier is guardian of the worthiest and noblest cause in the world, and the soldier himself, of course, is made to feel likewise. From the first day of his arrival at the barracks he is made to realize that he is a personage of worth, dignity, and responsibility. If, on first meeting an officer, he addresses him with the familiar *ty* which he has always used in his native village, the officer shows neither resentment nor disapproval. It is the officer, nowadays, who must set a good example for the soldier by employing always the polite form of salutation, *vy*, in addressing him. The officer must ever bear in mind the social origin and the home surroundings of the recruit and treat him with understanding and esteem, regardless of the blunders and indiscretions which he may commit in his early days in the army. No officer may call him a *durak* (fool) or any one of the many other ignominious epithets with which in the old days officers so freely belabored soldiers who were slow to carry out instructions. Nowadays an officer must never even shout at a soldier, and under no circumstances scold him. He must explain, persuade, help, encourage, but never insult, humiliate, or frighten. An officer invites the contempt of his colleagues, dismissal from service, and even harsher punishment if, for purposes of discipline, he as much as lays his hands on a soldier in public or in private.

No longer must the soldier address the officer as "Your Highness," "Your Nobleness," "Your Splendor," "Your" anything. Gone are all the old exalted appellations and salutations. Now it is always *Tovarishchi Commandir* (Comrade Commander). No matter what the rank of the officer, the form of address never varies. The officer in his turn addresses the soldier as *Tovarishchi krasnoarmeyetz* (Comrade Red Army Man). Unless he happens to be well acquainted with him and on friendly terms, the officer never calls the private by his first name or addresses him in the familiar *ty*. Nor does an officer disdain to eat at the same table with a private and out of the same kitchen. During the hours of drill, which are five a day, instead of eight and a half, as in the old times, soldiers and officers are required to maintain strictly formal relations, and the discipline is rigid. But after hours of service they may play together—football, chess, checkers, any game—rehearse a play for a theatrical performance or sit together before an open fire, sing and tell stories. When off duty the soldier is not obliged to salute the officers. Usually he does, as a matter of good-fellowship, but if he refrains nothing is said to him. Nowhere is he forced to behave like an inferior. If he enters a street car he may occupy any available seat, like any other citizen. If he is at a railroad station and wants to smoke, he need ask nobody for permission. When he goes to the theater he may purchase any seat he wishes. If he finds himself sitting next to his commanding officer, whether of the rank of lieutenant or of general, neither he nor the commander is discomfited. In many a theater in Moscow, Leningrad, and other cities even the boxes which in the old days were specially reserved for the Emperor are now occupied evening after evening by soldiers and sailors. Off duty, the Red soldier has no restrictions as to conduct other than those imposed by his own sense of honor. Thus in every way the Red soldier is made aware at all times of his personal dignity and his responsibility to himself, society, and the Revolution. Officers constantly remind him that they are not his masters but only teachers and friends.

As a result of this new relationship between officers and soldiers and the good-fellowship between them which it engenders, the old dread of military service has vanished among all classes and all nationalities in Russia. It has given way to an actual desire to serve in the Red Army. Youths of subject nationalities who in the old days had special reason to loathe military service, not only because they and their people were held under repression, but because the army was a mighty instrument of Russianization, are now as eager as any native youth to perform military service. For the new army offers fun, adventure, privilege, and opportunity to prepare for any number of careers, military and civil. Never in all my wanderings and contacts with these alien peoples—Poles, Jews, even gypsies—have I observed evidence of unwillingness to go into the army. Some of these nationalities maintain their own territorial armies in which their own language is official.

The change in the attitude of older persons toward the military has been likewise marked. Even men and women of deep family feeling no longer regard it as a calamity for their son to join the colors. Nor do women any longer weep when their sons, husbands, or sweethearts leave for the army. The reverse is often true: parents are glad to have a son become a soldier. It instantly raises their political prestige in the community, and makes possible the enjoyment of benefits which might otherwise be denied them. For one thing, their taxes are reduced. For another, it insures them against any adverse discrimination by their local Soviet. If they think themselves mistreated by local authorities they write to their soldier son, who often, through the intercession of army officials, is able to obtain redress for them.

Once while I was talking to a trade-union leader in

the city of Ivanovo a peasant entered the room shaken with grief. His younger son had just died following an operation in the hospital, and he had come to ask the trade union to supply a band for his son's funeral. The leader of the trade union replied that many of the workers were on vacation, and the band was temporarily dissolved.

"Please," begged the peasant, "tell the *tovarishchi* musicians who are at home that they must do it, not for my sake, but for the sake both of my dead boy and of my eldest son who is in the Red Army."

It was significant that he deemed it necessary to mention his soldier son.

Moved by this appeal, the leader promised to supply music for the funeral even though the regular factory band was unavailable.

In the summer of 1932, while traveling in the black earth region, I engaged a peasant to drive me to a collective farm five miles away. On the way the peasant grew friendly and talkative and proceeded to narrate his troubles. He had once joined a collective farm which had taken into membership neighboring railroad workers. These workers were so busy with their own jobs that they had no time to help with the work on the land. And they agreed to pay out of their earnings the cost of the extra labor that was needed. The peasants frowned on this arrangement and in the end withdrew from the collective farm. In retaliation the local Soviet refused to return to them their former lands. They were enraged, but there was nothing that they could do. My driver was earning his living by means of his horse and wagon. A few weeks before, he said, as he was taking two sacks of grain to the mill, the local chairman of the Soviet confiscated it because he had no receipt showing that he had met his grain tax. He argued, pleaded, and complained, but nothing came of it. Luckily, he continued, he had a son in the Red Army. So he picked up his documents, took them to the commander of the nearest military post, and begged him to help him recover the confiscated grain. The commander promised to take action at once.

What came of this particular complaint I never learned, as I did not see my driver again after he left me at my destination. In these days of intensified political conflict in the villages there is no doubt that many of the complaints of peasants to their sons in the army against rulings of local officials go unheeded. This is sure to be the case if the peasant in question is suspected of cherishing *koolack* attitudes. Yet peasants who have relatives in the army never cease to write to them of their troubles, and to bring up the fact that they have soldier sons whenever there is any conflict with local authorities. The effectiveness of such tactics is attested by the fact that many a peasant has escaped liquidation as a *koolack* by virtue of having had a son in military service. In one village which I visited several years ago an old peasant who had actually been liquidated and exiled was allowed to return home and had his house and his property restored to him, because his son, who had seen service in the army, had made a vigorous fight for his release.

In the summer of 1932 I was in the city of Kiev. I had come there at a time when the bread rations for Soviet office-workers were cut from one pound to one-half pound a day and for industrial workers from two to one and one-half pounds a day. The government shops were growing emptier and emptier, and the citizens were forced to supplement the ever dwindling government rations with purchases from peasants in the open market at prices ranging from ten to fifteen times as high as those of the government shops. Everywhere people were worrying about the failing food supply and wondering what would happen during the coming winter. But soldiers in the many neighboring army camps had no such worries. Their rations of bread had not been reduced. They ate meat every day and they had sugar, soap, tobacco, and other commodities of which there was a scarcity in the city.

Watch a military parade in Russia and you are at once impressed with the superb physical condition of the soldiers. They look clean, well fed, comfortably dressed in sturdy thick-soled boots, long overcoats, and warm caps. The magnificent appearance of the soldiers on the Red Square in Moscow during the parade on the fifteenth anniversary of the Revolution was in conspicuous contrast to that of the workers with their worn leather jackets, shiny overcoats, and shoes often run down at the heels.

The soldier is well cared for not only physically but also culturally. He is prepared to fight in time of war and to work and rule in time of peace. On his return home from service he is elected to membership in the local Soviet, to chairmanship of the collective farms, and to other responsible positions. In 1930 the army turned out one hundred thousand trained workers for the collective farms.

Whatever talent a soldier may have is given an opportunity for development in the many clubs and study circles maintained at his army post. There are six thousand so-called "Lenin Corners" in the army, which are essentially reading-rooms and recreation centers. There are more than a thousand societies for the study of politics, and an equal number of sports clubs. There are more than two thousand art organizations which embrace the arts of acting, writing, music, painting, carving, and sculpture, one thousand atheist societies, more than twelve hundred study circles in the field of general education or the liberal arts, and nearly six hundred groups for the study of foreign languages. The army has its own press, its own literature, and, above all, its own code of social and moral etiquette, which is as much a part of the soldier's training as is his rifle practice.

During a visit in the city of Kharkov I happened to be passing a coöperative store just after it had received a truckload of watermelons. Instantly a crowd of purchasers formed into a long queue, for watermelons in this store could be bought for about one-tenth the price charged for them in the open market. The queue had already attained considerable length when suddenly a man in work-clothes appeared and endeavored to take a place at the head. At once there was an outburst of protest, as everyone in the line demanded heatedly that the man take his place at the end.

"But I am a worker," shouted the man. The others laughed.

"I am a worker," he shouted again more fiercely and

resentfully than before. Once more some of the people in the queue laughed while others stormed at him.

Thereupon the man attempted to push his way into the store ahead of everybody. This insolent act so incensed some of the customers that they rushed at him, and after a fierce battle, accompanied by loud imprecations on both sides, the man was dragged out and flung into the street. The man was apparently quite sober and fully conscious of what he was trying to do. But he was one of those proletarians who had become so inflated with class egotism that he thought he could force exceptional privileges for himself in the face of the crowd's disapproval.

As I watched this scene I couldn't help thinking of the contrast between the social behavior of the most backward soldier in the Red Army and proletarians like this one. It is impossible to imagine a Red soldier ever allowing himself even the smallest liberties or privileges denied to other citizens. He would no more push himself in at the head of a queue than pull out his gun and shoot at the nearest bystander. In the army he learns to respect the populace as no Russian soldier in all that country's history ever learned it. Red soldiers are always courteous. They are the gentlemen of the country, ever conscious of the dignity of their position and the honorable conduct which it demands. In all my travels in Russia I have seen but one instance of drunkenness on the part of a Red soldier or sailor, and that one was at a peasant wedding in a village at which his brother was getting married. Neither in market places, theaters, railroad stations, nor in any other place at which crowds gather, have I ever seen a soldier in altercation with another soldier or with anyone else. Nor have I ever heard Red soldiers employing the gutter vocabulary so common to soldiers in the old days. From the moment he arrives at his post he is taught the social behavior, lacking in so many proletarians, that furnishes a living example in good manners and good citizenship for the civilian population.

It is no wonder that the morale of the Red Army is beyond reproach. If morale alone could make an army, one could say confidently that the Red Army is the best that Russia has ever had in all her history, and second to none in the world!

XVI

JAILS

WE TURNED off the main road and followed a narrow turnpike that was set with trees and cottages and at last halted in the midst of a cluster of buildings which were brightly lighted, not with lamps as in the near-by villages, but with electricity. We had now reached our destination—the prison farm, and as we alighted from our cars and surveyed the scene about us we felt somewhat dazed, like a person freshly aroused from sleep and wondering where he is.

It was hard to believe that the place we had come to was a prison. It neither looked nor felt nor smelt like one. Nowhere was there a wall, a barricade, a fortress, or anything excepting a few strips of barbed-wire fence. Nowhere a single soldier with rifle and fixed bayonet, such as guard entrances and passageways in all public buildings in Russia. Nowhere any heavy gate with a heavy lock and a portly attendant with a heavy key, suspended from a heavy chain, leisurely locking and unlocking the gate as people come and go. Nowhere a sign of a window or a door with bars. Nowhere in the outward appearance of things the least suggestion of rigor, compulsion, repression.

Only a short distance away was a public square brightly illumined with a hanging light, and there, suspended on a pole, a loud-speaker was squeaking out a lecture to which a large group of people were listening. Near the building at which we had halted other groups of people, chiefly men, were sitting or standing and chatting with one another with nothing in their appearance or manner to indicate that they were there against their will. Not one of them wore a special garb to distinguish him from any civilian in any village. If we had not been told that this was a prison colony we might have thought it was a prosperous commune or a collective farm.

Yet it was a prison colony. That was what we had been told in Poltava we were going to see, and that was what the people around us told us it actually was. Here for once was a place which had none of the rigor and the cruelty of the proletarian dictatorship. Here the dictatorship, unlike governments in other lands in similar institutions, actually overflowed with kindness.

From one of the attendants we learned the basic facts about the place. It had a population of 720 persons, of whom 140 were women. It was first started in 1930 and embraced twenty-five homesteads that had formerly been the properties of *koolacks*. What had happened to these *koolacks* and their families he didn't know and didn't care to discuss. The combined area of the confiscated homesteads was 300 hectares; in 1931 the government added 1,400 more and in 1932 increased the area to 4,000 hectares. Now it was one of the largest government farms in the vicinity and well equipped with implements, buildings, and livestock. There were three American tractors on the place, 700 pigs, of which 300 were sows, 230 cows, of which 170 were giving milk. There was a barber-shop, a bathhouse, and a community store, and though it was divided into two sections, there were only twenty attendants on it, five of whom were guards. These were scattered over the entire farm and did not always bother to carry guns with them. In all the time the farm had existed not once had a guard or anybody fired a gun. Not once did a guard have to flash a gun before an unruly inmate. Only one per cent of the prison population had ever attempted to escape, and all but one of these were eventually located by the police and brought back.

The offences of which the prisoners were guilty varied. Some of them were officials and clerks in government establishments who had accepted gifts of money or goods in return for favors which they conferred on their givers. Most of them were thieves. Some of them were *koolacks*; a few had committed murder. They were all treated alike unless they were guilty of breach of discipline, and now, after a day's work, they were in their civilian clothes enjoying themselves as best they could. Not one of them was barefooted, and all of them moved about as freely as if they were at home. What was even more astonishing, some of them were smoking cigarettes. In Moscow any number of people, workers and office employees, were constantly complaining of the difficulty of buying cigarettes. Boys and men with a flair for taking chances were "speculating," that is selling cigarettes in the streets, the cheapest brands at twenty copecks a cigarette. Once I saw one of these hawkers arrested, but that did not deter the others from continuing their "speculation." Yet here, in the prison store, they had cigarettes and tobacco and matches and, what was equally surprising, cigarette papers! These prisoners did not have to roll cigarettes in wrapping- or newspaper, as peasants in the villages usually did.

As we were talking to the prisoners and the attendants, they began to ask each other where the *agronom* (agricultural expert) was. In one voice they urged us to see the *agronom*, and several men dashed out to find him. Their insistence that we see him was an extraordinary thing. It meant that not only was this functionary held in high esteem but that the inmates and attendants thought him the most important personage on the farm. And so we lingered around waiting for him to make his appearance. As we surveyed the offices we were again impressed with the absence of anything suggestive of confinement and isolation. There were posters on the wall as in the offices of any collective farm or Soviet office. There were newspapers and books on the table. The windows were open and prisoners were looking in from the outside.

At last the *agronom* came. He was a tall, stocky man with a large head, a bronzed face, the usual Russian moustaches, and brilliant eyes that were overhung by thick lashes. He wore boots, a clean blouse, and a white cap, and had a lively manner. Born in Russia and a Russian citizen of German parentage, he had spent his life in association with farms. At one time he had been well to do, but the Revolution had, of course, deprived him of all his possessions. Originally he came to this farm to serve a sentence, and the prison director, on learning of his occupation, at once put him in charge of the place. He liked the work so well, for the opportunities it offered to carry out ideas he had always cherished, that, when his term expired and he was asked to remain as manager, he unhesitatingly accepted the offer.

He invited us to follow him, and a group of prisoners and attendants, two of them carrying lanterns, came along. Neither the *agronom* nor any of the attendants stopped them. They seemed as welcome on this excursion as we were. We walked across a field soaked in dew and came to a place where there were several new buildings, some already finished and others in process of construction. Here were barns for pigs, for cows, for horses, all made of brick with large windows and large doors and lighted by electricity. Fresh from villages and collective farms where we had been listening for days to tales of woe about excessive grain collections and loss of stock because of lack of fodder, it was cheering to see the stalls here filled with huge white sows and even larger boars and innumerable litters of young pigs. Some of these were newly born and were still sucking. Others had already been weaned from their mothers, and still others had grown to a size at which they leapt up to the partitions on the approach of a human being, to sniff and grunt vociferously in anticipation of a gift of food. The partitions were whitewashed and the stalls were bedded with sparkling straw. Water was ready at hand, as was everything else to make them comfortable. Here were pigs that could hold their own with any of their breed in Kansas or in Iowa. The percentage of mortality among them was strikingly low and not once had they been struck by an epidemic—a rare condition on the newly organized large farms in Russia, whether collectives or state owned. Some distance away was a row of cowsheds, and here too evidence of order was manifest. The cows were out to pasture for the night, but the calves were kept in—scores of them—bull and heifer calves, sleek and fat and shiny with care and contentment.

Clearly this farm was not merely a place of confinement for evildoers. It was one of the choicest agricultural enterprises in Russia. Here were order, forethought, knowledge. Here were superb management and magnificent results and one more testimony to the possibilities of large scale farming when properly conducted. If the 210,000 collectives and the 5,000 state farms were equally fortunate in equipment, in management, and in discipline, Russia would not have been harassed by food alarms and shouts of mistreatment and privation in the villages.

We traversed another field and came to another row of buildings, some likewise finished and some still in process of construction. These were new dormitories for the prisoners. We walked through all of them. Built of brick, with high ceilings and large windows, with nowhere a sign of bars or locks or any other steel contraption intended to impose limitations on the movements of the people, they were the equal of the best apartment houses on the more prosperous collective farms and in the factory districts. One of these was already in use. It was divided into several large rooms, each intended for from six to twelve persons. There were beds here neatly made up with sheets, blankets, and pillows. The windows were large and clean and, true to peasant fashion, were closed. There were tables and chairs, and the walls were hung with displays of posters and pictures of Bolshevik heroes. In the near future, we were informed, every room would be furnished with a large mirror. Again it was difficult to believe that this was a prison. So much care and effort were being expended to make the inmates comfortable. I could not help thinking of the many villages I had visited in White Russia, in the old provinces of Ryazan, Tambov, Voronezh, Vladimir, where peasants lived in their one- or at most two-room huts, often sharing these with poultry and pigs and always infested with flies and other insects, with scanty furniture and the air so heavy with pungent odors that after a prolonged stay I would suffer from a headache. But here these prisoners were living in airy and well-lighted dormitories.

Then we proceeded to the community kitchen. It was long past supper-time, and the open pavilion which adjoined the kitchen and served as a summer dining-room was now vacant, but some of the workers in the kitchen were still on duty, washing and cleaning up for the day. All peasant kitchens in Russia, whether of individual families or collective farms, have in summer their insufferable quotas of flies, and this kitchen was no exception. The cooks complained that they didn't like it but had found no way of exterminating them. They didn't have enough flypaper, of which, as of other things, there was an acute shortage in the country. Yet in spite of flies the kitchen gleamed with cleanliness—pots, plates, kettles, washed and dried, were put away on shelves, and the floors were swept clean, with nowhere a scrap of food, bones, potato-parings or other débris.

The workers in the kitchen were Ukrainian women who, like Cossack women, are famed for the high quality of their housekeeping, and they kept this community kitchen as clean as they would their own at home.

A small, talkative, sunburned woman was the chief cook, and on our appearance she expressed regret that we hadn't come earlier so we could have eaten supper with them. She assured us that it would have been a simple supper but we might have enjoyed it. There was still some soup left, and we might taste it and also their bread. Hastily she poured soup into a plate and offered it to us with bread. It was thick potato soup, seasoned with fat, and the bread was the half-dark, Ukrainian bread, rich in nutriment and taste, the like of which it is hard to obtain in Moscow. With that melodious intonation which is so distinctive of Ukrainian speech, the little woman again expressed regret that we had come too late for supper. But if we stayed over until morning we might breakfast with them. Their meals, she continued, were simple, as peasant meals always are—bread, soups, vegetables, *kasha*, meat every other day, and tea several times a day, though rarely with sugar.

Such a menu may sound meager to Westerners, but in Russia, among the peasantry, meals never are highly diversified, and what counts is not variety but quantity, and there was no shortage here. Indeed meat every other day was more than some of the best collective farms we had visited enjoyed, and as for sugar few of them had received any for months, and what little some of them had on hand they kept for children and for the sick.

We proceeded to the office, and by this time the number of inmates who had joined us made a sizable crowd, with more and more of them gathering around, some of them as before peeping in through the windows. They not only listened to the conversation but now and then took part in it, and neither the *agronom* nor any of the keepers reprimanded them or showed resentment or regarded their participation as an intrusion. The *agronom* held the center of the stage, and his speech teemed with plans and purposes for the near future. Since the coming of the Five Year Plan everything in Russia, he assured us, had to be planned in advance so that it could be linked up with and fitted into the higher plan of the country. In all of their plans on this farm, first and foremost was the consideration of food for themselves. Never did anyone from the outside interfere with these plans. Always they managed to keep abundant supplies on hand, and they had no worries about the coming year. They were expecting a shortage of sugar and tea, but of everything else—which came from their own land, grain and vegetables—they had more than sufficient for their own needs. They also grew some fruit, and their flourishing livestock would supply them with all the animal fats they might need. The summer previous the weather had been against them, they hadn't had enough rain, but their crops turned out better than they had hoped. The coming year, with any luck at all, they would have a large surplus to sell to the city. The year previous the farm had made a profit of 82,000 roubles!

In the presence of the prisoners, and sometimes with their help, the *agronom* and the attendants proceeded to outline the daily regimen of the community. The prisoners worked on a system of wages of which there were for the present three categories, the highest for skilled workers, men and women who could operate machines, and the lowest to people inexperienced in farm work. Half of the wages the government collected to defray cost of maintenance and education, and the other half the prisoners received regularly every month. They might dispose of their earnings as they chose—save, send home, spend in the local store on tobacco, sweets, or anything else that might be for sale. They worked ten hours a day in summer and eight in winter, and they followed the six-day week, that is they worked five days and rested on the sixth. When their day's work was done they might do as they pleased—visit one another, listen to the loud-speaker, read, go to the bathhouse, the barber-shop, play games, and if their behavior was good they might go to a near-by village. Always visitors from villages might come to see them after work hours. They were encouraged to pursue some cultural interest. Those who were illiterate might attend classes in reading, writing, arithmetic. Those who had a love for dramatic self-expression might join a dramatic club. Those who liked music might go to a concert or rehearsal of the local orchestra, which was made up of two accordions and two guitars. Those who were especially interested in agriculture might take courses in grain-growing and in the breeding of live-stock. Regularly once a week they had motion pictures. They had their own Red Corners, in which there was a library and a reading-room which were open evenings and on the days of rest.

But these were not the only privileges they were enjoying. Though without permission they might never go off the premises of the farm, unless under a penalty for infraction of rules, the privilege of maintaining contacts with the outside world was never withheld from them. On the day of rest they might go to Poltava and remain there as long as they chose, provided they returned before bedtime. Like workers in a factory and in an office they were entitled, on good behavior, to an annual vacation. The length of this vacation was officially limited to seven days—that is the local administration had no power to make it longer; but on appeal to the prison board in Poltava it might be extended to a whole month. During this vacation inmates might go wherever they pleased. Wherever they went they were under no obligation to report to the police or undergo registration or inspection other than is prescribed for all citizens. They were as free as any factory worker or any civilian who is off on a vacation—the government acts on the assumption that they will not violate the trust reposed in them and, at the end of their vacation, will, of their own accord, return to the farm. If they fail to do so they are searched for and brought back. But the punishment for this violation of trust is never more severe than the denial, for a certain period, of the right to leave the farm and to make purchases in the store.

More extraordinary than all the above rights of comfort and good fellowship is the Soviet Government's regard for a phase of human life which in other countries is hardly accorded any cognizance in the prevailing systems of penology. I am referring to the sex needs of the prisoners. Of course prostitution is barred and promiscuity is frowned upon—as it is in all other communities in the country; and the government makes no effort to supply sources of satisfaction. But it offers no interference with a prisoner's personal effort to obtain it. If a man or woman wishes to cultivate the friendship and love of a member of the opposite sex among their own numbers or among the population in a near-by village or in Poltava, the government offers not the slightest objection or interference—on the contrary it encourages such relationships. If a prisoner falls in love with a girl on the outside he may see her after working hours. She may come to visit him and they may stroll around in the fields, sit out in the moonlight, and talk and sing as freely as if they were in their own homes. If they decide to get married, they obtain only the blessings of the authorities, and on the day of rest and during vacations they may spend all their time together. If a prisoner is already married and his wife wants to visit him, she may do so. She may come and stay with her husband during his day of rest and they are accorded all the privacy that a marital union requires. As the attendants and *agronom* explained, the more normal and the more satisfying the life of the prisoner is, the more readily he responds to corrective measures, and the more eager he is so to behave that he will suffer no curtailment in any of the privileges that he enjoys when on good behavior.

Let not the reader imagine that this prison farm is an exception. Since the coming of the Five Year Plan several hundred such farms have been opened all over the country. This one may be exceptional only as a farm enterprise. At every step it shows evidence of skilled and efficient management. But the principles of penology practised here are universal under the Soviets, not only on farms but in the cities. Vindictiveness, punishment, torture, severity, humiliation, have no place in this system. The Soviets are acting on the assumption that it is not the criminal who is under obligation to society but that society is under obligation to the criminal. Implacable environmentalists, they believe that under normal conditions of living the human animal, unless in a pathological state of mind, would not commit anti-social acts. Now and then one meets a Soviet penologist who will grudgingly admit that biology may have something to do with a person's social behavior or misbehavior. There have been instances when Soviet courts, in trying bandits who had been previously under sentence, have come to the conclusion that they are beyond redemption and have imposed on them a death sentence. In such instances of course Soviet courts stress their belief that such bandits have become a political menace. As a matter of principle all Soviet jurists assume that it is environment which makes criminals. When they say environment they mean capitalist environment or capitalist features in their environment which they have not yet been able to wipe out.

That is why the sentences for ordinary crimes are light. There is no capital punishment in the Russian criminal code except for political offenses. Nor are there any life sentences. Ten years is the highest sentence a criminal ever receives. For any offense which requires sterner punishment they order the death sentence, and a criminal with a ten-year sentence hardly ever serves a full term. On good behavior, which is easy in Soviet jails, as easy as in Soviet schools, the sentence is pared down. Constant amnesties on the occasion of revolutionary holidays bring further reductions. During the period of confinement criminals experience no other hardships than the enforced separation from home. Unless they violate the light discipline that they must observe they never are made to feel the yoke of the stigma of prison life. There are no chain gangs. There are no severe compulsions. There is no lockstep. There are no striped or any kind of uniforms. There are no limitations to the amount of literature or correspondence they may receive. Indeed the prison exists not for punishment but for ministration. This ministration divides itself roughly into three parts—work, education, recreation and social life. Work comes first. In everything in Russia work comes first. It is the great badge of honor and quality. It is the great healer of all ills and wrongs. It is the basic justification of human existence. But work, as already specified, is supplemented with education and recreation so that the prisoners can ever think of themselves as the equals of people on the outside and as members of a new society that wants to fit them into its new scheme of things.

That is why the word *turma*—which literally means prison—has dropped out of usage. The young generation never hears it mentioned. It has been supplanted by the word *ispravdom*, which means house of redemption.

When a prisoner leaves his place of confinement his

record doesn't count against him. Factory managers never ask him whether or not he has been in a house of redemption. If they should happen to know and, on that account, refuse him a job, they would be severely reprimanded and sometimes dismissed. Nor are the high honors of membership in the trade unions or in the party held from such a man. Much, of course, depends on his social origin. If he descends from a family of clergymen, *koolacks* or former traders, the doors of these are not easily opened to him. Not because he was in prison but because of the sins of his father. Should he expiate his sin in the prescribed manner through labor and exemplary social behavior, membership in the above-mentioned societies is open to him. The mere fact that he was in a house of redemption is never held against him.

Late in the evening we returned to Poltava. It was dark and damp and cold, and all around life had come to a standstill. Save for the whine of a lonely animal and the chug-chug of our wobbly automobiles, there were no sounds. Not even dogs barked, a rare phenomenon in the Ukraine, where dogs never seem to tire of barking. I was riding with a Soviet official, a man of about forty who looked at least ten years younger. He wore a khaki outfit and high boots and was one of those rare Bolsheviks who, instead of shaving his head, actually took pride in his haircut. He had been working in the city of Kharkov, the capital of the Ukraine, but had been sent to Poltava to rectify the blunders his predecessor had committed. He was a seasoned revolutionary—versed in party history, party doctrine, and ever ready for any task to which the party might assign him. He had been on the revolutionary firing line, as he expressed himself, since the outbreak of the Revolution. During the civil war he fought against the Germans, the Ukrainian White Armies of Makhno and Petlura and other White leaders. At one time the Germans and the Whites had offered a high premium for his head, but he had run off to the woods and his enemies never found him. He was always a league ahead of them, and from his place of hiding he organized a network of underground spies and partisan bands and continually harassed the armies of his enemies. He had become a sort of Robin Hood of the country, and peasants came to him with petitions, with reports, with gifts. He was a handsome, finely built man, with a straight back, square shoulders, and a rollicking laugh, and he talked away with unbridled gusto of his career, of the Revolution, of his own and of Soviet Russia's future. He talked with special enthusiasm of the prison farm. He was on its board of directors and was immensely pleased with the progress it had made. People, he avowed, were learning to be good citizens on that farm, and that was what the Soviets needed more than anything else at the moment, citizens who would know how to work and would be willing to work and would not grumble when face to face with difficulties and privations. That was why they tried so much to make the prisoners comfortable and educate them. If he had ever learned that an attendant had spoken a harsh word to a prisoner, called him *durak* (fool), or *svolotch* (scamp), or some other insulting epithet, he would demand the man's discharge and would bring him to trial and insist on severe punishment. Prisoners, he continued, were misguided people, unfortunate in their environment, in their condition of living, and had to be retrieved through wholesome treatment and good care and education.

Yet when he touched on the subject of *koolacks* his good humor vanished. *Koolacks* were enemies of the Revolution and deserved no mercy. If *koolacks* or any enemies of the Revolution deliberately set out to foment trouble, to stir up sentiment against grain collections, collectivization, or any measure of the Soviets, there was not much use bothering with them. Anyone who was in the way of the Revolution had to be swept aside. Exile to the far north for *koolacks* was no punishment at all but in a way an act of kindness. It gave them the opportunity to do something new and useful without exploiting anybody and the chance to sweat themselves out of their parasitism; in time they might regain citizenship and would enjoy the fruits of the Revolution on a plane of equality with anyone who worked and did not exploit. Of course they were undergoing hardships—so was everybody everywhere; and if theirs were greater—what of it? They were enemies, weren't they? But up north they were building new towns, new factories, a new society, and in time they would enjoy amply the results of those labors.

The attitude of this official was the attitude of all revolutionaries. The ordinary criminal is to them only an accident of time and circumstance. Even the courts treat him with a certain leniency. I was attending a trial in Stalingrad, in the days before the Five Year Plan, of a peasant and his wife who were accused of murdering with an axe a friend of theirs, a middle-aged woman from a neighboring village who had stopped with them for the night. Both confessed to the crime and did not shrink from describing in detail the manner in which they had murdered the woman. They admitted that they did it for money. They thought that, in so much as she was on her way to Stalingrad to make purchases for the shop which she owned in the village in which she lived, she had much money with her. But in the course of the trial the court ascertained that they never had committed any crime before and had little land and never employed any hired labor, and so they got the maximum prison sentence which was ten years.

A few days later in the same court a man was tried for having been on the publicity staff of Denikin at the time this White general had occupied the city. The prosecuting attorney admitted that since the coming of the Soviets this man had done valuable and valiant work for them. He had been a lawyer in the old days and a social worker and had given all his time to helping the local Soviets in numerous tasks. He had worked honestly and well. But he had helped Denikin. The man in his turn pleaded guilty to the charge but protested that he was helpless. Denikin made him work under the penalty of severe punishment, and Denikin, he reminded the court, did not hesitate to string up people on telephone poles. Yet the court confiscated his property, leaving nothing to the wife and children, and imposed on him a sentence of three years in jail. The prosecuting attorney was vehement in demanding a much heavier penalty.

This is always the case with political offenders. Journalists who attended the Shakhta trial, when leading engineers in the coal industry were tried for sabotage, remember only too vividly the ferocious zest with which Krylenko, the state prosecuting attorney, sought the blood of engineers, even of men who in the opinion of the foreign press were as innocent of the charge as any of the jurymen or the presiding judge.

I have never visited a political prison. Once during a stay in Tiflis I made inquiries as to whether it would be possible to see the incarcerated Mensheviks, but friends discouraged me from pursuing my quest. Political offenders are regarded as deliberate enemies of the state and naturally are accorded more severe treatment. If there is a political prison anywhere in Russia comparable in its ministrations to the prison farm near Poltava I have never heard of it. Now and then stories come out of political prisons which have none of the cheer and promise of the ordinary city prison or prison farm. But an ordinary criminal is to the revolutionaries an evil-doer by accident. They believe that if properly treated, taught to read, to write, to work, to play, he will develop a social sense and a revolutionary consciousness and thus become an asset to the new society. They at any rate accord him abundant chance to become such an asset.

XVII
MAN

THE REMAKING OF THE HUMAN PERSONALITY

IN A PLAY which I saw recently in London one of the characters says to the woman he loves: "Men cannot take orders from women; I cannot." As I listened to these words I could not help thinking of Russia and the new Russians; of how strange such words would sound to them, how joyously they would pounce upon them as one more proof of the decadence of the capitalist civilization that discriminates against women in so many human relationships and in so many fields of effort. Reared in the practice of sex equality, these new people in Russia are accustomed to seeing women in positions of high authority in educational, industrial, judicial institutions. These women executives often command large numbers of men, yet now it is only an occasional older person who ever grumbles at the need for taking orders from a woman. They see women literally flooding the medical profession with their offices and clinics. Nor are the women and men who throng them displeased because the medical service they receive is not being dispensed by a man. It never occurs to these new people that women are inferior to men, except perhaps in physical strength; and when they hear words like those quoted above, they feel all the more confirmed in their belief that so-called exploitation of women, like exploitation of workers and of colonial peoples, is inherent only in capitalist civilizations.

In the same play from which I have quoted there are two young persons who are in love with one another. Poor and with no prospect of being able to marry for some time, they yet hunger for intimate association with each other, but cannot muster the courage to override convention and yield to this hunger. The resulting emotional strain is too much for them, especially for the man. They quarrel, nag one another, and finally break up. Again I could not help thinking of the New Russians and how different would be their behavior under similar circumstances. If they found themselves in love yet unable to be married for some time, they would not allow respect for convention to drive them into boredom and agony and finally into separation. They might break up—unhappy love affairs are not rare in the land of the Soviets—but it would not be because of emotional tension. Emotionally they are among the most emancipated people in the world.

Anyone who has been in intimate contact with Russian humanity cannot help noticing, especially on first coming out of the country, the difference between the behavior there and that of people in other lands. He listens to the speech of friends, overhears stray bits of conversation in the street, in a restaurant, in a hotel lobby, and he says to himself, "Russians would never say that." He observes the actions of people of other lands, and again he says to himself: "Russians would never do that." He is continually contrasting things and people. He does it almost unconsciously, and the more he compares and contrasts the more firm is his conviction that the Revolution has created a new human being —or at least a human being with a new form of behavior.

If he be an open-minded person and one sensitive to human adversity he does not readily dismiss the shortcomings of the Revolution. He thinks of the lowered standard of living of the masses, of the dispiriting queues waiting everywhere in shops and postoffices, of the troubles in the villages, of the endless and grinding sacrifices that everybody is called upon to endure, of the recantations which outstanding persons who disagree with the ruling group are obliged to make. These last are especially puzzling and irksome to the impartial observer. He cannot help feeling that men of the intellectual stature of Trotsky, Bukharin, Rykov, Tomsky and others, even Kamenev and Zinovyev, do not pen recantations out of a sincere conviction of wrongdoing. He knows that it is impossible for a man of intelligence to root out of his mind the heresies of which he is accused as easily and quickly as a farmer can pull a carrot out of the earth! Why, he wonders, must the ruling group employ this procedure, in method reminiscent of a horrid age which they themselves cannot help despising, a procedure that is bound to engender so much bad faith and even more bad feeling. Many are the questions which perplex the honest onlooker. Many are the Soviet practices which dishearten him.

Yet when he encounters the new culture that the Revolution is creating and observes the new human being that is emerging out of it, he stands in awe of its transcendent powers. He sees the process of transformation take place before his very eyes, and he can find nothing in all human history that is comparable to it. So he is no longer impressed with the pronouncements of scholars, business executives and statesmen who stoutly proclaim that such a transformation is impossible. He knows better. He has seen too many living examples of it—is, indeed, constantly rubbing shoulders with them. He may not approve of the nature of this transformation, but he cannot close his eyes to its overpowering reality.

We have already seen what the new sex morality with its altered conception of the family has done to the new Russian. Consider now how atheism has changed his personality.

In the company of a group of young Russians I once witnessed a performance of Chekhov's *Uncle Vanya.* At the end of the play, when the visitors from the city leave the country estate and Uncle Vanya and his niece Sonya remain alone, broken up and desolate over their unrequited love, Sonya gives utterance to the following words, perhaps the saddest that Chekhov has penned: "We shall go on living, Uncle Vanya. We shall live through a long, long chain of days and weary evenings. We shall patiently bear the trials which fate sends us. We shall work for others, . . . now and in our old age, and have no rest. And when our time comes we shall die without a murmur, and there beyond the grave we shall say that we have suffered, that we have wept, that life has been bitter to us, and God will have pity on us. And you and I, uncle, dear uncle, shall see a life that is bright—lovely—beautiful. We shall rejoice and look back at these troubles of ours with tenderness, with a smile, and we shall rest. . . . I have faith, uncle, I have faith, passionate faith."

I have never seen a performance of this play where, at this particular passage, the older people in the audience did not hold their handkerchiefs to their eyes and sob quietly. It brings back to them so much of their old world, with all its pain and travail, its ecstasy and sadness. But my companions were hardly moved. They were more amused than touched by the weakness and futility of the characters that passed before them. They had no sympathy for their sorrows and no regret for their defeats. Least of all could they sympathize with Sonya's religious fervor and her consolation that "God will pity us." In the discussion that took place at the club-house to which we later adjourned they maintained boldly enough that dependence on God—on a being supposedly more powerful and more wise than one's self—weakens and ruins a human being. They saw in religion no romance, no beauty, no adventure. They laughed at the very notion of a God or a supernatural power consciously guiding the destinies of nature and man. They would not even admit that something might be said for religion as an art, or as a source of solace for the heart-broken and the defeated. Let those who maintain that man cannot live without religion or faith in some supernatural power, in something wiser and stronger and better than himself, consider these new Russians, who, without such faith, are living full lives untroubled by any consciousness of emotional frustration, or spiritual incompleteness.

Not only religion, but race consciousness also, is vanishing from the life of new Russia. This latter phase was vividly impressed upon me by a recent visit to Hitlerite Germany, where the very air is heavy with a haughty and vehement race consciousness. There race has become a passion, an ideal, a symbol. Everything Aryan or of Aryan origin is good and glorious. Everything non-Aryan is vile and ruinous. But in Russia race is neither an ideal nor a passion, nor is it a symbol of anything worthy. For the new Russian, there are no "good" or "bad" races: Negro, Mongol, Semite, Aryan —all are alike to him, and any attempt to assert racial superiority meets violent resistance. A good illustration of this is the present attitude toward anti-semitism. Not yet completely dead, this once wide-spread prejudice still smolders in places, and occasionally flares up into open hostility against Jews. But no sooner does it appear on the surface than it is vigorously stamped out. The heavy hand of Russian law, instantly raised against it, falls severely upon the person or group supporting such hostilities. A few years ago, shortly after my return from Russia, I heard the drunken leader of a night club orchestra in Berlin shout "Verfluchter Jude" at the manager of the place. And nothing happened. Nobody stirred; nobody protested; neither the guests nor the attendants nor the manager himself. To me, fresh from Russia, this seemed an odd and unbelievable occurrence. In Russia under similar circumstances something would have happened. The guests—even one of the waiters or porters, if nobody else, would have been sure to reprimand the musician. They would have demanded documents, reported him to his trade or factory union, or summoned a policeman and had the offender arrested on the charge of "hooliganism." If the offended person were a Negro, a Chinese, a Persian, or one of any other race, the procedure would be no less prompt and severe. In the ethics of the new society, race prejudice or any assertion of racial superiority is held to be a relic of savagery from the old order which must be fought until it is wiped out.

But not all of the new Russian's reactions are negative. His waning consciousness of God and of race is being supplanted by an even more powerful class-consciousness. Indeed, this humanitarian concept is the chief pillar of his new faith. He has divided the world into two groups: heroes and villains. The heroes are the exploited, or the workers; the villains are the exploiters, or the capitalists. The villains are fat, crass and foul. The heroes are lean, dignified and noble. Everywhere the Russian sees capitalists and workers thus depicted—in cartoons, in plays, in motion pictures—until he comes to think of them only in this way. The capitalist has no virtues that he need respect; the worker, no vices that he need condemn. The capitalist always wallows in luxury; the worker always swelters in misery. If in some other land there are workers who do not swelter in misery but on the contrary enjoy quite a fair degree of modern comfort—possess a radio, a house of their own, perhaps an automobile and an insurance policy—then they are either unimportant exceptions, or else victims of a vicious capitalistic plot which permits the elevation of a few workers to superior comforts in order to inspire false hopes in the others and thus deaden their class consciousness and their revolutionary ardor. No other explanations are acceptable, for they would be contrary to the basic tenets of the proletarian creed.

In the face of such dogmatic principles, it is no wonder that the new Russian manifests such a sturdy spirit of super-righteousness; that he cannot see why a *koolack* should ever be pitied or a political offender treated with leniency. Justice for the sake of justice he abjures as a mere legend or chimera. It is always either capitalist or proletarian justice. He will recognize none other. If a mob outside a courthouse in Scottsboro seeks to rouse the jurymen's prejudices in order to insure a verdict that will result in the death penalty for accused Negroes, that mob consists of the vilest scoundrels in the world. But if, while Soviet engineers are on trial in a Moscow court on charges of sabotage, masses of workers parade before the courthouse loudly demanding the death penalty for the accused, those masses are performing a heroic duty. If an American university expels a professor for voicing radical opinions, it commits a heinous offense. But if a Soviet university expels a professor whose interpretation of his subject is not sufficiently Marxian, it is performing an honorable act and is a credit to the new society. Thus it goes. The new Russian seems incapable of detaching himself from his own immediate cause and purpose. All of his liberalism in the realm of sex and race avails him nothing in his appraisal of political values. It is as if passion for the idea had burned out of him compassion for the human being. That is why he has grown so indifferent to the sacrifice that accompanies his continued class war. Especially is this true if he is a member of "the Party." Then he is like a soldier on a battle field, bent on only one task, the defeat of his enemy.

But the most striking and challenging feature of the Russian's new ideology is his aversion to the acquisition of material wealth. For countless ages, it has been assumed that such acquisitiveness is the mainspring of human action, and that without it man would stagnate and decay and his civilization would collapse, until this belief has become practically a dogma. Scholarship has exalted it; religion has sanctified it in the main, though not always without reservations. With rare exceptions, man has come to accept it as an unquestioned law of human behavior, as the one thing that is and must be if man is to survive and to push on to higher social attainments. But the new man in Russia now repudiates this concept. He has set out to eradicate the acquisitive faculty from his society and root it out of his human personality. He will hunt and harry it as if it were the carrier of a vile plague.

Not that the Russian of today frowns on material incentive or on the enjoyment of material satisfactions. He is no ascetic. The hardships he now endures are not a matter of choice. He accepts the joys of the flesh and hopes for a time when in his society these will be more or less evenly distributed among all working folk, among the men who labor with their muscles as well as those who labor with their brains. This hope is, indeed, a source of constant comfort and encouragement to him.

I have yet to meet a Russian youth who even now does not covet a bicycle of his own, a fountain pen, a camera, a flash light, a good woolen sweater. I have yet to meet a Russian youth, however profoundly revolutionary, but who, on observing my portable typewriter, does not express a desire to possess one for himself. Any foreigner who has mingled with Russian men and women, including Communists, knows how greatly they are intrigued by his clothes and shoes and how desirous they are of possessing similar clothes and shoes.

One has only to consider the course of events in the Russian villages during the last few years to become acutely aware of the importance of material incentive in the life of the many-millioned peasantry. It is because the peasant has deemed himself poorly compensated for his labor that his work on the land has been so faulty. One has only to observe the immense turnover of labor in Soviet factories to appreciate how adversely lack of proper material returns is affecting the industriousness of masses of Russian workers. In a speech delivered in June, 1932, Stalin severely denounced the whole conception of equality of material reward at this stage of the Revolution. He warned Communist managers and directors that unless they based compensation on kind and quality of work, they would be inviting on themselves endless troubles. Communists no longer are limited in their salaries to the sum of 225 rubles a month, as they formerly were. Now there is no limit to the salary they may receive, though there is an unwritten understanding that they must not be among the highest-paid workers in the country. When the Soviets decorate a man for distinguished service they often bestow on him some material reward—a trip abroad, or to some far away and notable place in the Union, a new apartment, a monetary allowance, a gold watch. It is not always merely a pin and a ribbon. One evening I passed a store in Moscow which displayed in its window an array of sweaters, shirts, shoes, suits of clothes and fine silk and satin fabrics that were almost as good as those in any of the Torgsin or gold ruble stores. I wondered if Russian shops were at last being abundantly supplied with consumption goods. But on closer scrutiny I discovered that the merchandise in this store was for sale only to shock-brigadiers—for workers who had distinguished themselves in their factories. Obviously, the Soviets are applying material incentive with no little vigor.

But material incentive is one thing and acquisitiveness is another, though outwardly they may appear to be the same. For the new Russian, material incentive has as its purpose well-being, but no accumulation. The desire to acquire possessions for their own sake, or for some future enjoyment, or for the enjoyment of others, even of one's own children, he regards as a grievous sin. He has stripped wealth of all possible advantages. Even if its acquisition were possible in Russia, which at present it is not, it would afford the holder none of the satisfactions that it provides in the western world. It would bring him neither power, nor prestige, nor distinction, nor a sense of triumph, nor even security. It would be only a weight about his neck, a burden that would bruise his flesh.

Whatever one may say of the Russian leaders, the desire for riches is one thing of which they cannot be accused. There have been exceptions, naturally, but these have occurred only among minor party officials, who have always paid dearly, sometimes with their lives, for giving way to their acquisitive impulses. Outstanding leaders in every country enjoy better living conditions than those of the workers; and though this is true to some extent of Russia's leaders, they fare none too well in this regard when judged by western standards. They may occupy commodious, well-furnished apartments, but even in this respect they are not as well situated as are the outstanding foreign engineers. I have never known an official anywhere who had at his disposal as spacious and luxuriously furnished an apartment as that, for example, of Dr. Alcan Hirsch, chief consulting engineer to the chemical industry. Russia's great men may be having all the butter and cheese and meat they want, and certainly they do not have to wait their turn for weeks before they can buy a pair of shoes, an overcoat, or anything else of which there is a shortage in the country. But these are about the only special privileges they have, and even these are available to any foreigner who can pay for them in foreign money and to any foreign engineer in the employ of the Soviet government.

And how different are the Soviet state receptions from those of other lands! Among the Russians, there are no expensively gowned bejeweled ladies displaying their country's wealth. Indeed, the only array of elegance to be found at these functions is provided by the foreign diplomats. Kalinin, the president of the Soviet Union, will attend in a business suit, the quality of which is conspicuously shoddy. Except for Litvinov, the Commissary of Foreign Affairs, who travels about much in foreign lands, none of the Russian officials wear clothes which any of the foreign diplomats would consider fit to own. Even the military uniforms lack the layers of gleaming silver and gold braid which distinguish the military attire of so many other lands. Watch a Russian parade on the Red Square in Moscow and you will see, among the small group of officials gathered to review the procession from the top of the Lenin Mausoleum, not a single one wearing a hat. They are dressed casually in leather jackets, or long heavy overcoats, in boots or low shoes, just like workers on their rest days —sometimes not even as well.

I cannot imagine Stalin wearing a modern hat or conventional evening dress. If a hostess were to call him on the telephone and request him to wear a black or white tie, I think he would be most astounded. I am sure he would not know the significance of either; and if told, he would chuckle with merriment, so absurd and artificial such a convention would seem to him. During my travels in Russia I have spent much time in the homes of factory directors and managers of state farms, and I have never found them living in as good style as do tourists, for example, in Soviet hotels of the so-called "second category." Whatever the failings or the virtues of Russian leaders, material aggrandizement is not one of them. There is nothing they abhor more or combat more fiercely.

With the personal profit motive removed, what now are the incentives that call forth the worker's best efforts? First, of course, there is that great need of all mankind, the desire for security. Allied with this is the equally old and powerful fear of public disapproval. The Russian worker doesn't want his name posted conspicuously in a list of slackers. Conversely, he, like everyone else, craves the approval of his fellows; he likes to see his name written in the honor roll for good service. For the same reason he is willing to work hard for promotion. The desire for distinction, for power, above all, for achievement, are all primal forces which have lost none of their power to drive men forward. All too readily do we of an acquisitive society tend to underestimate the urge to achieve and to create. In the light of Russian experience these natural objectives loom up as the most real and powerful stimuli in human behavior.

Only slightly less striking than the atrophy of the acquisitive faculty in the new Russian is his wholehearted objectification of so much of his life. He ties himself with numberless bonds to some definite purpose or project—factory, farm, school-house, trade union, party organization—sometimes to all of these, and always above all to the idea behind them, until his very ego is identified with this idea and his whole being transmuted into its objectives. Hence he finds it hard to understand—and harder still to sympathize with—people who live exclusively within themselves and are preoccupied with problems and conflicts that concern primarily their personal lives. For this reason such characters as Eugene O'Neill has created in "Strange Interlude" or in "Mourning Becomes Electra" are to the Russian strange and alien, far stranger and more alien than they could ever be to any westerner who finds it difficult to appreciate their reality. For that matter, many Russian characters are equally incredible to him, Dostoyevsky's Karamazovs, or even Leo Tolstoy's, and nearly all of Chekhov's heroes and heroines, in fact any portrayal of people who are always in conflict with themselves, puzzle and distress him. Why do they brood and lament and despair so much, he wonders. With all his heart he would agree with the words of Chekhov's Dr. Astrov when he says: "Those who will live a hundred or two hundred years after us will despise us for having lived so stupidly and so tastelessly." And his heart echoes the loquacious student Trofimov: "I am strong and proud. Humanity is advancing toward the highest truth, the highest happiness which is possible on earth, and I am in the front ranks." Of course Trofimov is not and never will be in the front ranks. He can only talk about being there. None the less, the new Russian would applaud him for speaking the language of action, for displaying enthusiasm and purpose, for his interest in something outside of himself.

And so whatever the shortcomings and perversities of the Revolution, in its task of reconstructing the human personality it has achieved triumph after triumph. It has fashioned a new man with a wholly new outlook on the world and his own position in it. For good or for ill this new man has lost all faith in God and all fear of God.

He has lost all fear of sex.

He has lost all fear of money.

He has lost his old fears of the family.

He has lost the old fear of insecurity.

Not that he is now enjoying abundant security. Most assuredly he is not. He is beset by a multitude of wants which the new society cannot at present satisfy. Under the best of circumstances it will be several years, for example, before he will have all the meat and all the dairy foods that he may want to eat. He is acutely aware of the wretched service that the new society now offers him in shops, in hotels, on railroads. Again and again he cries out against the bureaucracy and stupidity which so often prevail in Soviet offices and paralyze Soviet administration. But he has unshaken faith in the creative powers of the new society and in its capacity to overcome all existing difficulties and eventually to bring him all the security that he might need, whether in old age, in sickness or in time of unemployment.

A highly regimented individual, the new man in Russia brims over with a body of prejudices and dogmas all his own. How violently he can hate and how cruelly he can punish! He may not be the type of humanity that the outside world would care to emulate or would even approve of. But here he is, a robust personage, with an aim and a mission and a mentality all his own, a product of a new idea and a symbol of a new society.

PART III
FOR NEW ADVENTURES

XVIII
SIBERIA

STEPPE rolling as far as the eye could see and merging now into forest and now into sky; patches of silvery birch gliding past like gleams of lightning; clusters of somber evergreens fading away like passing shadows; here and there a hillock; a lake sinking from view with a sparkle; herds of cattle browsing in rich grass; haystacks brown with age; pigs rooting diligently in a meadow threaded by a narrow stream; *muzhiks* ploughing with one or two horses and digging up soil as fat and as black as in the Ukraine or in Iowa; now and then a man or woman trudging along a footpath and pausing to look with shaded eyes at the train; now and then a village sprawling on a hillside or a hut with smoke curling out of a round black chimney —

If the loquacious conductor had not told us that we were in Siberia, we should never have known it. Neither the lay of the land nor anything in the surroundings and the scenery was different from what we had observed in the territory left behind us. The sun, too, was as hot, the sky as blue, the air as balmy. And yet the mere knowledge that this was Siberia brought the passengers to the window, all but the two Russian officials who kept to themselves. Most of the passengers were non-Russians, and they gazed out upon the Siberian scene with an intentness that betrayed inner cogitation.

No doubt they had all read of Siberia. Certainly they had heard much of it. Not only in the Russian, but in other living languages, the word had acquired a sinister connotation, had become a symbol of something irretrievably bleak and hard. There are men and women all over the world, and especially in America and England, who at the mention of the word envisage endless steppes or forests with gangs of prisoners marching in deep snow to the tune of clanking chains, or toiling in a far-off mine under constant guard of keepers unsparing of rod or even of gun. Who, indeed, that has read Dostoyevski's *Memoirs of a Dead House* can ever dissociate Siberia from cruelty and anguish? Who that has perused George Kennan's *Siberia and the Exile System*, the classic record of Czarism's vengefulness on its foes, can erase from his mind the innumerable woes that are depicted there?

For generations the Romanovs had been using Siberia as a dumping-ground for the unruly and the disaffected. During the nineteenth century alone more than a million of Russia's sons and daughters had been cast overboard there. Not only bandits or murderers, but Nonconformist church-folk and political offenders, the flower of Russia's intelligentsia, men and women, many of them mere boys and girls in their teens and fresh from the high-school classroom or the college lecture-hall, trudged the snowy wastes to some far-away dungeon or prison mine or to some aboriginal settlement in the arctic wastes. No wonder Siberia had become a symbol of torture, desolation, and martyrdom.

But the Siberian countryside, as it unfolded to our eyes through the windows of the swiftly moving Trans-Siberian express, was bathed in sunshine and fragrance and verdure. It bore nowhere a trace of anything gruesome or even severe; it was a picture of rugged and lovable splendor.

"Does it get very cold here in winter?" asked the Frenchman, a little man with a bald head, fiery eyes, and a squeaky voice.

"Cold enough," retorted the conductor, "so you won't want to venture outdoors without felts and sheepskins."

"And do they still send exiles to this country?" asked the paunchy German engineer who was on his way to Tokyo.

"Well —" The conductor's face contorted into a grin. He paused as if to weigh his words before uttering them. That is the way of folk in Russia when they speak to foreigners who are strangers to them on subjects that relate, however remotely, to the policies and practices of the government. They are cautious in their choice of words. They do not always round out their thoughts. They leave much to the imagination—that is, all but the lowly *muzhik*, and he not only speaks but shrieks his mind freely to anyone who will listen.

"*Katorga*—hard labor—of course has been abolished," the conductor finally explained, "but, as for exiles, there are still some." He smiled as if to say, "You know what I mean." True enough, the old Siberian dungeons and mines and torture-chambers are now a thing of the past. They were done away with long before the Communists smashed into power. But exiles continue to wend their way to the Siberian cities and villages—a new type of exile, themselves often proletarians, many with records of heroic struggle for proletarian emancipation, Mensheviks, Social Revolutionaries, and, of course, multitudes of *koolacks*.

We plied the conductor with questions, and he answered them readily enough, though at times with visible signs of irritation if not of indignation. Since he was a Siberiak, a native Siberian, the grandson of a fugitive serf, it irked him to find us so ignorant of the country he loved. "Why," he finally complained, "do foreigners invariably ask the same questions about Siberia—questions about cold, exiles, wolves? As if these were all there was of interest or importance to the country. Why, Siberia is a wonderful land," he intoned with pride; "wait, citizens, wait until you see Siberian flowers, taste Siberian honey, sample Siberian butter, feast on Siberian fish. Wait, citizens; there are surprises in store for you."

This was in 1927, when Siberian fields, recovered from the ravages of the civil war, once more began to bloom; certainly there were surprises in store for us. They came one after another. After we had passed Tyumen, at station after station, the first persons to greet passengers as they came off for an airing were flower-venders, principally boys and girls. They would crowd around us and thrust their bouquets into our faces—daisies with heads larger than any I had ever seen, wild roses, buttercups, primroses, pansies—gorgeous bouquets at the price of from one to three copecks each. So cheap and so abundant were flowers that even the passengers in the "hard" coaches, proletarians, *muzhiks*, minor officials, bought endless quantities of them. There were two women in our sleeping-car, one a German on her way to join her husband, an engineer in Soviet mines, and the other a Russian bound for Harbin, and we kept their compartment deluged with flowers. I doubt if this act of gallantry cost any of the men more than twenty-five cents. It seemed incredible that Siberia, the land of supposed desolation, should grow such a profusion and variety of flowers and of such extraordinary beauty and fragrance. And not only along the Trans-Siberian Railway. I was out once on an excursion with a group of university students, engineers, about a hundred miles from a railroad. At one point our dilapidated Ford truck crashed into a ditch, and we scattered over the countryside in search of a *muzhik* with horses to pull us out. In company with a trio of students I ascended a hill, and there below us on a sloping stretch of steppe I saw flowers—blue, golden, violet—a riotous splash of color.

Wherever there are flowers, there are sure to be bees, and Siberia is noted for its honey. Certainly honey could not be cheaper than in Siberia at the time I visited it. Peasant women were selling it at railroad stations, not in comb but in pretty little kegs made of birch-bark with neat, tight-fitting covers, and at six or seven cents a pound! We ate so much honey that we were sick.

"How can they afford to sell it so cheap?" wondered the Frenchman. When I put the question to one of the women peddlers, her reply, as that of a Russian and a peasant, was memorable. "People have not any money and won't pay any more; so what's the use of asking." Strange words these were for a *muzhik* woman, since any Russian petty trader had always made it a cardinal principle of business, if not a hobby, to ask a customer at least double the amount he expected to obtain. If only *izvozchiks* (cabmen), especially in Moscow, would follow the example of these Siberian honey-peddlers! Then, I am convinced, even atheistic Bolsheviks would begin to believe in miracles.

Nor do flowers and honey exhaust the bountifulness of Siberia. At every station at which the train stopped, the foods for sale in the buffets, in the booths, and even in the baskets of the peasant hawkers would tempt the appetite of the most dyspeptic or the most surfeited person. Eggs, honey, butter, cheese, berries, sausages, whole roasted chickens and geese and little pigs, breads, biscuits, cakes, everything but fruit. Not even in the rich Volga basin had I seen a greater abundance and variety of food at prices so low. A whole roasted chicken, hot from the fire, twenty-five cents; a whole goose or little pig, a dollar and sometimes even less; butter, ten and fifteen cents a pound; eggs, less than two cents each. The farther we got into Siberia the greater was the profusion of food and the lower the price. At Lake Baikal, spoken of as the Baltic Sea of Siberia, I bought a whole basket of smoked fish for fifty cents, and what a feast we had with the roasted chicken and little pig and the two bottles of Caucasian port that some of my co-travelers bought! Passengers on this train ate as I had never known even Russians to eat.

At every train stop they would pour out in mobs, load up their arms, pockets, and sometimes even their bosoms with all manner of food, and proceed to devour it, so as to be ready for more and more at the next stop.

Nowadays travelers in Siberia find nowhere such displays of food at the railroad stations. The forces which have brought European Russia to its present shortages of meat and dairy products have operated in Siberia not less but even more violently. But the agricultural riches of its lands remain unimpaired. In the old days, in spite of backward methods of tillage, Siberia could boast of as fine wheat lands, as superb herds of sheep and cattle as any part of old Russia. In 1896 a group of Danes introduced modern methods of butter-making, and within a decade Siberia acquired fame all over Europe for its butter. In 1909 daily a trainload of refrigerating cars sped towards the Baltic seaboard with cargoes of butter to be shipped to Paris and London and other parts of Europe. In 1909 Siberia had an output of 140,870 tons of butter. The soil is there for wheat and other cereals, for pasture, for hay.

Only twelve million people live in Siberia—and in area it is larger than the whole of non-Russian Europe and America put together. In the north spread the *tundras*, the treeless steppes that freeze to a depth of a score or more meters and that thaw only a few feet on the surface during the brief summers. These *tundras* are not entirely barren. Since the moss and grass that grow there in summer make good fodder for reindeer, aboriginal tribes wander about with herds of these animals. The Soviet Government, perhaps taking a clue from

Vilhjalmur Stefansson, has had a commission investigating the region with a view to cultivating the reindeer industry as a new source of food.

Back of the *tundras* begins the *taiga*, the forest belt which stretches with some breaks all the way from the Urals to the Pacific Ocean. Larches, cedars, pines and, in the southern fringe, poplars, aspens, and other leafy trees, spread for thousands of miles. It is this *taiga* that casts both a glamor and a dread over Siberia. What legends cluster about the word! What tales have come out of there! What adventures and desperadoes the *taiga* has swallowed and spewed forth! Exiles and convicts have always fled there for freedom only to find, alas how often, nothing but death. There are men in Siberia, old and wrinkled, with hair turning white, who make frequent pilgrimages to the *taiga* as to a sanctuary and, like medieval saints, lose themselves for months in its wilderness. Even the hideous Rasputin sought spiritual revelation there. Countless tales have been written about the *taiga*, its grandeurs and terrors, its dramas and mysteries, its griefs and joys. When I was in Krasnoyarsk, I read in a newspaper of the discovery by a Russian scientist of a village of Old Believers somewhere in the heart of the *taiga*. These people had been living there sundered from the outside world since the days of Peter the Great, having fled there to escape religious persecution. When found, they had not heard of the World War, of the Revolution, of the death of the Czar, and they were not happy at being located and at the possibility of being drawn back to civilization.

Tundra, *taiga*, steppe, lakes, rivers among the mightiest in the world and, all but the Amur, pouring into the

Arctic Ocean! Human beings cannot live in a land of geographic features so pronounced without acquiring a distinctive quality, a certain sternness and severity in both character and physique. The Siberian certainly has acquired such a quality. He considers himself as of a group, if not a race, all his own. Russian, of course, he never called himself by that name in the old days, and he does not do so now. He is a Siberiak—a Siberian—and, even when also a Bolshevik and not supposed to cherish special local loyalties, he glories in the word. To him it implies qualities of valor and hardihood that the European Russian does not possess. He is, of all Russians, the sturdiest. No wonder the Siberian troops proved the most courageous in the late war.

There may be peasants in Siberia other than the new migrants who wear *lapti*, but one seldom sees them. Such houses as clutter the villages of White Russia and a huge slice of Great Russia—low hovels with thatched roofs with few and small windows, with ovens without chimneys and with ceilings and walls shiny with smoke-stains—I never saw anywhere in Siberia. The Siberian peasant may build a one-room house, but it will have large windows and shutters to fit—painted, both of them, even if the walls are not; and in summer on Sundays and holidays he will have his doorways and window-frames draped with leafy twigs and his tables and window-sills splashed with flowers.

Above all the Siberiak, even the peasant, is an adventurer, a darer of the Fates. The very conquest of Siberia at the end of the sixteenth century had its roots in a wild adventure, and it is no accident that Cossacks achieved this conquest. Cossacks, these age-old rovers and plunderers, these men of flaming hates and fierce lusts, who took life as readily as they gave their own. Even after the emblem of the Czars had been planted in its soil Siberia continued to be a land of adventurers; for only such succumbed to its fierce lure. True, a few years after its annexation the Czars began to send convicts there, and later political exiles, but these often had to turn adventurers to escape madness or death. Most of the population went there, of course, of its own accord, some to escape service in the army, some to break away from the yoke of serfdom, some to avoid religious persecution, some to dodge detection by the criminal police, some in search of gold, some in quest of a new god or of an answer to the riddle of life or of solace from misfortune, most of them in pursuit of a new home and material betterment. Mystics, murderers, peasants, pilgrims, quacks, they all went there, the sturdiest of the race and the most desperate. They still go there, many, very many, to escape new conflicts and new tyrannies—go, an endless procession of them. When off the railroad, they travel, not in covered wagons with a trundle-bed inside and a kerosene stove, but in little carts without covers and filled with straw and offering no shelter from rain and snow; or else they march on foot.

Wherever there is bold adventure there is certain to be desperation. There is that in Siberia. In the old days hunting of gold-miners was a diversion and a profession in some parts of the country. *Gorbachestvo*, a word used originally to designate the search after escaped convicts, came finally to be associated with this form of man-hunting. Kuznetsov, one of the oldest living former exiles, builder of parks and museums, narrated to me several tales, harrowing enough, of this form of "sport." The hunter would search for the man returning with the precious metal from some Klondike and would shoot him with no more hesitation or compunction than if he were a beast of prey. There are villages in Siberia inhabited solely by criminals or their descendants, and hardly a holiday passes but there are murders there. When I started for a trip to the northern country, friends and even officials in the city of Irkutsk warned me to be watchful, for there was no telling what might happen to me on the Siberian highways. Things always did happen there. Again and again the chauffeur of the truck on which I made the first lap of my journey pointed out to me wooden crosses at the edges of the road. Every cross, he informed me, marked the spot of a murder. In one place I counted six such crosses.

Yet in spite of her natural grandeur, the hardihood of her people, and her agricultural wealth, Siberia remained a backward land with but few cities strung along or around the Trans-Siberian and resembling overgrown villages more than urban communities. In Irkutsk, the oldest Siberian city, a few blocks away from the main avenue the streets are not even cobbled, and after rain pigs wallow in mud puddles as in the most squalid villages. In Chita in summer the wind blows up clouds of a hot sand that blind the eyes and scorch the face. Not a city in Siberia built in the old days had drainage or a centralized water system or decent pavements and sidewalks. There might be a pretty mansion of a governor or mayor or some other functionary, or an imposing house of a merchant, or an impressive gymnasium building, and for the rest, off the business streets, rows of straggling houses and low log huts—just as in a village. No one in Siberia had ever planned a city or bothered to modernize it. A city just grew, planless and chaotic, with now and then an educated exile or group of exiles, or some functionary of taste, of his own accord and on his own account seeking to infuse into it in spots a semblance of culture. Trotsky once said that Siberia was the epitome of Russia's backwardness, and surely there was no part of Russia with the wealth and glamor of Siberia that was so pathetically neglected in its development.

Now Siberia is entering a new age. Evidence of changes in the form of visible improvement in external appearances and in daily comforts is lacking. The cry for commodities of all kinds is as loud there as in other parts in Russia. But the Offensive launched by the Five Year Plan is an Offensive of science, the machine, socialization, and there is scarcely a community in Siberia that has not felt its impact.

It is a far cry from Ghengis Khan to the Five Year Plan—a jump of seven centuries; but it was this ancient Mongol warrior who first brought the machine to Siberia. A very primitive machine it was—only the forge. In the intervening years Czars toyed with the idea of developing Siberia but did little to carry it out. There was of course the laying of the Trans-Siberian railway, a most ambitious enterprise, the largest single-track railway in the world. There was also the building of some factories, foundries, and railroad shops. There are in Siberia to this day thirty-three factories that are from 153 to 200 years old. They are primitive in equipment but so solidly built that they still function. Only with the coming of the Five Year Plan did the work of industrializing Siberia in the modern manner earnestly begin, and unless present plans are thwarted by war, mismanagement, or some unforeseen calamity, Siberia is on the road to becoming the most highly industrialized territory on the Asiatic mainland.

In a way the industrialization of Siberia has become a matter of life and death for Russia. The Russians know only too well how handicapped they are in a war in the Far East or Central Asia with their base of supplies thousands of miles away from the battlefield and with only a single-track railroad to transport men, food, ammunition. They have not forgotten the lessons of the Russo-Japanese war, and as long as Japan remains a potential enemy they cannot rest secure unless they make themselves industrially ready to meet an attack should it ever come.

The chief centers of the industrial offensive in Siberia are Magnitogorsk in the Urals and Kuznetsk at the foothills of the Altai mountains. The climate in both places is rigorous and requires the hardiest of men to do the work in industry. But their geographic location has a priceless military advantage. So far removed are they from potential enemies, east and west, that they are practically immune from attack, except in the event of a complete conquest of all Russia, which no nation or group of nations has ever come within range of achieving.

The primary reason for locating steel plants in these regions is because of the presence there of natural re-

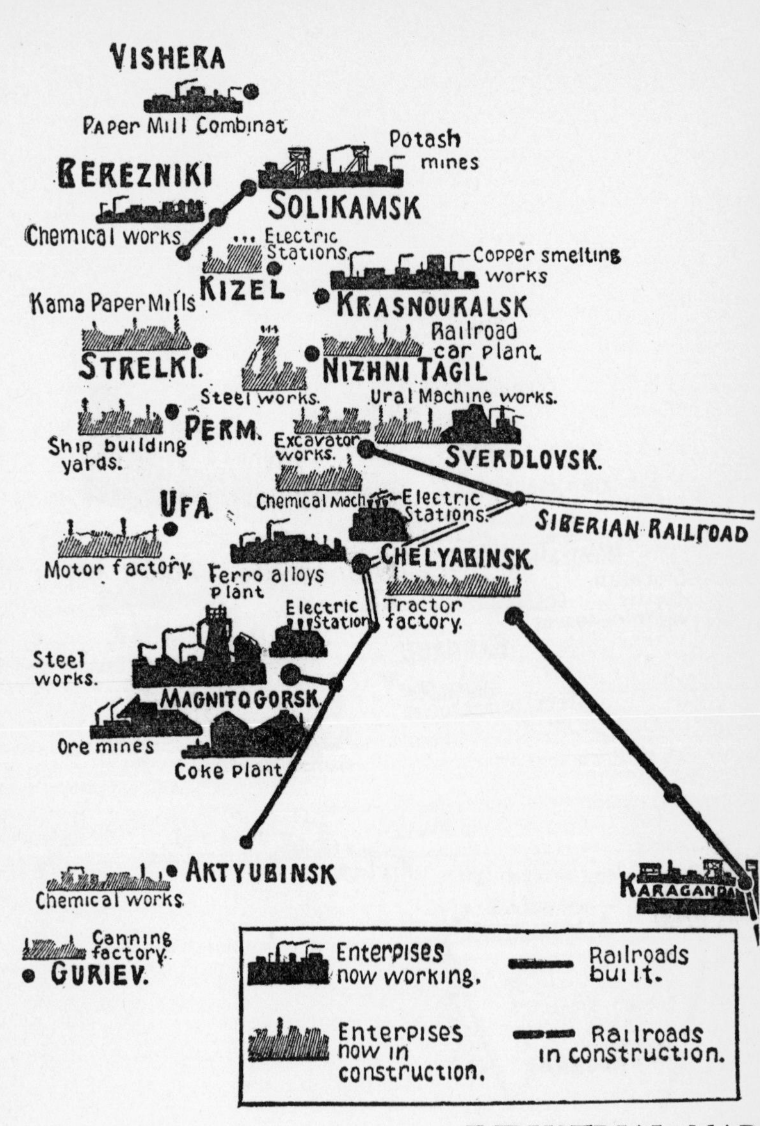

INDUSTRIAL MAP

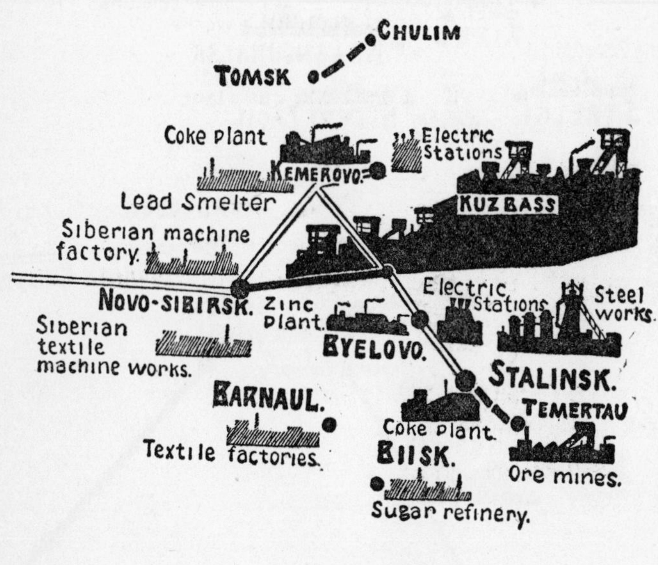
CHULIM
TOMSK
Coke plant
Electric Stations
KEMEROVO
KUZBASS
Lead Smelter
Siberian machine factory.
NOVO-SIBIRSK.
Zinc plant.
Electric Stations
Steel works.
Siberian textile machine works.
BYELOVO.
STALINSK.
BARNAUL.
TEMERTAU
Coke plant.
Textile factories.
BIISK.
Ore mines.
Sugar refinery.

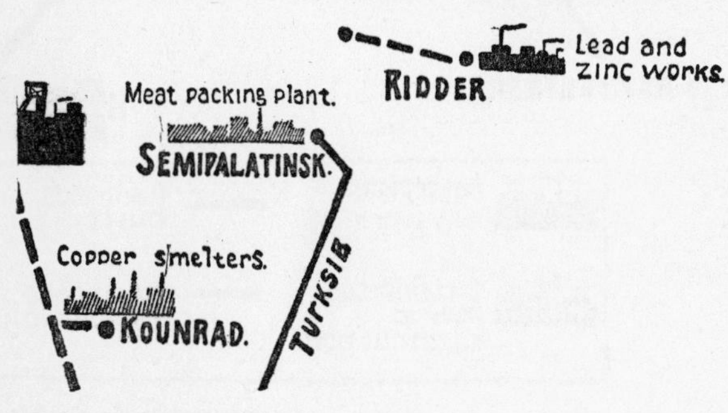
Lead and zinc works.
RIDDER
Meat packing plant.
SEMIPALATINSK.
Copper smelters.
KOUNRAD.
TURKSIB

OF SIBERIA

sources. Magnitogorsk is rich in iron, Kuznetsk in coal. They are separated by a distance of about two thousand kilometers, and they exchange coal and iron with one another. The haulage involved in this exchange makes the production of steel more costly than it would have been had the iron and coal been near one another. But the Russians are acting on the assumption that, no matter what the cost, it is better to make at home all the steel they might need in time of peace as well as war than to depend on foreign imports. More and more do they want to make themselves independent of such imports. Besides, the whole of Siberia and particularly the Urals are still only meagerly explored, and they are hopeful that new stores of coal and iron will be discovered within closer proximity to the new steel plants.

Both Kuznetsk and Magnitogorsk are products of the Five Year Plan. It was only on July 30, 1929, that the first train arrived in Magnitogorsk. Until then the territory was a wild region, sparsely inhabited by Russian settlers and wandering nomads and as untouched by the machine age as the *tundras* of the north. Kuznetsk was likewise a wilderness with three primitive villages scattered over its domains. These villages had to be moved twenty versts to prepare the ground for work on the plant. Neither Magnitogorsk nor Kuznetsk is completed. But the Russians, inspired by architectural and engineering specifications, speak of Magnitogorsk as the largest steel plant in the world with an annual capacity, when completed and functioning efficiently, larger than that of Gary, Indiana. Kuznetsk is much smaller, with a planned capacity of 1,100,000 tons a year. Both plants were built by American engineers, Magnitogorsk by the McGee Company of Cleveland, with occasional aid by John Calder, the builder of the tractor plant in Stalingrad, and Kuznetsk by the Hugh Frayne Company of Chicago.

The two plants are to be the pivotal points in the industrialization of a territory which, exclusive of the *tundras* and the *taiga* in the north and the waste lands in the south, covers an area of 2.8 million square kilometers, and extends to Turkestan. Within its zone, according to Soviet estimates, lie 20 per cent of the known iron reserves of the country, 90 per cent of the copper deposits, 71 per cent of the lead, 94 per cent of the zinc, 71 per cent of the fuel, chiefly coal, and rich stores of gold, platinum, nickel, potash, magnesium, and other minerals.

Already a network of industrial enterprises has sprung up in this territory, some already finished and some in process of construction. There is Sverdlovsk, the capital of the Urals, with its chain of factories, mostly new but some inherited from the old régime and rebuilt. The more important new factories are the ones for the manufacture of heavy machinery, of excavating apparatus and of mechanical equipment for chemical plants. There is Cheliabinsk with a plant nearing completion for the manufacture of 60 h.p. ten-ton caterpillar tractors with an initial capacity, unless plans miscarry, of 20,000 units a year, and with an ultimate capacity of 60,000 units a year. There is Nizhny Tagil with a steel plant of its own and a plant for the manufacture of railroad cars with a planned annual capacity of 54,000 four-axle freight cars a year. There is Berezniki within the arctic circle with its vast chemical works.

I have enumerated these enterprises without pretending to exhaust the list and merely to indicate the magnitude of the program the Soviets have undertaken. Difficulties and set-backs they have encountered at every step. As in other parts of Russia, inexperience, incompetence, poor transportation, cocksureness of Russian engineers, who now and then disregard the advice of trained foreign experts, and inferior living conditions, have again and again brought to grief the construction and the operation of blast furnaces, open hearths, and other industrial mechanisms.

But the Offensive for a new modern Siberia goes on with no abatement in energy and zeal. The Soviets are resolved to make it a land of railways, canals, power-stations, factories, highways, large-scale farms, modern cities—in short a new world for a new humanity.

If they succeed Siberia will become the most industrialized country on the Asiatic mainland and will exercise a more powerful influence on the destiny of this mainland than any other existing force.

XIX
REVOLUTION

THE COLLAPSE OF WORLD REVOLUTION

NOTHING that has happened in Russia since the coming of the Soviets has so infuriated the outside world as the Bolshevik idea and advocacy of world revolution. Dismayed as the world might have been at the Bolshevik defiance of the tenets of Western civilization—the attack in Russia on religion, private property, the individualistic family—this after all was an internal affair which concerned only the Russians themselves. But when, in the days of their early triumph, the Bolsheviks proposed to inflame the world with civil war and proceeded again and again to appeal to industrial workers of other nations to seek salvation in the overthrow of their governments and the establishment of Bolshevik dictatorships, the outside world grew fiercely resentful. I can think of nothing that has stood so much in the way of official good fellowship between Russia and other nations, and particularly between Russia and America, as the movement for world revolution.

The Soviet Government, as such, professes to be out of the orbit of this movement. Its job, it has maintained, is to defend Russia's national interests. In its pursuit of a nationalistic policy it has more than once outraged Bolshevik morality. Again and again it has followed a course quite opposite to that of the Communist International. At one time it worked to keep a king in power—King Amanullah of Afghanistan. When the Kellogg Pact was signed the Communist International beheld in it another nefarious scheme of the bourgeoisie to lull the proletarian world into false quiescence, and the Communist deputies in the parliaments in which they were represented denounced it and voted against it. Yet the Soviet Government almost invited itself to be one of its first signatories.

Nor has the Soviet Government ever taken up the defense of Communists in other countries, no matter how sternly they were repressed. Kemal Pasha in his early years in power did not deal gently with Communists: nor did Mussolini. The Communist International anathematized them both. Yet there are no countries with whom the Soviet Government has maintained such friendly relations as it has with Italy and Turkey. Whatever the personal feelings of individual Soviet leaders may have been toward Mussolini and Kemal Pasha for their persecution of Communists, they never allowed these to obtrude into any of their official relations with either ruler.

Recently a minor incident occurred in Moscow which bears significantly on the strictly nationalistic nature of the Soviet Government. A Moscow film company had invited a group of American negroes to come to Russia and make a picture portraying the oppression of negroes in the South. The name of the picture was to be *Black and White*. There was to be a lynching in it, and it was to end in a white girl marrying a black man. It was to contrast all the way through the Communist and the Southern bourgeois attitude toward the negro. A prominent American engineer heard of it, and he was interested enough to express his opinion to a leading member of the Soviet Government that such a picture would foster hostility toward the Soviets in America. Shortly afterwards an announcement was made in the press that the making of the picture was postponed, and those of us who have learned to read between the lines of Russian pronouncements are convinced that it will never be made, or, if it is, it will not be the picture that was originally planned.

In its pursuit of a nationalistic policy the Soviet Government has again and again clashed with the interests of world revolution and has bothered neither about the Communist International nor about the Communist Parties in other lands. Witness Germany.

Bolsheviks of course, whether in or out of the Soviet Government, cherish as much faith in the inevitability of world revolution as they ever have. It is as cardinal an article in their faith as is immortality of the soul in the faith of the Fundamentalist.

Yet events have occurred in Russia and the outside world which have markedly cooled their ardor for the movement. There was a time when no Bolshevik of importance would deliver a speech, no matter what the occasion or the subject he discussed, without first giving a survey of the international scene, and pointing out situation after situation in place after place testifying to the rising tide of the proletarian revolution. Always he would seek to impress his hearers with its ever-present and far-reaching reality and vitality. But in the speeches at the last Communist Congress in January, 1933, there was scarcely any reference to the rising tide of proletarian supremacy. Bolshevik after Bolshevik spoke of the widespread depression, and of the inability of capitalism to lift itself out of the confusion and paralysis into which it had sunk. But not one proclaimed triumphantly as in former years that the world revolution was coming to the surface.

Even the Communist International has lost its old-time belligerency. It still issues protests against repression of workers and Communists. It still holds meetings and prints resolutions, and calls on workers of the world to make ready for the final reckoning with capitalism. But gone is the old fire and the old tempestuousness. It no longer even treats the world to exciting oratory. Since the departure of Zinovyev and Bukharin from leadership it has fallen on dull and innocuous days. The men who now guide its destinies have no thunder and no lightning in them. Their speeches are mere repetitions of old phrases without a trace of brilliance, novelty, or pomp. Its followers, of course, explain its decline on the ground that it is biding its time, waiting for the "imminently revolutionary situation" to burst forth into the open. Quite so. But this is acknowledgment of resignation, and at least of temporary paralysis. Let the reader remember that when the Bolsheviks first leaped into power they had no notion that they would be the only proletarian government in the world. They were firmly convinced that other nations —especially those engaged in the World War—would follow them. They were sure that they were starting not a national but an international revolution. Their prophet Marx had warned them that no single nation could possibly carry out a proletarian revolution, especially a nation as backward industrially as old Russia was. I often wonder what Lenin and his followers would have done had they been convinced at the very outset that the revolution they were contemplating would die, as it subsequently did, on the Russian frontier? World revolution, as the Bolsheviks visioned it at that time, was indispensable to the preservation of their power in Russia. It was, they thought, a question of life and death to them. For that reason alone, they strove mightily to fan it into being wherever they could.

But when Lenin realized that he had erred, when he saw the uprisings in neighboring countries ending in the slaughter of the proletarians, he retreated to the so-called *Nep*—which once more legalized private property and private enterprise. Afterwards, for a number of years, the Bolsheviks floundered about without a definite internal or external policy. They were desperately hoping that the revolution would still sweep the world and come to their rescue. Unless this happened they did not see how they alone could attain the ends in the name of which they had made their own revolt. Their convulsive fear of an outside attack only fanned their eagerness for the spread of Bolshevism in outside lands. But with the *débâcle* of the Bolshevik cause in China in 1927 their last hope for immediate world-wide action collapsed.

Here, then, they were, ardent crusaders for world revolution with none in immediate sight anywhere, and with the Marxian theory of the impossibility of building a Socialist society in one land threatening them with failure. Something had to happen to cut this Gordian knot in their philosophy. Along came Stalin and very ruthlessly proceeded to do the necessary cutting. He enunciated the doctrine that one nation, especially a nation like Russia, with its immense resources and its vast territories, a nation that is really a world in itself, can build Socialism within its own domains. Stalin had to wage a fierce war with Trotsky and other Bolshevik leaders to get this doctrine officially accepted and acted upon. But he won his war, and now Russia is marching full steam ahead in the belief that she can build the new society alone, regardless of whether or not other nations join her.

This change of front marks a turning-point in Bolshevik philosophy and even more in the destiny of Russia. It brushes aside the notion that immediate world revolution is necessary for the preservation of the Soviet régime; hence the achievement of it no longer presents for the Bolsheviks the momentous problem that it did in the days preceding the enunciation of Stalin's theory.

At present no movement on earth seems so devoid of hope as world revolution. Wherever it flamed up it was quickly quenched in blood. In Hungary, in Germany, in the Baltic States, in China, it was the same story. One would have imagined that the world-wide depression would give it a fresh impetus. Never has the world witnessed so much unemployment, and never has capitalist society been in such a state of confusion and distress as in the past few years, and yet, instead of advancing, the movement of world revolution has actually been receding. In America and England, in spite of propaganda, parades, and the existence of millions of jobless men and women, the Communist parties in the last elections failed to muster sufficient support to elect a single functionary to the national parliaments. There certainly is no sign anywhere in these Anglo-Saxon lands of labor turning to Communism. The objective conditions, according to Communist theory, seem as never before to favor the growth of Communist sentiment, and yet, like a plant in arid soil, such sentiment does not get sustenance from the national soil.

Next to Russia, Germany had the largest Communist Party in the world and yet it was powerless to interfere with Hitler's sweep to power. Communists, of course, are never at a loss for an explanation of their setbacks. They now propound the theory that Hitlerism will only pave the way for their triumph. Maybe. They have said the same about Italy when Mussolini rose to power. Yet nothing has happened in Italy to justify their optimism or their prophecy. Communists may succeed Hitler, but then somebody else may, some other group may gain ascendancy in Germany. One thing is clear: the Communist International has become convinced of the impotence of Communists alone to fight back the tide of reaction that is sweeping over Europe. It has had to swallow pride and belligerency and actually follow Trotsky's counsel and urge Communist parties to cooperate with the Second International and other labor groups and present a united labor front against the common enemy. All the more remarkable is this change of heart in the Communist International, as it has always bestowed its most vitriolic epithets on the Second International and branded its leaders as vicious hirelings of the bourgeoisie.

Surely these events call for a re-appraisal of the Communist threat to inflame the world with revolt and to impose on it proletarian dictatorships such as Russia has consummated.

Bolshevik leaders have been credited with being astute propagandists. In reality they have shown themselves woefully incapable of understanding other peoples and the conditions under which they are living. Implacable predeterminists, they have been appraising the outside world in terms of the psychology and the living conditions of old Russia and of the formulas and slogans of Marx and Lenin. They have allowed nothing for difference in political experience, social background, emotional response. But these are differences, immense and stirring, and of no small value in the interplay of social forces.

Let the reader ponder over the background out of which Bolshevism sprang in Russia. Here was a nation occupying one-sixth of the earth's area and boasting a population of 160,000,000 people, 120,000,000 of whom were peasants. At least three-fourths of these peasants could neither read nor write; one-third of their number possessed no land of their own; very few of them found it possible to enter high institutions of learning or attain to any rank in the army or in civil service; and at least half of them lived in dismal one-room huts together with their pigs and chickens and sometimes even with their cows. Clearly Russia was a feudal land with a hidebound caste system, its supreme ruler, the Czar, surrounded by an aristocracy socially accomplished but intellectually stagnant. So jealous was this aristocracy of its prerogatives that it held back the industrial development of the country, and, in so doing, retarded the formation of the middle class which makes up the backbone of a modern nation. One must always remember that the distinguishing features of the old Russian society was the comparative absence of a middle class.

When the war descended on Russia in 1914, it instantly brought to the surface all the weaknesses and contradictions of the old régime, which in time, under the increasing strain of the war, fell under the sheer weight of its impotence.

After the Czarist government fell, there was no group in the country powerful enough to hold the nation together on the basis of the old condition, so that when the Bolsheviks promised land to the peasants and peace to the soldiers, both of which groups were in a desperate mood, they swept away all opposition and leaped into power. If Russia had had a middle class of any size, the Bolshevik Revolution might never have become an active fact, or, if it had, it surely would have failed.

For this has been actually the fate of Bolshevism in all lands having even a semblance of a middle class. There are in Europe a number of countries, once parts of Czarist Russia, which were more backward economically than any of the leading industrial nations of the world, yet more advanced than was Russia proper. Even in these countries, badly shaken as they were at the end of the World War, the middle classes found it possible to sweep back the tide of Bolshevism which threatened to engulf them. In such lands the revolution, after a temporary triumph, ended in a holocaust for the Bolsheviks. Weak as the middle classes were in Finland, Esthonia, Latvia, they managed to fight off the proletarian onslaught. In each of these lands aggressive groups launched civil wars that shook the old order to its foundations but ended in the defeat and slaughter of the Bolsheviks. True, the White Armies in these lands received support from foreign invaders. But so did the White Armies in Siberia, in Archangel, in the Caucasus, in the Ukraine. Yet it availed them nothing. The Bolsheviks smashed through to victory. If, therefore, countries whose middle classes are vastly inferior in power and resources to those of industrialized nations were able to check Bolshevik revolutions, what possible chance of success has such a revolution in any large middle-class country?

I am using the word revolution in a Bolshevik sense—meaning a class struggle, a civil war, with a resultant proletarian dictatorship. I can conceive of no other revolution in the Bolshevik meaning of the term. The Communist manifesto on this point is explicit enough: "We traced the more or less civil war raging within existing society up to the point where the war breaks out into the open revolution, and where the violent overthrow of the bourgeoisie lays the foundation of the rule of the proletariat." The emphasis in this pronouncement must be placed on the words "the violent overthrow of the bourgeoisie."

The chief error the Bolsheviks have made, and with them the Communists the world over, is in their failure to appreciate the nature, the size, the powers of the modern middle class. To begin with, this class in its process of development and expansion keeps an open door. Unlike the old Russian aristocracy it does not shut itself off from the rest of society by artificial barriers. It cannot keep out newcomers who, taking advantage of competition or education, lift themselves into its ranks. It is therefore no exclusive society. It does more—it infects a host of allied groups with its ideas of a standard of living, its ambitions, and its social ideas: the intelligentsia, the bulk of the farmers, the upper layer of the industrial workers, such as comprise most of the unions of the American Federation of Labor or the German trade unions, and, above all, government employees, from policeman to teacher, from legislator to ordinary office clerk. Not that there are no exceptions made up of members of the middle classes throwing in their luck with the proletarian groups. Neither Marx nor Engels nor Lenin nor Trotzky nor Stalin are proletarians. But it is not the dramatic exception that counts, but the frame of mind of the class *en masse*. Indeed the middle class is a composite of many classes with differing intellectual achievement and economic background, but with a common and united abhorrence for efforts to dislodge them by violence from their position, their privileges, their beliefs, their usages.

And it has formidable power in its hands. It dominates the schools, from the lowest to the highest, the police, the army, the navy. It is held together through numerous organizations of one kind or another: secret societies, country-clubs, chambers of commerce, church unions, trade bodies. It has its hands on the guns, the aeroplanes, the poison-gases, and all other weapons of modern warfare. Withal, unlike the old Russian aristocracy, it has no false pride and is not afraid to soil its hands with menial tasks, or to strike with its own fists at a foe threatening its existence. What chance have industrial workers against such a formidably organized body? There is, of course, the theory that capitalism is destroying the middle class. "Society," says the Communist manifesto, "is as a whole splitting up more and more into two great hostile camps, into two classes directly facing each other—the bourgeoisie and the proletariat. The lower strata of the middle class, the small tradespeople, shopkeepers, and retired tradesmen generally, the handicraftsmen and peasants, all these sink gradually into the proletariat."

Do they? In this day and age, with the machine constantly displacing man-power, they could not sink into the ranks of the proletariat even if they wished it. They could find no jobs in industry. The small shopkeeper may lose his business, but he seldom seeks economic rehabilitation in a proletarian pursuit. Germany since the end of the war has gone through crisis after crisis, including inflation which has wiped out the savings and the other possessions of vast bodies of people, and there is no evidence anywhere that these ruined business and white-collar folk have sought salvation in industrial jobs. They could find no such jobs. Certainly neither in England nor in America is there a perceptible inflow of small business men or office workers into factories. Somehow they manage to float around within the orbit of middle-class occupations. They remain essentially white-collar folk. Immense after all is the number of men that modern business and modern government require for the operation of their respective enterprises.

But whatever adjustment the ruined business man or the white-collar man without a job may make, with rare exceptions they do not flock to the banner of the proletariat and become champions of the proletarian revolution. They certainly do not do so *en masse*. They cling to political allegiances which are hostile to a proletarian civil war and the enthronement of the proletarian dictatorship, and for a very simple reason—such a dictatorship has nothing or little to offer them which would offset the prodigious losses they would suffer through the new shift in political power.

There are three stages that a proletarian revolution must pass—the destructive, when the industrial workers fight for power; the restorative, when the proletarian dictatorship seeks to heal up the wounds of the civil war and reëstablishes the normal functioning of the economic machinery of the country; and the reconstructive, when it begins to rebuild civilization on a Socialist basis. In a highly industrialized nation a revolution may skip the second stage, or pass through it quickly. It never can skip the first. If the proletarian revolution could start with the third or restorative stage, it is conceivable that large groups of the middle class would give it their support. In Russia this stage has been marked by the Five Year Plan, which, in spite of rigid regimentation, has relaxed its severities toward the engineer, the artist, and others who in the outside world would be regarded as members of the middle class. Their salaries have been increased, their children are being admitted to the higher institutions of learning on a place of equality with proletarians. They have received official recognition through the building of their own clubhouses and their own vacation resorts. The Russian Revolution emphasizes now, not equality, but inequality of income, which means inequality in standard of living. And, what is even more significant, the preceding years of the Revolution had ground out of them many of their old beliefs and old attitudes. It has really remade their personalities. But even in this restorative period, with new liberties and new opportunities for the white-collar man, the proletarian dictatorship is ever on its guard and smites down ruthlessly anyone it suspects of disloyalty. Witness the recent execution in Russia of thirty-five agricultural experts, and the arrest of the British engineers and twenty-five of their Russian aides. The dictatorship provides for the white-collar man but it never relaxes its vigilance over him.

But what can the middle class expect from a revolution during the period of the civil war or in the early years of the proletarian dictatorship? It will have no voice in either. It can expect only discrimination, distrust, disfranchisement, loss of properties, of social position, and continuous subjection to a rigorous discipline. Able as members of the middle class might be to fill positions of responsibility, the dictatorship would suspect them, and often rightly, of disloyalty, and would keep them from such positions. Or, if such positions were given to bourgeoisie, it would be only under the strictest supervision. Incumbents would have to remake themselves before they could be trusted. They would have to undergo a period of servitude, reorganize their habits and usages, and re-create their very personalities just as they have had to do in Russia. If they did not, they would encounter, at every step, recrimination and frustration. In return for these forced sacrifices they would be promised a happy society in the future. At best the dictatorship could say to them: "You and all that you represent have to be unmade and liquidated so that future generations may have a free and abundant world to live in." Even if they had faith in the fulfillment of the promise, they could not resign themselves to their own effacement. If they survived and got accustomed to the new usages, by the time the revolution reached its reconstructive stage they might become settled and willing enough to carry on under the dictatorship. But knowing, as they must, the hardships and privations they must endure in the early stages of the revolution they would not be likely to offer it support. They would be sure to shoulder a musket and keep the dictatorship from coming into power. They would support, not the revolution, but the counter-revolution.

In one other respect the Bolsheviks fail to comprehend the nature of the middle class or else deliberately shut their eyes to it. I am referring to their spirit of nationalism and patriotism. Here, too, the Bolsheviks superimpose their own Russian psychology on outside peoples. The Russian masses never were patriotic. Some years ago, while journeying about in villages in the part of the country where I was born, I heard peasants say again and again that they wished the Germans, who had been there during the war, had never left. They would have made good rulers and that was what *muzhiks* needed. Russian peasants never had thought in terms of national interests. The only groups that stirred their loyalties were their families and their villages—the only groups to which they were bound by sentiment and self-interest. There was nothing in their lives or in the lives of industrial workers to instil loyalty to the nation. They really did not know Russia. They identified the country with the Czar and the government, and these were something outside their lives and aloof from them. They never had even cultivated a love for Russian culture. They knew so little about it. That was why after the overthrow of the Czar neither Rodzianko nor Kerensky nor Milyukov could play on their emotion of patriotism. The Bolsheviks did not even try. They were not interested in patriotism, and they knew well enough that appeals in that direction were as futile as curses at the weather. But Mussolini could play on the patriotic feelings of the Italian people, so could Hitler in Germany, and Horthy in Hungary. Indeed, patriotism was the main force that helped these men obtain the support they needed to put themselves into power.

The middle class in every country is patriotic. It identifies itself with national interests and national movements. Communists, of course, disavow patriotism. They put class above nation. But that does not weaken the power of patriotism over men, and the belief that their welfare is bound up with the welfare of the nation and not with that of any distinct class or group. The intelligentsia, or a part of it, may lampoon and denounce patriotism, or an excess of it, but in an emergency national loyalties get the best even of them. The last war testified to that convincingly enough. And, of course, in time of a class struggle the one big weapon that the bourgeoisie can be counted upon to use is patriotism, and a most formidable weapon it is! One can imagine what would happen in America, in England, in France, in Germany, in any large middle-class country, in time of an effort of the proletarian to put himself by violence in power! Patriotic passion would flame so hot that it would fairly burn up the rebellious mass!

Indeed, the Bolsheviks, viewing the world in terms of conditions that obtained in old Russia, do not appreciate the possible consequence of a revolution in a strongly middle-class country. They forget that it was the very backwardness of Russia which made it physically easy for them to conquer their enemies. With the exception of a few northern cities, there is in Russia scarcely a community which could not be self-sustaining in an emergency. If the revolutionaries conquered Moscow, the remainder of Russia might feel the impact of the conquest, yet could go on living on its own resources. But if New York were cut off from the rest of America, almost every inhabitant of that city would feel the catastrophic effect of the forced separation. Moreover, in Russia, because of its industrial backwardness, there was comparatively little to destroy. Had all its industrial mechanism been wiped out, the country could still have gone on.

But consider a similar situation in America, where, because of the wide diffusion of its middle class, the revolution would have to cover every inch of territory from coast to coast. Assume for a moment that the revolutionaries could muster a sufficiently powerful army to launch into warfare; the fight between them and their enemies would be so desperate that in the end, no matter who was victor, there would be no fruits of victory. If such a war were to break out in New York City the revolutionaries, naturally enough, would attempt to seize the strategic buildings, the big banks, post offices and telegraph agencies, the arsenals, the important business blocks, and the chief government institutions. They would be fighting with modern weapons—that is, with machine guns, aëroplanes, poison gases. To engage in conflict without such equipment would be suicidal. Their enemies would strike back with weapons no less deadly. In the pursuit of such a civil war, provided that it assumed serious proportions, the destruction of life and property would be so colossal that in the end hardly anything or anybody would be left. This alone, it seems to me, precludes all possibility of a Bolshevik civil war in a modern highly industrialized society.

I am not assuming that Communism or certain communistic ideas have not the power to cure the wastes, confusions, and distresses incident to capitalist society. They may well have, and, if so, sooner or later they will dominate the world. But, judging the world as it is now constituted, this domination will not come through a class struggle and civil war. The proletarian in a highly organized middle-class country must always remain too weak to make his conquest of power with his own hands, and there are no immediate advantages he can offer to lure other groups to his aid; and, even if there were, the ensuing conflict, if it reached serious proportions, would create so much havoc that by the time it was over it might convert the whole industrial community into a heap of wreckage. So closely intertwined are the modern machine and the modern community in all their parts and processes that damage in one place means whole or partial paralysis all along the line. Unlike a feudal agricultural society, a modern industrial community simply cannot stand the strain of a civil war fought in the modern manner.

If Communist ideas gain their dominance in the world it will be through some method other than the class struggle and the proletarian dictatorship. It is not inconceivable that Fascist or some other middle-class dictatorships will, of their own accord, make Communist ideas their own. Already the Communist idea of planned production is agitating their minds, and not only theirs, but those of the whole capitalist world. If they, and other rulers, cannot introduce planned production in a competitive society, they will curb competition just as capitalist governments more and more are beginning to curb the rights and privileges of individual enterprise.

There is only one reservation that one is bound to make in any discussion of world revolution, and that is the unforeseen shift of influence, emotion, and power in time of war. Zinovyev once declared that Bolshevik revolutions must sweep the world. They may do so in time of peace, but it is far more likely in time of war or after a war. Communists hold that war is a concomitant part of capitalist society. Territorial aggression; fights for markets, for fields of investment, for spheres of influence, for national honor, and all other causes of war, are, they insist, as inseparable from capitalist practice as is the urge for profit and accumulation.

The Russian Bolsheviks were confident that the last war would lead to world revolution. But it did not. World revolution died on the Russian frontiers. Then they evolved the theory of temporary stabilization of capitalism through imperialism and colonial exploitation. They have no more doubt of the eventual doom of capitalism than of the eventual triumph of the proletarian dictatorship. They confidently look to some future war which will so unsettle the capitalist world that it will never be able to put itself together again. It will, they hold, crash to ruins, and out of its débris will spring the proletarian revolution.

Prophecy on this point is futile excepting for a Communist. But judging the world as it now is, world revolution seems to be the most hopeless idea afloat—if peace continues. If war comes, anything may happen—proletarian dictatorships, fascist dictatorships, monarchical dictatorships, and even the extermination of all Communists and all capitalists.

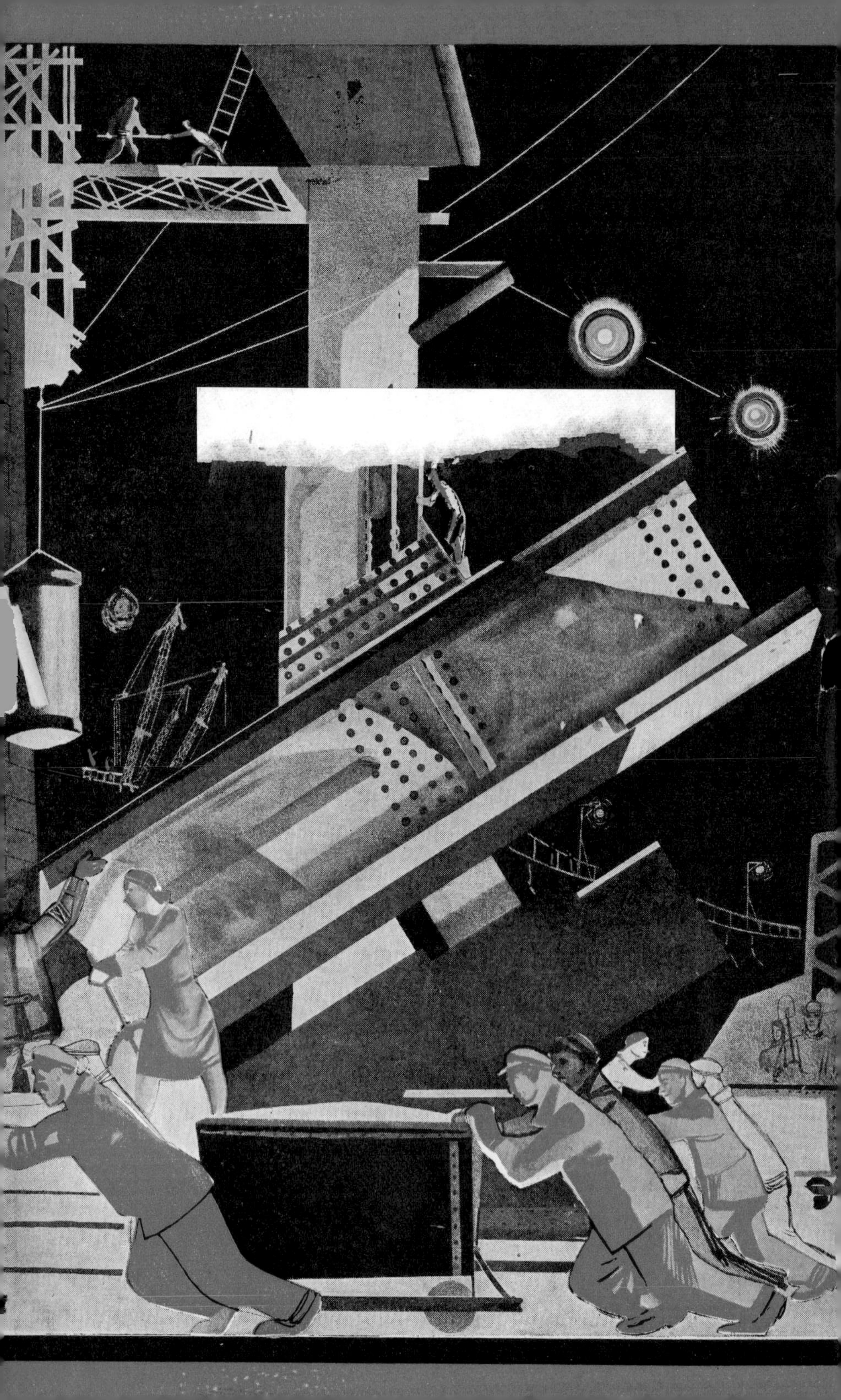